ANTHROPOLOGICAL SERIES
NUMBER 5

INDIANS IN PENNSYLVANIA

Paul A. W. Wallace

Second Edition

Revised by William A. Hunter

Illustrated by William Rohrbeck

Y0-AGO-410

Commonwealth of Pennsylvania
Pennsylvania Historical and Museum Commission
Harrisburg, 2005

Commonwealth of Pennsylvania
Edward G. Rendell, *Governor*

Pennsylvania Historical and Museum Commission

www.phmc.state.pa.us

Indians in Pennsylvania

Foreword

Since its original publication in 1961, the late Paul A. W. Wallace's *Indians in Pennsylvania* has been one of the best and most popular histories of the Indians of Pennsylvania. Of the many books published by the Pennsylvania Historical and Museum Commission, it has been the best seller. After twenty years and more than twenty thousand copies in print, we decided to publish a new edition, incorporating the revisions that further scholarship made advisable. Mr. William A. Hunter, who was Chief of the Division of History of the Commission when this book was published and who was also an authority on this subject, carried out the task of revision most admirably. The reader can be assured, however, that this is still Dr. Wallace's famous book, both in content and in spirit. It is hoped that the book will be a useful tool for historians, teachers and interested readers, and that it will provide a sound foundation for those who wish to learn more about these first inhabitants of Pennsylvania.

HARRY E. WHIPKEY, *Director*
Bureau of Archives and History

Paul A. W. Wallace

Although Dr. Paul A. W. Wallace (b. 1891, d. 1967) was a native of Canada and a graduate of the University of Toronto, he spent most of his scholarly career in Pennsylvania. He was associated with Lebanon Valley College, and was for many years Chairman of the Department of English. Wallace also served as editor of *Pennsylvania History*, the quarterly journal of the Pennsylvania Historical Association. He was a consultant to the Pennsylvania Historical and Museum Commission (PHMC) from 1951-57, and historian at the PHMC from 1957-65. His numerous publications include: *Indian Paths of Pennsylvania; Pennsylvania: Seed of a Nation; The White Roots of Peace; The Muhlenbergs of Pennsylvania; Conrad Weiser, 1696-1760.*

ISBN 0-89271-017-9 paperbound
ISBN 0-89271-018-7 clothbound

SECOND EDITION
Copyright © 1981 Commonwealth of Pennsylvania
First Printing 1981
Second Printing, 1986
Third Printing, 1991
Fourth Printing, 1993

Preface to the Second Edition

The popularity of Dr. Paul A. W. Wallace's *Indians in Pennsylvania* dates from its first appearance in 1961 and has continued through twenty years and four subsequent printings. In the meantime continuing research has added to our information and modified some of our interpretations, and no doubt will continue to do so, but it would not have altered Dr. Wallace's interest in the Indians or his great respect for them.

The prime purpose of republishing *Indians in Pennsylvania* is to satisfy the continuing requests for an evidently useful book; the occasion also affords an opportunity to update some factual content while retaining the author's original outlook and interpretation. For help in the preparation of this revised edition, Dr. Barry C. Kent, State Archaeologist and Chief of the Archaeology Section of the William Penn Memorial Museum, deserves special thanks for his professional advice, and Mr. Harold L. Myers, Associate Historian of the Pennsylvania Historical and Museum Commission, for his editorial suggestions.

Particular appreciation is due the members of the Commission and its then Executive Director, Mr. William J. Wewer, for their authorization and support of the present publication; Mr. Harry E. Whipkey, Director, Bureau of Archives and History, and Dr. John Bodnar, Chief, Division of History, who were directly involved in planning the work; and Mr. Myers, who supervised its editing and production. Mrs. Joanne Bornman of the Division of History typed the manuscript.

WILLIAM A. HUNTER

Acknowledgments

Acknowledgment is herewith made to the following persons and institutions for permission to quote from books and manuscripts as indicated: Cornell University Press, for *Indian Affairs in Colonial New York*, by Allen W. Trelease; the John Day Company, for *The Maple Sugar Book*, by Helen and Scott Nearing; Dr. Amandus Johnson, Governor of the Swedish Colonial Society, for Lindeström's *Geographia Americae;* the Michigan Historical Collections, University of Michigan, for C. C. Trowbridge's "Account of Some of the Traditions, Manners and Customs of the Lenee Lenaupee or Delaware Indians"; Archives of the Moravian Church, for John Jacob Schmick's report of November 18, 1766, in the Bethlehem Diary; the University of Nebraska Press, for *The World's Rim*, by Hartley Burr Alexander; the University of Oklahoma Press, for *Civilization: As Told to Florence Drake by Thomas Wildcat Alford.*

The author wishes also to thank *Pennsylvania History* for permission to use passages from his article, "The Iroquois: A Brief Outline of Their History," which appeared in *The Livingston Indian Records (Pennsylvania History*, XXIII, 15-28).

For the reader who wishes to explore this subject further, there has been included a short bibliography of works concerning Indian life and culture.

PAUL A. W. WALLACE

February 10, 1961

Contents

Illustrations

Maps

Indians in Pennsylvania

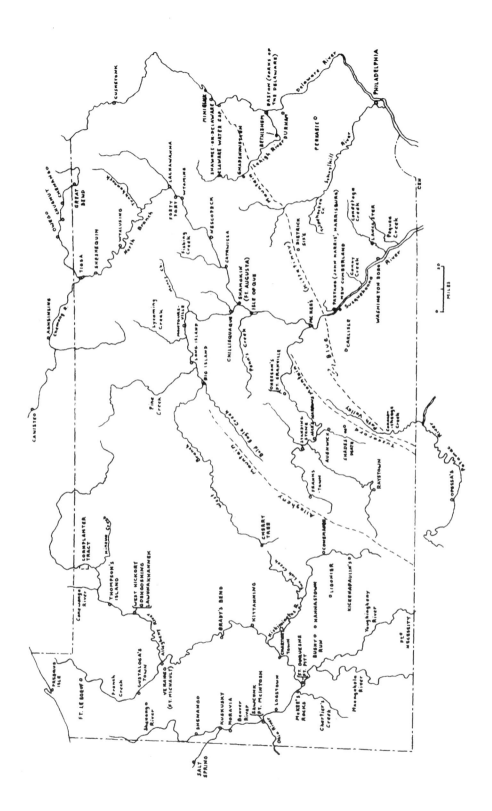

1

The Origin of Pennsylvania's Indians

IMMIGRATION FROM ASIA

THE DELAWARES who, as far back as the white man's memory goes, were the Indians most closely associated with Pennsylvania, called themselves *Lenni Lenape* (pronounced Len-nee Le-nah-pay), which means the Real (or Original) People. If the name sounds arrogant, we should remember that all nations like to think themselves unique. We who live in "God's Country" should not have difficulty in understanding this, nor should Englishmen who sing:

> When Britain first at Heaven's command
> Arose from out the azure main. . . .

Other Indian nations gave themselves comparable names. *Illinois* means Real Men; *Ongwe Honwe* (Iroquois), Original People: names which suggest priority over all other peoples on earth. "We are 'the

3

People,'" said Emerson Metoxon (an Oneida) to me, with a twinkle in his eye. "The rest are only Indians."

The human race, however, did not originate on this continent. No trace has been found here of man's parent stock. We may leave aside also (for lack of sufficient evidence) theories that would trace the American Indians back to the lost Atlantis, to the Egyptians, to the Welsh, to the Lost Ten Tribes of Israel, or to islands in the South Pacific.

The ancestors of the American Indian came from Asia. People of differing physical types, so it is thought, crossed Bering Strait in a succession of migrations to the New World. They came in bands, crossing from Siberia to the Seward Peninsula of Alaska before, during, and after the last Ice Age. From Alaska many of them moved south, some by a route roughly corresponding with that now taken by the Alcan Highway from Fairbanks, Alaska, to Edmonton, Alberta. They spread out all over the two Americas, leaving a trail of spear points from Alaska to Tierra del Fuego. Certain of those Asiatic immigrants were the ancestors of our Pennsylvania Indians.

By what route Indians first crossed the Plains is not known, nor how long ago it was that they first entered Pennsylvania. Archaeologists tell us that man has probably been on this continent for at least twenty-five or thirty thousand years and in Pennsylvania for between twelve and eighteen thousand. The Indian is a well-naturalized American.

DEVELOPMENT OF CULTURE ON THIS CONTINENT

The first migrations to America were made by a primitive people, bringing from Asia little on which to build a civilization except language, the mastery of fire, a few tools, and simple forms of social organization based on kinship and the local band. These early-comers had no pottery and they knew nothing about farming. The great agricultural discoveries which were to constitute the Indian's chief gift to mankind were made on this continent.

Early man in Pennsylvania left no records on stone, clay, or parchment to tell us who he was and what he did. For his prehistory—the thousands of years he lived in America before the white man came to make written records—we must rely chiefly on the findings of archaeologists. These carefully trained scientists dig their evidence out of the ground: fragments of stone, bone, and pottery, and (very rarely) wooden tools and containers or cordage and fabrics. From a close study of such objects and the places where they are found, archae-

4

ologists have learned much about the way the Indian developed his material culture.

Simple as aboriginal culture may appear when we compare it with modern ways of living (with refrigerators, television sets, and jet planes), its evolution was complex and progressive. The Indians changed from a hunting to a diversified economy, from a life of roving in search of game to village and town life based upon farming.

Eleven thousand years ago the Indian lived a nomadic life, hunting big game with a stabbing spear, roasting his meat, and wearing clothes made of animal skins. Eight thousand years ago he was still a nomad, but within recognized family territories. His diet was improved by fishing and the gathering of roots, nuts, and berries. Six thousand years ago he had added a spearthrower to improve the reach of his weapon. He traveled the rivers in canoes, and added shellfish to his diet.

More than three thousand years ago in Pennsylvania he was cultivating the ground. Indian corn or maize has been called the mother of civilization in America. Its cultivation for food freed men from hunting. It gave them time to sit and think, to attend council meetings, and so to develop political forms.

Before the beginning of the Christian era, the Indian was living in a village leading a more or less sedentary life, making pottery, stewing his meat, and enjoying trade with distant tribes. He had adopted the bow (apparently a new contribution from Arctic-Asiatic culture), and he chipped flint expertly to make arrowheads. His diet was now based on maize culture. He grew tobacco and used it, not only for pleasure, but also as incense in elaborate religious ritual. Before the white man came, the Indian population was increasing, town life had developed, hunting had declined, and farming had become intensive. Then came Columbus, Jacques Cartier, and the *Mayflower*. In the scramble that ensued the Indian population was decimated by gunpowder and European diseases.

When the white man arrived, the Indians were far less primitive than their Asiatic ancestors had been. On this continent they had advanced to comparatively high forms of culture. Yet if we judge Pennsylvania's aborigines by European standards and *on material grounds alone*, they were primitive. That does not mean that their men and women were inferior in physique, brain power, ethics, or capacity for further development. It means only that they had fallen behind in the mechanical arts, which provide a convenient, if superficial, ladder on which to measure the ascent of man. In toolmaking, they were still of the Stone Age.

5

Ellsworth Huntington in *The Mainsprings of Civilization* suggests eight criteria by which to measure progress in material civilization:

1. The development of tools, in numbers and precision.
2. The raising of cereals.
3. Irrigation.
4. The taming of animals.
5. The construction of advanced forms of houses.
6. The making of good highways.
7. The smelting of metals.
8. The use of pictographs or letters.

The Indians of Mexico, Central America, and the Andes were well advanced in all these categories at the time of Columbus' discovery of America. But the picture changes as we come north. For whatever reason, the Indians of the northeastern United States fell short of the southern Indians and of the Europeans.

It does not appear to have been lack of initiative or ingenuity that held them back. It was rather the smallness of their population. They had not yet developed a city life, which, with its commerce and book-keeping, is the usual spur to the invention of a written language. Pennsylvania's Indians made no use of metals, and their only domestic animal was a wolflike dog. There was in fact little need or opportunity to domesticate other animals. There were no wild horses in America; wild sheep and the Rocky Mountain goat were to be found in the West and vast herds of bison roamed the plains, but in Pennsylvania there were no sheep or goats and the bison was rare. Where bison were plentiful they were easier hunted in the wild than cared for in captivity, and this was true of animals in general. Furthermore, Indians had little use for draft animals: they had no commerce in bulky goods and their agricultural work was done with the hoe rather than the plow. Even if there had been animals that in course of time might have been bred to domesticity like European cattle, good pasturage in Pennsylvania (before the introduction of "English grass") was not everywhere available.

> The woodland pasturage was soon exhausted [writes Stevenson Whitcomb Fletcher]. It was mostly of coarse species, principally wild rye (*Elymus* sp.) and broom straw (*Andropogon* sp.). Grazing prevented these from re-seeding....Cattle might eke out a meager existence on tree and brush browse, particularly red maple, but this was a desperate expedient.[1]

On the other hand, the Indians were far advanced in the raising of cereals. Their corn was so highly domesticated that it could not seed

[1] *Pennsylvania Agriculture and Country Life, 1640-1840* (Harrisburg, 1950), 154.

itself but had to be planted anew each year. Their houses were well constructed. Their paths, though unpaved, were well routed for distant travel by moccasined men and women. As for irrigation, they had little need of it, the population being small and water abundant.

Their most serious handicap may have been the absence of a written language. They had pictographs, it is true. On the inner bark of peeled trees their pictographs recorded simple events such as the exploits of hunters and warriors. For this purpose they used conventional figures which everyone, whatever his tribe or language, could understand. When woven into wampum belts, pictographs assisted the memory. They helped recall the terms of treaties. But such methods were not capable of preserving the exact information on which science depends nor of conveying ideas from age to age with any precision.

When the white man came, the Indian was quick to see the superiority of metal tools and at once set about getting them. The fur trade, which was his means to that end, all but ruined him, as we shall see. When he came to himself and developed, as the Cherokees did, a written language of his own, it was too late. The white man, impatient as man has always been with those who are a little behind in the race for material goods, brushed him aside, as we see in the "Trail of Tears": the forcible removal of the Cherokees from Georgia in 1838.

Pennsylvania's Indians, when the white man arrived, were in that stage of development which archaeologists call the Woodland Epoch. They lived in towns, made good pottery, dressed in soft and beautifully decorated leather garments, and expressed an artistic instinct in the carving of ornaments, the weaving of feather blankets, and the singing and dancing that accompanied their imaginative religious ritual. They had developed, moreover, a system of social restraints which, except for the cruelties committed during war, produced a high degree of gentleness and harmony in their relations with one another.

In the clash between the races, atrocities were committed on both sides, a circumstance that has colored social attitudes ever since. It is well for white men, as they read about the early American Indians (and people in other parts of the world now emerging from centuries of thoughtless exploitation by white men), to heed the advice of Dr. Hartley Burr Alexander in his preface to *The World's Rim:*

> We judge our own humanity by its white pages, not by its black, especially when we are concerned with what most gives us courage to live or what most deeply explains our understanding of life. We should assess the thought of another race by stand-

7

ards no less generous, nor can our hope for humanity anywhere rest upon a lesser truth.[2]

[2] (Lincoln, Nebraska, 1953), xi.

2

The Susquehannocks and Their Western Neighbors

AT THE OPENING of the seventeenth century, several distinct Indian peoples inhabited the three great river valleys of what is now Pennsylvania:

1. On the Delaware River the Lenape or Delaware Indians occupied the lands south of the Blue or Kittatinny Mountain, and a kindred people, the Munsee or Minisink Indians, had their home north of the Delaware Water Gap.

2. On the Susquehanna River the Susquehannocks (also called Minquas or Andastes) held the lands below the mountain and had formerly lived higher up on the North Branch.

3. On the upper Ohio the situation is obscure, for the original residents were destroyed or driven out before white explorers visited the region; but traces of palisaded villages,

in southwestern Pennsylvania especially, prove their existence. Lacking any certain names for these Indians, students refer to them as the "Monongahela people." Another group important to Pennsylvania history, but living at that time outside her geographical limits, was the Iroquois, the Five Nations. Their territory lay to the north, extending in a belt across upstate New York from the Hudson to the Genesee by way of the Mohawk River and the Finger Lakes.

We shall leave the Delawares for more detailed study in later chapters, while we discuss here briefly the Susquehannocks and their western neighbors.

The Susquehannocks

When in 1608 John Smith sailed up the Susquehanna River to the fall line (Deposit, Maryland), he met there a body of sixty Susquehannock warriors. At his invitation, they had made the two-day journey from their settlement near present Washington Boro in Lancaster County, Pennsylvania. He left a lively account of his impressions of that meeting. If it be read with a little caution (Smith did not lie, but he leaned over backward to avoid understatement), it is an excellent introduction to these people, who had as yet been little touched by the presence of white men on this continent.

> But to proceed, 60 of those Sasquesahanocks came to the discoverers with skins, Bowes, Arrowes, Targets, Beads, Swords, and Tobacco pipes for presents. Such great and well proportioned men, are seldome seene, for they seemed like Giants to the English, yea and to the neighbours: yet seemed of an honest and simple disposition, with much adoe restrained from adoring the discoverers as Gods. Those are the most strange people of all those Countries, both in language and attire; for their language it may well beseeme their proportions, sounding from them, as it were a great voice in a vault, or cave, as an Eccho. Their attire is the skinnes of Beares and Woolves, some have Cassacks made of Beares heades and skinnes that a mans necke goes through the skinnes neck, and the eares of the beare fastned to his shoulders behind, the nose and teeth hanging downe his breast, and at the end of the nose hung a Beares Pawe: the halfe sleeves comming to the elbowes were the neckes of Beares and the armes through the mouth, with pawes hanging at their noses. One had the head of a Woolfe hanging in a chaine for a Jewell; his Tobacco pipe 3 quarters of a yard long, prettily carved with a Bird, a Beare, a Deare, or some such devise at the great end, sufficient to beat out the braines of a man: with bowes, and arrowes, and clubs, sutable to their greatnesse and conditions. . . . They can make neere 600 able and mighty

men, and are pallisadoed in their Townes to defend them from the Massawomekes their mortall enimies. 5 of their chiefe Werowances came aboard the discoverers, and crossed the Bay in their Barge. The picture of the greatest of them is signified in the Mappe. The calfe of whose leg was 3 quarters of a yard about: and all the rest of his limbes so answerable to that proportion, that he seemed the goodliest man that ever we beheld. His haire, the one side was long, the other shore close with a ridge over his crown like a cocks combe. His arrowes were five quarters [of a yard] long, headed with flints or splinters of stones, in forme like a heart, an inch broad, and an inch and a halfe or more long. These hee wore in a woolves skinne at his backe for his quiver, his bow in the one hand and his clubbe in the other, as is described.[1]

Like the great Elizabethans, of which company he was a belated member, Captain John Smith (1579-1631) was intoxicated with words. We must not expect his measurements to tally exactly with those of science. A man's calf that tapes twenty-seven inches owes something to the imagination. But it is a mistake to think him an impostor. (See Marshall Fishwick's article, "Was John Smith a Liar?" in *American Heritage*, October, 1958.) Smith did actually see the things he said he did. But, in order to make his readers see them, he splashed down lively impressions in a manner that betrays the artist as well as the adventurer. When he likened the speech of these warriors to a great voice sounding in a vault, he was trying to share the excitement he had felt when listening to a flow of language so different from the clipped English speech he was familiar with. He used a simile that comes to our own minds today when, at Onondaga, let us say, we hear a kindred Iroquoian tongue spoken by a people who love language. When he tells us that these well-proportioned men "seemed like Giants to the English," we need not take him to mean (as an early historian of Maryland, George Alsop, did in 1666) that they were seven feet tall. Susquehannock graves give no indication that these people were tall according to modern standards.

[1] Lyon G. Tyler (ed.), *Narratives of Early Virginia, 1606-1625* (New York, 1907), 87-89.

11

The Susquehannocks lived in stockaded villages, each headed by a chief. Their typical longhouse, like that of the Iroquois north of them, was from sixty to eighty feet in length, having a door at each end, a corridor down the middle, and bunks lining the sides. Each family (mother, father, and children) lived round a hearth in the corridor, with a smoke hole above it. Several families occupied the longhouse, being separated from each other by bark partitions between the bunks.

In contrast to Europeans, the Susquehannocks and other Indians of Pennsylvania had a "matriarchal" society. That is, they traced descent through the mother, not the father. Married men lived with their wives' families. All the "fires" or families in a longhouse were under the authority of an elder matron.

John Smith called these people "Sasquesahanocks." That was not the name they gave themselves, but one John Smith apparently picked up from his Indian interpreter. It derives from the name of the river itself, which according to Delaware Indians meant "muddy river," a term more suited to its lower courses than to the parts most familiar to Pennsylvanians.[2]

Other names have been given them. The Delaware Indians called them *Minquas*—a name they applied to Iroquoian peoples generally—, meaning "treacherous." This name was adopted by early Dutch and Swedish settlers. (As *Mingo* it was later applied to Iroquois Indians—not Susquehannocks—living in the Ohio country.)

The French called the Susquehannocks *Andastes* and *Gandastogues* ("people of the blackened ridge pole"). The name *Gandastogues* has been preserved in such Lancaster County names as Conestoga Indian Town, Conestoga Manor, Conestoga Creek, and the Conestoga wagon.

In his map of Virginia, 1612, John Smith showed six towns: Sasquesahanough (the town from which came the warriors he met), Quadroque, Attaock, Tesinigh, Utchowig, Cepowig, but this may reflect some misunderstanding: The last two names seem to refer to "mountain" and "river." All that it is safe to say is that in 1608 there were Susquehannocks living in a large town, Sasquesahanough, on the east side of the Susquehanna River at Washington Boro, Pennsylvania, about half a mile north of a low-water ford (later known as the Blue Rock Ford) which crossed the river, here a mile and three quarters wide, to a point above the mouth of Canadochly Creek. From this place trails ran west to the Potomac and the Monongahela.

The Susquehannocks were an alert, well-organized, military people, and great traders. Driven from the North Branch by their Iroquois

[2]Paul A. W. Wallace (ed.), *Thirty Thousand Miles with John Heckewelder* (Pittsburgh, 1958), 369.

12

neighbors, they established themselves on the lower Susquehanna in a very advantageous situation for trade with European settlers on Delaware and Chesapeake bays. According to current archaeological evidence, a large Susquehannock community such as John Smith described had existed on the lower Susquehanna as early as 1580. They also had a settlement on the upper Potomac River, their hunting and trading activities extended into the Ohio country, and they were in touch with the Huron people in Ontario. In 1669 Iroquois Indians warned the French that if they tried to descend the Ohio River they would be in danger from the "Andastes."

The Susquehannocks differed sharply from the Delawares in that they possessed a superior political and military tradition. In this respect they were like the Five Nations north of them and the Hurons still farther north. These three nations were members of the Iroquoian linguistic family, whose territory extended in an unbroken block from Lake Huron to Chesapeake Bay and also included the related Tuscaroras (who later joined the Iroquois) in North Carolina and the less closely related Cherokees in the southern mountains. The Hurons (Wyandots) with their affiliated tribes (Petun or Tobacco Nation, Neutral, and Wenro) held the land from the Georgian Bay to Niagara and a little beyond. The Iroquois Confederacy controlled the territory between Lake Ontario and, roughly, the northern bounds of what is now Pennsylvania. The Susquehannocks at one time or another commanded a large part of the drainage area of the Susquehanna River, both the North and West Branches. When the fur trade developed, these three Iroquoian powers—Huron, Iroquois, Susquehannock— were able to cut off the coastal tribes, whose forest wealth of fur-bearing animals was soon exhausted, from the rich hunting lands of the interior, and so to seize the position of middlemen in the trade.

The story of the ensuing Beaver Wars, during the course of which the Susquehannocks were driven out of Pennsylvania (to reappear later in a small band of so-called Conestogas), will be found in Chapter 13.

THE MONONGAHELA PEOPLE

The early Indian groups in the upper Ohio Valley and northward to Lake Erie are very poorly known. Dutch and Swedish settlers who traded with the "Minquas" on the Susquehanna also had some contact with the "Black Minquas" who lived beyond the mountains; and the French in Canada knew of the Eries or Cat Nation who lived somewhere on the south side of Lake Erie. Any connection between these little known people and the village sites in the valleys of the Monongahela and the Ohio-lower Allegheny is so far unproved; but archaeological study of those sites provides our fullest and most precise knowledge of the Indians who once lived there, and since no tribal identification can be made, we shall follow the archaeologists' example in referring to these early residents as "Monongahela people."

Whoever they were, whatever their relation to Indians known in recorded history, the culture of the Monongahela people was evidently derived in part from the highly developed Indians of the Mississippi Valley. To judge from the graves, post molds, and refuse pits of the Monongahela people, they were the most highly advanced Indians known to have inhabited the upper Ohio Valley. They had disappeared before anyone came to record their institutions; but archaeologists have been at work, and some of the externals of their culture have been described by Dr. William J. Mayer-Oakes in his *Prehistory of the Upper Ohio Valley.*[3]

The Monongahela people lived in stockaded villages, situated often in commanding positions on hilltops. Within the stockade, dome-shaped (beehive) houses were arranged in a rough circle. House construction was simple. Saplings were driven into the ground in a circle about twenty feet in diameter. The tops were bent inward till the ends met and were lashed together. The frame was then covered with bark or mats made of rushes.

These people lived by agriculture, their diet being supplemented by hunting and fishing. The staple foods were the traditional Three Sisters: corn, beans, and squash. Attached to the houses were post-lined storage pits where dried corn and other foods were preserved, either to tide over emergencies or, in good times, to provide leisure for the food gatherers. Boiled victuals, of which their meals chiefly consisted, were eaten out of pottery bowls. Spoons for this purpose were made of elk antlers.

That they were an artistic people is seen in the many handsome stone and pottery tobacco pipes of which fragments have been found, and in well-designed ornaments of shell, stone, pottery, bone, or even cannel coal.

Of their political and social organization we know nothing with any certainty. We do not know what name they gave themselves, what language they spoke, nor what divisions there were among them.

Their trail, after they disappeared from these parts, has never been picked up. We do not know whether they moved away of their own choice or were wiped out by war or disease. Some think they may

[3](Pittsburgh, 1955).

14

have been destroyed by epidemics originating with white men. The Indians had established no immunity to European diseases and were defenseless against measles, smallpox, syphilis, and tuberculosis. Such diseases, brought by ships touching on the Atlantic coast, spread like forest fires into the interior, wiping out whole tribes that had not yet even been "discovered."

Others think the Monongahela people may have been destroyed by the Susquehannocks from the east or by the Senecas from the north. It is possible that the long war between the Susquehannocks and the Iroquois (of whom the Senecas were a part) for the furs of the Ohio Valley may have made this middle ground untenable by neutrals.

The important thing to remember is that the disappearance of these people during the early years of the seventeenth century left whole sections of western Pennsylvania bare of inhabitants. When the Iroquois-Susquehannock war was over, these lands were occupied by bands of other Indians, among them the Delawares and Shawnees who had been pushed out of their homes in eastern Pennsylvania.

THE BLACK MINQUAS

The Dutch and Swedes, who commonly referred to the Susquehannocks as Minquas, traded also with the "Black Minquas" ("who are thus named because they wear a black badge on their breast, and not because they are really black"), whose special importance was that they could supply beaver pelts, which were in dwindling supply near the settlements. In 1653 the Swedish governor reported a decline in the trade "since the Arrigahaga [Eries] and Susquahannoer (from whom the beavers come) begin to fight one another"; but in 1662 the Minquas reported that two hundred of the Black Minquas had come to help them against the Iroquois. Augustin Herrman's map of Virginia and Maryland, dated 1670, contains fuller but still vague information: The "Black Minquas" lived beyond the mountains on "a very great River," almost certainly the Allegheny-Ohio, from a branch of which they had a portage to a branch of the Susquehanna; "but the Sasquahana and Sinnecus [Seneca] Indians went over and destroyed that very great Nation." That there were some survivors of this destruction, however, appears from a report received in Maryland in 1681 that a "Nation called the black Mingoes are joined with the . . . Sinniquos."

THE ERIES

South of Lake Erie was the home of a people known to the French as the Eriehronon or Cat Nation—named, not for the wildcat as commonly supposed, but for the raccoon (as some think) or the panther. The Eries were of Iroquoian stock, related to the Hurons and Susquehannocks as well as to the Senecas and other members of the Iroquois Confederacy. Little is known about them except their impact on other peoples. No white man visited their country until after their dispersion in 1655-1656, but the Jesuit missionaries received reports about them from the Hurons, Neutrals, and Senecas.

We do not know whether they were a single nation, a confederacy, or a neighborhood of separate peoples thrown together by the chance of war. The location of their towns and the extent of their hunting grounds are matters much discussed by historians, archaeologists, ethnologists, and linguists. But we know that they were an entity of some kind with a geographical base, and that the Iroquois conquered them in 1655-1656.

Our only clues to their home come to us from the French, who did not themselves know the country. In 1648, the Jesuit Relation records that "This lake, called Erie, was formerly inhabited on its southern shores by certain tribes whom we call the Nation of the Cat; they have been compelled to retire far inland to escape their enemies, who are farther to the west." Note that the Eries are not described as a single, unified tribe, that they no longer lived on the lake shore, and that their enemies, living farther west, could not then have been the Iroquois. By 1654 they and the Iroquois were at war, however; and the story of an Iroquois war party that arrived at an Erie town in canoes that they used as ladders to scale the palisade offers a tantalizing possible clue to the town's location. By 1656 the Eries were conquered or dispersed; but as late as 1682 a Jesuit missionary at Onondaga reported that six hundred of the Cat Nation had voluntarily surrendered to the Iroquois.

While there are obvious parallels between the histories of the Black Minquas and the Eries (both Iroquoian peoples), this does not prove that they are the same people, but it does suggest that the names may overlap. The relation, if any, between them and the Monongahela people remains unknown.

We conclude this brief description of the Eries with a passage from Father François Le Mercier, dated September 21, 1654:

> They [the Iroquois] informed us that a fresh war had broken out against them, and thrown them all into a state of alarm; that the Ehriehronnons were arming against them (these we call the Cat Nation . . . .). They informed us that a village

16

of Sonnontoehronnon Iroquois had been already taken and set on fire at their first approach . . . . They declared, in a word, that all the four Nations of the upper Iroquois were on fire; that they were leaguing together, and arming to repulse this enemy. . . .

. . . .

The Cat Nation is very populous, having been reinforced by some Hurons, who scattered in all directions when their country was laid waste, and who now have stirred up this war which is filling the Iroquois with alarm. Two thousand men are reckoned upon, well skilled in war, although they have no firearms. Notwithstanding this, they fight like Frenchmen, bravely sustaining the first discharge of the Iroquois, who are armed with our muskets, and then falling upon them with a hail-storm of poisoned arrows, which they discharge eight or ten times before a musket can be reloaded.[4]

[4] Reuben Gold Thwaites (ed.), *The Jesuit Relations and Allied Documents*, 73 vols. (Cleveland, 1896-1901), XLI, 81, 83.

3

The Delawares:
Physical Appearance and Dress

THE LENNI LENAPE or Delaware Indians were a loose confederation of Algonkian bands which, at the opening of the seventeenth century, occupied a continuous territory from Delaware Bay to
the Blue (or Kittatinny) Mountain and from the Atlantic coast to the
Delaware-Susquehanna watershed. Their lands included most of
present Delaware, all of New Jersey south of the Raritan River, and, in
Pennsylvania, the Delaware River drainage area south of the Blue
Mountain. Their nearest neighbors, who also spoke Algonkian lan-
guages, were the closely related Munsees on the upper Delaware, the
Wappingers (or Opies) on the lower Hudson River, the Mahicans
farther up the Hudson, and some small groups on Long Island. (Some
of these neighbors, Munsees especially, later joined with the Delawares.) The Nanticokes, in Maryland, were their southern neighbors.
The destruction of the Susquehannocks in 1675 opened the way for the
Delawares—those in Pennsylvania especially—to make settlements on
the Susquehanna and to supersede their former neighbors in the fur
trade.

The Delawares called themselves Lenape, "real people" (Lenni

Lenape is a more emphatic form). Their popular name derives from that of the river, so called by the English in honor of the Baron De La Warr, first governor of Virginia. Unacquainted with tribal divisions and names, early explorers referred to the regional natives as "Delaware River Indians." Shortened to "Delaware Indians" and then to "Delawares," the name continued to be used for these people, even after they were far removed from the Delaware River.

PENN'S DESCRIPTION OF THE DELAWARES

The first good description of the Delawares comes from William Penn's letter to the Free Society of Traders in 1683. He was writing in a more scientific age than Captain John Smith's, and after much longer and closer observation of the Delawares than Smith had had of the Susquehannocks. Penn's account, though enthusiastic, is discriminating. In the following selected passages he gives us his early impressions of the Delawares, their outward appearance and inner qualities, their sports, and their dining habits. It is a more penetrating appraisal than the speed and ease of the style might suggest, and it will serve as a good general introduction to these people as they were nearly three hundred years ago:

> For their Persons, they are generally tall, streight, well-built, and of singular Proportion; they tread strong and clever, and mostly walk with a lofty Chin: Of Complexion, Black, but by design, as the Gypsies in England: They grease themselves with Bears-fat clarified, and using no defence against Sun or Weather, their skins must needs be swarthy; Their Eye is little and black, not unlike a straight-look't Jew: The thick Lip and flat Nose, so frequent with the East-Indians and Blacks, are not common to them; for I have seen as comely European-like faces among them of both, as on your side the Sea; and truly an Italian Complexion hath not much more of the White, and the Noses of several of them have as much of the Roman.

When Penn came to deal with them, he was impressed by two things, their revengefulness and their open-hearted generosity:

> . . . They are great Concealers of their own Resentments, brought to it, I believe, by the Revenge that hath been practised among them; in either of these, they are not exceeded by the Italians. . . .
> . . . But in Liberality they excell, nothing is too good for their friend; give them a fine Gun, Coat, or other thing, it may pass twenty hands, before it sticks; light of Heart, strong Affections, but soon spent; the most merry Creatures that live, Feast and Dance perpetually; they never have much, nor want much:

19

Wealth circulateth like the Blood, all parts partake; and though none shall want what another hath, yet exact Observers of Property. Some Kings have sold, others presented me with several parcels of Land; the Pay or Presents I made them, were not hoarded by the particular Owners. . . . We sweat and toil to live; their pleasure feeds them, I mean, their Hunting, Fishing and Fowling, and this Table is spread every where; they eat twice a day, Morning and Evening; their Seats and Table are the Ground.[1]

At the time Penn wrote those words, the Delawares had been in contact with white men for some seventy-five years, and in close contact for almost sixty, the Dutch having built Fort Nassau opposite the mouth of the Schuylkill in 1624. During that time the material culture of the Delawares had undergone some change. The use of English cloth, tools, and weapons had become common. Yet it is doubtful if their inner culture had changed much from what it was in 1608 or even 1497, when John Cabot first saw the coast of North America.

In bodily appearance and clothing the eastern Indians of whatever tribe were all very much alike. There were some differences in dress, especially in the matter of ornamentation, which served to identify the wearer's nationality. But fashions in clothing were international then as they are now. In describing Delaware costume and physique, therefore, we are describing most Indians of this area.

PHYSIQUE

David Zeisberger in the winter of 1780-1781 described the North American Indians as of medium height. On the other hand, Francis Daniel Pastorius (founder of Germantown), writing in the 1690's, said, "They are generally tall of stature,"[2] and a great many other early travelers said the same. If these latter are right, it does not mean that the Indians of three hundred years ago were taller than most Americans are today. It means only that the white man since that time has added several inches to his stature, thanks very largely to an improved diet. In the old days the Indian's diet was probably better (in quality if not in quantity) than the white man's. But the white man has now caught up.

The Indians differed little from Europeans in their anatomy, but they had finer bones, a lighter frame. They were broad-shouldered

[1] Albert Cook Myers (ed.), *Narratives of Early Pennsylvania, West New Jersey, and Delaware, 1630-1707* (New York, 1912), 230, 232-33.
[2] *Ibid.*, 433.

20

and strong, but their muscles were smoother and more gracile. They were slender-waisted, wiry, quick on their feet, and capable of long endurance as well as of sudden bursts of energy.

They had broad cheekbones and well-shaped but usually not prominent noses, in this differing from the hawk-nosed Indians of the Plains. Their eyes were dark. Their hair was black and straight. Like the gypsies, they were brown-skinned. "Redskin" is a misnomer. "Some are light brown," wrote Zeisberger, "hardly to be distinguished from a brown European, did not their eyes and hair betray them."[3]

CLOTHING

Delaware clothing was simple and less out of key with modern taste than with Victorian. The men wore a belt, a breechclout (equivalent to our bathing trunks), and moccasins—in summer as a rule, nothing more. Small children wore nothing at all.

The belt was made of deerskin or wampum, sometimes highly decorated. The breechclout was a length of soft deerskin passed under the body between the legs, brought up inside the belt, and folded out over it so as to hang down, front and back, like a small apron. The moccasins were of laced deerskin, decorated with porcupine quills and wampum. For cool weather there were other vestments. A robe made of skins—deer, bear, beaver, raccoon—or even of woven turkey and goose feathers, was thrown over the shoulder: sometimes over both shoulders, but more commonly over the left shoulder only, in order to leave the right arm free. The upper ends were tied together. The robe was worn with the fur next to the body in winter, outside in warm weather. In sewing skins together for a long garment, care was taken to set the hair all one way so that the rain would run off.

In place of the robe, or under it, a deerskin jacket might be worn. It reached a little below the knee. Leggings of fringed buckskin fastened with thongs to the waist-belt descended from above the knee to below the ankle.

These garments, decorated with designs in wampum (shell beads) or porcupine quills, made a handsome wardrobe. The gaudy green, red, blue, and black blankets which the white trader introduced made at best a cheap substitute.

Women's clothing was much like the men's except that the women wore a knee-length skirt, made by folding a rectangular piece of deerskin over the waist-belt and doubling it on the right side. Ornaments

---

[3] David Zeisberger, "A History of the Indians," *Ohio Archaeological and Historical Society Quarterly*, XIX (1910), 12.

of deer antlers and wampum hung round the neck, wrist, and ankle. In later years, the trader's brass and silver trinkets were much prized, and Indian women wore little bells round their ankles and silver trinkets that tinkled as they walked.

Among the Indians there was little or no "keeping up with the Joneses," yet they took pride in their personal appearance. The vermilion pot with its bright red paint, shell tweezers for pulling out hair on the face, and bear's grease for the hair and for the body were household necessities. In northwestern Pennsylvania, petroleum (later known as Seneca Oil) was used as an ointment. Bear's grease and petroleum had an odor unpleasant to Europeans, but it must not be thought that the early Indians were a filthy people. They kept themselves cleaner than most white men of that day. Delaware young people were accustomed to a daily swim in the stream; and their elders, when tired or ill, took steam baths in a "sweat lodge" to restore them. Well or ill, they seldom let a week go by without one or two visits to the sweat lodge.

Dressing the Hair

Women let their hair grow long. George Henry Loskiel, the Moravian, writing in the late eighteenth century, tells us that in his day nothing was more shameful for a woman than to have her hair cut off. "The Delaware women," he wrote, "never plait their hair, but fold and tie it round with a piece of cloth. Some tie it behind, then roll it up, and wrap a ribband or the skin of a serpent round it, so as almost to resemble a bag-wig."[4]

In earlier times they used deerskin and wampum rather than cloth and ribbon on their hair. To give hair a gloss, they applied bear's grease.

The Scalp Lock

The men, wrote Loskiel, "never suffer their hair to grow long, and some even pull so much of it out by the roots, that a little only remains round the crown of the head, forming a round crest, of about two inches in diameter."[5] That was the scalp lock. It was carefully tended in time of war as a symbol of manhood and a defiance to the enemy. Even in peacetime, and especially in preparation for a dance, it was

[4] *History of the Mission of the United Brethren Among the Indians in North America*, 3 vols. (London, 1794), I, 52.
[5] *Ibid.*, 48.

22

not unusual for a young man to shave his head with a sharp flint stone or to pluck out the hairs.

Fashions in scalp locks differed from tribe to tribe. Men might be neglectful of them during a period of peace, but on the approach of war scalp locks appeared everywhere. Men shaved their heads and greased the lock to make it stand erect. When they "put the plume on," an eagle plume, that was equivalent to mobilization. The eagle plume was not the long feather worn for decoration, but a fluffy white spray. It was believed that this would confer the eagle's courage on anyone who wore it.

THE BEARD

Indians with beards were rare but not unknown. Hair grew sparsely on their faces. They got rid of what little they had by taking a pair of mussel shells which had been sharpened on a stone and pulling the hair out by the roots. John Heckewelder, a Moravian missionary who lived among the Delawares for many years during the second half of the eighteenth century, has given us a vivid picture of the process:

> This they do in a very quick manner, much like the plucking of a fowl, and the oftener they pluck out their hair, the finer it grows afterwards, so that at last there appears hardly any, the whole having been rooted out. The principal reasons which they give for thus plucking out their beards and the hair next to their foreheads, are that they may have a clean skin to lay the paint on, when they dress for their festivals or dances, and to facilitate the *tattooing* themselves, a custom formerly much in use among them, especially with those who had distinguished themselves by their valour, and acquired celebrity. They say that either painting or tattooing on a hairy face or body would have a disgusting appearance.[6]

FEATHERS

Long feathers were worn by men in the hair for adornment. The number of feathers and the angle at which they were worn are said to have indicated the tribe a man belonged to. The Delawares usually wore only one or two feathers in the headdress, never the Siouan war bonnet with its showy circlet and tail, which today is mistakenly assumed to have been worn by all Indians. Women did not wear feathers at all in their hair.

Feathers were frequently put to more practical use. "They also make

[6] *History, Manners, and Customs of the Indian Nations Who Once Inhabited Pennsylvania and the Neighbouring States* (Philadelphia, 1876), 205.

very fine and beautiful quilts of painted bird feathers," wrote Peter Lindeström in his *Geographia Americae* (based on notes made by him, 1654-1655). "In the first place they tie them with meshes like nets, yet very fine; then they fasten the feathers in the meshes, so neat and strong that not one feather can come loose from it. . . ."[7] This work was usually done by old people, requiring as it did the patience and dexterity by which age compensated for loss of youthful ardor.

FACE PAINTING

Painting the face was a universal custom among both men and women. Every color they used had a special meaning. White was a symbol of peace; black of evil, grief, and death. Warriors streaked their faces with black and sent black wampum to their allies as a summons to war.

Women, Loskiel tells us, liked to paint a round red spot on each cheek. They also reddened their eyelids, and sometimes used red on the rims of their ears and on their temples. Nice women were restrained in the use of paint, but men of all sorts laid it on thick. "Every one follows his own fancy," wrote Loskiel, "and exerts his powers of invention, to excel others, and have something peculiar to himself. One prides himself with the figure of a serpent upon each cheek, another with that of a tortoise, deer, bear, or some other creature, as his arms and signature."[8]

"Here and there," wrote Zeisberger, "black spots may be introduced, or they paint one-half of their head and face black, the other red."[9]

John Heckewelder tells of an Indian friend who painted his face so ingeniously that, when seen from one side, his head looked like an eagle with round, pointed beak, while from the other it seemed to be the snout of an open-jawed pike.

In wartime, black was applied on a vermilion base to both face and body in bars and zigzags. Sometimes a warrior's eyes were circled in black to make him more fearsome. Streaking the face with black was a ritual preparation for war, public or private. Mushemeelin blacked himself thus before killing Jack Armstrong at the Juniata Narrows (since that time known as Jack's Narrows) near present Mount Union, Pennsylvania.

Dr. Frank G. Speck has told us that "The proper native source of red for face painting, which the Delawares believe to have been created

[7] Peter M. Lindeström, *Geographia Americae, with an Account of the Delaware Indians* . . . (Philadelphia, 1925), 221-22.
[8] *History of the Mission*, I, 49.
[9] "History of the Indians," 87.

for their use by the Great Spirit, is Blood-root (Sanguinaria cana-densis)."[10] Loskiel noted that "Near the river Muskingum a yellow ochre is found, which, when burnt, makes a beautiful red color."[11] Wood ash or black shale, such as is found (and still used as a paint base) in the old Indian quarry near Muncy, Pennsylvania, was a common source for black paint.

TATTOOING

The process of tattooing [wrote Heckewelder], which I once saw performed, is quickly done, and does not seem to give much pain. They have poplar bark in readiness burnt and reduced to a powder, the figures that are to be tattooed are marked or designed on the skin; the operator . . . quickly pricks over the whole so that blood is drawn, then a coat of this powder is laid and left on to dry. Before the whites came into this country, they scarified themselves for this purpose with sharp flint stones, or pricked themselves with the sharp teeth of a fish.[12]

The face was tattooed as well as the body. Most men were content to carry on their persons simple pictures of animals, birds, and snakes. A certain famous Munsee warrior, on the other hand, made his skin portray the story of his whole adventurous life. Heckewelder describes it thus: "Besides that his body was full of scars, where he had been struck and pierced by the arrows of the enemy, there was not a spot to be seen, on that part of it which was exposed to view, but what was tattooed over with some drawing relative to his achievements"—a spectacle which, in its total effect, "struck the beholder with amazement and terror."[13]

The same warrior, who in his middle years became a Christian and was baptized by the Moravians under the name of "Michael," made a striking end. Loskiel writes:

The serenity of his countenance, when laid in his coffin, made a singular contrast with the figures, scarified upon his face when a warrior. These were as follows: upon the right cheek and temple, a large snake; from the under-lip a pole passed over the nose, and between the eyes to the top of his forehead, ornamented at every quarter of an inch with round marks, representing scalps: upon the left cheek, two lances crossing each other; and upon the lower jaw the head of a wild boar. All these figures were executed with remarkable neatness.[14]

[10] *A Study of the Delaware Indian Big House Ceremony* (Harrisburg, 1931), 71.
[11] *History of the Mission*, I, 49.
[12] *History, Manners, and Customs*, 206.
[13] *Ibid.*
[14] *History of the Mission*, II, 189.

25

Nose and Ear Decoration

Some Indians pierced the nose and wore, suspended below the nostrils, a piece of wampum, a pearl, or a sparkling stone. The Senecas, especially, liked that kind of finery. Andrew Hesselius wrote in his diary for August 23, 1721:

> Among all the sorts of adornments I saw at any time worn by the savages of [the] five nations, no one is more absurd than the nose ornaments used by these Senikoes. The gristle between the nostrils they have bored through, and in this hole they have a small piece of brass wire in form of a ring from which they suspend a flat three-cornered sebano-stone [wampum bead] downwards of a breadth of two fingers. This stone is unceasingly dangling right before their mouth and the lips [so] that they cannot eat or drink without the greatest inconvenience unless they are to hold up the stone with one hand.[15]

The Delawares did not practice nose cutting, but it was fashionable among them to cut their ears. Indians have naturally long and well-

shaped ears. Like the ancient Chinese artists who idealized their portraits by lengthening this feature, the Delawares tried to outdo nature by distending and cutting the ear lobes, as may be seen in St. Mémin's crayon portrait of a Delaware Indian. To the loose ends they attached pearls, feathers, flowers, and other such ornaments.

Cutting the ears was a painful operation, often ending in serious disfigurement. In summer the ear strips and loops might be torn by the bushes; in winter they were apt to be frozen and to drop off. Until late in the eighteenth century, after the fashion of ear cutting had been discontinued, Indians with torn ears were a common sight.

[15] Notes on a Visit to America, Am 211, Historical Society of Pennsylvania, Philadelphia.

4

Delaware Villages and Houses

THE INDIANS OF PENNSYLVANIA, when the white man first knew them, were not nomads. Agriculture, the foundation of their society, attached them to the soil. Their cereal diet was supplemented, it is true, by fish, flesh, and fowl. That, in the absence of domestic herds, gave importance to the hunter. But before the coming of the white man, who created a demand for European goods and a fur trade (monstrous in its effects on native life) to satisfy it, the small hunting territories adjoining every village sufficed to meet each family's needs. Hunting, therefore, caused little disruption of normal living.

The Delaware confederation being very loose, the effective unit of government was the self-contained local community, which consisted of one or two small villages. In all Indian life the local community was important; among the Delawares it was supreme.

Unlike the Iroquois, the Delawares do not appear to have lived in palisaded towns. Their villages or hamlets were open, each containing perhaps half a dozen houses, sometimes in clusters, more often scattered over a comparatively wide area.

27

In choosing a village site, the Delawares looked for three things: a good water supply, good drainage, and warmth for the winter. They liked their homes to be near a lake or navigable stream, facing the sun on gently sloping river bottom lands or terraces above flood level. They did not occupy their villages all year round. There were seasonal migrations, each family having its town and country house. Early in October, for instance, the men, sometimes accompanied by their wives, went off to cabins in their family hunting territories. These extended back from the village or from some well-known landmark as far, it might be, "as a man walks in a day" or a day and a half.

Such seasonal movements can be followed fairly closely. In spring there was planting to attend to in the small fields adjoining the village. In June and July, the men went into the woods for deer hunting. They were back in time for harvest and the Green Corn Festival. In September and October, they moved again to the hunting territory and remained there, on and off, for the winter. In January, deer hunting gave way to bear, fox, beaver, and raccoon hunting. In February, when the sap began to run, those fortunate enough to be in the sugar maple country, moved into the sugar bush, whole families together, selecting sites for sugar-boiling camps. In March or April, there was pigeon nesting. Back they all came to the village in time for spring planting.

The village was quiet during the day, few sounds being heard except that of women pounding corn in wooden mortars—a daily task—or the howl of an Indian dog. This latter was of a primitive breed, now extinct, which, though a true dog, did not bark, but howled like a wolf.

At night from the houses came the sound of voices engaged in storytelling or conversation. The Indians were past masters in the art of conversation, which provided entertainment and their best means of self-improvement. The voices were quiet, and one seldom heard the sharp dissonance of interruptions, such as is usual in white society. The Indians loved talking, and they often sat up all night over it.

Some evenings, when the villagers had gathered for a "social dance," a latecomer might hear from a distance the pad of "stomping" feet (a soft sound, not to be confused with the more boisterous "stamping"), together with the pulse of the turtle rattle and the wistful, haunting melodies of songs the women sang in accompaniment.

Agriculture gave a measure of permanence to Delaware village life, but exhaustion of the soil (corn is very hard on it) and depletion of the firewood made it necessary every now and then to move the village. Among the Susquehannocks and Iroquois, who lived in large towns and cultivated the soil more intensively, a move was necessary every ten or twenty years. The same came to be true of the Delawares after they had left Pennsylvania and set up large communities in Ohio. But it is doubtful if the Delawares in their early homeland on the Delaware River needed to move so often. Not only were their villages smaller than those of the Iroquois and with houses farther apart, but the Delawares fertilized their soil with fish scrap, fish being abundant in their home waters.

HOUSES

Early visitors to the Delaware River have not left detailed descriptions of the Indians' houses, but it seems clear that the Delawares did not build "longhouses" like those for which the Iroquois are famous: "In the eighteenth century the Delawares typically lived in one-family peaked-roof bark houses in unplanned, unstockaded villages."[1] William Penn wrote that "Their houses are mats, or bark of trees set on poles, in the fashion of an English barn, but out of the power of the wind, for they are hardly higher than a man."

Other Algonkian tribes of the neighborhood, however, are known to have built circular, beehive houses like those of the Monongahela people described on page 13. It has been supposed that the Delawares, too, must have used them. It is suggested by William W. Newcomb that the beehive house may have served the Delaware for his hunting lodge in winter.[2]

Whatever its shape, the smaller house with only one fire came to be used more and more in Indian villages as time went on. By the eighteenth century the bark-and-sapling house of the Delawares had all but disappeared. Their typical dwelling by that time was often a small rectangular log house with moss or earth to stop the chinks. These late dwellings derived from the log cabins introduced by Swedish pioneers and copied by other white settlers. Such houses were much more substantial. A surveyor in western Pennsylvania in 1785, commenting on the remains of an Indian village abandoned some ten years earlier, wrote that "there were some cabbins, which would have been useful to [white] settlers."[3]

A 1756 description of the Delaware town of Kittanning notes a thirty-foot "long house where the frolics and war dances are held"— probably the "Big House," whose use is described on page 72.

[1]Ives Goddard in *Handbook of North American Indians*, Vol. 15 (Washington, 1978), 229.
[2]*The Culture and Acculturation of the Delaware Indians* (Ann Arbor, 1956), 25.
[3]Andrew Henderson in *Pennsylvania Archaeologist*, XXVI (1956), 176.

THE WAYSIDE CABIN

The wayside cabin used by the Delawares and other Indians when traveling was a simple structure, much like the Boy Scout lean-to. It could be put up in a few minutes. Four stakes were driven into the ground, about three feet high on one side and five or six feet high on the other, to make a sloping roof. The stakes had forked tops, across which poles were laid. To cover this frame, large sheets of bark were fastened on three sides and on the top. The high side, which faced away from the wind, was left open, and in front of it a fire was built. Balsam boughs or rushes made a soft mattress for the night. The cabin might have a length of six, nine, or more feet as desired; and it was wide enough to allow the men inside to sleep with their feet toward the fire.

On main trails the traveler might find many of these cabins. If it began to rain, he had only to stop at one of them, and turn up any bark he found lying on the ground to see that no snakes were harboring there. Then he spread fresh balsam on the ground, built a fire, and retired snugly until morning or until the rain ceased.

THE SWEAT LODGE

Every community had its sweat lodges ("sweat ovens"), one for the men and another at the opposite end of town for the women. The sweat lodge was used by young and old as a cure for various diseases and for a general sharpening of the wits in preparation for some important conference.

The sweat lodge was usually built beside a stream. One end might be sunk into the bank, the rest of the structure being roofed by bark and earth. Steam was produced by pouring water on hot stones. Persons specially assigned to this task heated the stones (each about the size of a turnip) in a fire outside the lodge, bringing in fresh stones as needed to replenish the steam. The patient remained inside for half an hour or an hour, drinking a concoction specially prepared for him, while the sweat rolled off his skin. When he came out, he plunged into the river, or, in wintertime, rolled in the snow. Loskiel tells us that for the best effect this alternation of hot and cold was repeated three times.

The use of the sweat lodge was a community matter. A public crier made announcement when all was ready. Then the villagers trooped round, each with his kettle into which was poured a potion to promote perspiration and at the same time to quench thirst. Some persons brought their own potions for the cure of particular diseases.

5

Delaware Occupations

DIVISION OF LABOR

BETWEEN MEN AND WOMEN in the Indian world, there was a
fair division of labor. "Delaware women," wrote Loskiel in his
History, "live as well as the situation of an Indian will permit." The
man, because of his greater physical strength and his freedom from
the burden of child rearing and nursing, attended to the more strenu-
ous and dangerous duties. He cleared the land, felled the trees (by
girdling and then hacking them down with his stone ax), built and
repaired the house. He made the fish dam, attached the "fish basket,"
and gathered the catch. At certain seasons of the year he went out
hunting to provide food and clothing for the family. He made canoes,
war clubs, bows, and arrows. He went to war to defend his home. But
he left the management of the house to his wife and the chief matron
of her lineage, and he listened to the advice of these women in matters
of peace and war.

The Delaware woman was far from being a slave. She had a
relatively higher, more respected position in the community than her

sister in Europe. She was complete mistress in her home. She owned the house, its equipment, and the fields attached to it. In case of divorce, she kept the children. In public affairs, her advice was powerful. "In terms of blood-money (the custom of payment to prevent the taking of blood-revenge)," writes John Witthoft in "The American Indian as Hunter," "a woman was worth twice as much as a man; where the family of a killer had to make formal payment of the victim, Indian law determined that the sum must be doubled if the slain were a woman."[1]

Her duties were commensurate with her privileges, and she bore her responsibilities without complaining. She nursed the children, made the pottery, tanned the hides, dressed the game her husband brought, kept the fire burning, made the bread, provided her husband and family with two good meals a day, and kept a kettle of soup on the fire for possible visitors. She gathered the firewood, fetched the water, and made clothing for herself and the family. She plowed the ground, planted the corn, cultivated it, gathered it, and ground it into flour or meal.

But the Indian woman with her corn-pounder and hoe is not a figure to be pitied. Her housekeeping was not exhausting. Household furniture in the longhouse consisted chiefly of earthenware, wood, and bark receptacles of different sizes for various uses: pounding corn, cooking, eating, storing. Gardening (farming in those days was little more) was everywhere looked upon as woman's work. It was believed that women had invented agriculture, and that the Corn Mother cooperated best with her own sex. Besides, the fields were small, the work was light. Tending the corn patch was a cheerful part of community life. The women sowed, cultivated, or reaped at their own time and their own speed, enjoying a neighborly chat with friends as they worked. In later years, as men's preoccupation with hunting and war grew less, the husband took on more and more of this "women's work" as his own, thus keeping the balance of labor even.

FOOD AND COOKING

The Delaware woman spent a good deal of time and ingenuity in the preparation of food. Though she is said to have yielded to the Iroquois woman in the fine art of moccasin decoration, she was unsurpassed as a cook. Her two meals a day were prepared with a nicety that astonished Europeans.

The staple foods were the Three Sisters: corn, beans, and squash. The species of squash they ate was what we call the pumpkin, though

[1] *Pennsylvania Game News*, XXIV, No. 2 (February, 1953), 15-16.

not the variety that goes into our Thanksgiving pies. The diet was not so narrow as it might seem to be. There were many other foods available, and these were combined with the Three Sisters to provide variety. Besides fish, flesh, and fowl, there were insects. The Moravians observed that fried locusts were enjoyed by the children. In addition to the staple vegetables, there were potatoes and wild peas. There were chestnuts, hickory nuts, hazelnuts. There were also wild grapes, wild plums, crab apples; cranberries, huckleberries, strawberries, blackberries, gooseberries, whortleberries, bilberries, raspberries. Of cranberries and crab apples they made preserves.

They tapped the maple trees and boiled the sap to syrup and sugar. There has been some question whether the white man learned the art of maple sugar making from the Indian or the Indian from the white man. Helen and Scott Nearing in *The Maple Sugar Book* assure us that the debt is to the Indian. Here is some of their evidence:

Marc Lescarbot, in his *Histoire de la Nouvelle France*, 1609, wrote that when the Indians were thirsty they got juice from the trees and distilled it into what he found to be "a sweet and very agreeable liquid." Sebastien Rasle, a missionary to the Abenakis, observed in *Lettres édifiantes et curieuses*, 1724, that the forest contained plenty of sugar in fluid form. The Indian women, he said, in spring "busy themselves in receiving it into vessels of bark, when it trickles from these trees; they boil it, and obtain from it a fairly good sugar." Robert Beverley in his *History and Present State of Virginia*, 1705, said that the Indians boiled eight pounds of sap down to one pound of sugar. He added: "Though this Discovery has not been made by the English above Twelve or Fourteen Years; yet it has been known among the Indians, longer than any now living can remember."[2]

Lewis Morgan saw evidence, in the religious festival known as the Maple Sugar Dance, of the antiquity of maple sugar making among the Indians.

Early European travelers in America found Indian sugar a great curiosity. They observed that Indians drew the sap from the trees into bark receptacles or hollow logs, and boiled the liquid by dropping in hot stones. The process could be speeded up in cold weather by letting the sap freeze in the container. When the ice, which was almost all water, was skimmed off, the syrup left behind was found to be more sugary.

Thomas Wildcat Alford, in telling of his youth among the Shawnees, described customs that were probably ancient also among the Dela-

[2] Helen and Scott Nearing, *The Maple Sugar Book* (New York, 1950), 22-25.

33

wares. Of sugar making he had this to say: "Sugar and syrup were made from sugar maple, but when our people were not in the country where sugar maple grew they substituted soft maple, box elder, and even hickory sap for the sugar maple sap, though of course the product was not so good."[3]

The Delawares used maple or other sugar in many ways, mixing it with their corn bread and even seasoning their meat with it. They sweetened melted bear's fat with a strong infusion of maple sugar, and dipped their roasted venison into it.

At home they were delicate in their eating, and the women were particular about cooking. Not only had they many recipes, but they were skilled in regulating their fires, selecting the right woods for different dishes and different tastes. Some Delawares liked their meat rare, some liked it well done. Lindeström tells us they ate their meat half cooked. Zeisberger, on the other hand, says: "Food which they prepare must be well cooked and well done; they do not like anything rare or raw. Meat and even fish must be so thoroughly cooked that they fall apart."[4] It is not the time element that explains the discrepancy between these two reports, but local custom or private taste.

The Delawares were neat and cleanly in their cooking. "They often laugh at the white hunters," wrote Heckewelder, "for baking their bread in dirty ashes, and being alike careless of cleanliness when they broil their meat."[5]

They had many ways of preparing food. They roasted meat on wooden spits, boiled it in earthen pots, or broiled it on clean coals. Pumpkins they stewed in pots covered with large leaves to keep in the steam.

Indians made corn the basis of most of their meals. But they used corn of so many varieties, cooked in so many different ways and in such a multitude of combinations (with chopped meat, shredded fish, ground-up nuts, powdered sugar, and so on) that there was no monotony.

Loskiel tells us that both the Delawares and the Iroquois dressed Indian corn in twelve different ways:

1. Boiling it in the husk.
2. Parboiling it, rubbing off the husk, and boiling it again.
3. Roasting the whole ear in hot ashes as it came off the stalk.
4. Pounding it small and then boiling it soft.

[3] Florence Drake, *Civilization: As Told to Florence Drake by Thomas Wildcat Alford* (Norman, Oklahoma, 1936), 41.
[4] "History of the Indians," 14.
[5] *History, Manners, and Customs*, 196.

34

5. Grinding it as fine as flour by means of a wooden mortar and pestle, clearing it from the husks, and making a thick pottage of it.

6. Kneading the flour with cold water, making a cake about a hand's-breadth round and an inch thick, enclosing this in leaves, and baking it in hot ashes under live coals. That was their bread.

7. Mixing dried bilberries with the flour to give the cakes better relish.

8. Chopping roasted or dried deer's flesh or sometimes smoked eels, and boiling this with the corn.

9. Boiling coarsely ground corn with fresh meat.

10. Letting unripe corn swell in boiling water, drying it, and laying it by for later use as soup or salad.

11. Roasting the whole corn when well grown but still full of juice.

12. Roasting corn in hot ashes till it became thoroughly brown; then pounding it to fine flour, mixing it with sugar, and pressing it forcibly in a bag.

When hunting or on the warpath, they carried with them a supply of this last, which they called *psindamoakan*. A mouthful or two— equivalent to one or two tablespoonfuls—was sufficient nourishment for a day.

No table was set for an Indian meal. The food was placed on the ground, the diner sat on a rush mat. His equipment was a wooden spoon, a stone knife, and a clay bowl. Water was the principal drink. Loskiel reports that the Delawares prepared also a drink of dried blueberries, sugar, and water, which he found "very agreeable."

Etiquette based on religious scruples forbade the Indian's throwing the bone to the dog. Instead, he dropped it into the fire. There was a prejudice against eating ground hog, hare, or wildcat; and no Delaware would dream of killing, much less of eating, Grandfather Rattlesnake.

John Heckewelder one day questioned the wisdom of this rattlesnake taboo and told an Indian friend that white men killed rattlers. When the Indian inquired if, in consequence of this "declaration of war," the snakes did not sometimes retaliate by killing white men, Heckewelder had to admit that this was so. "No wonder," said the Indian. "You have yourselves to blame." He warned Heckewelder to leave the rattlesnakes alone and not to carry this "war," with the danger of reprisals, into the Indian country where up to that time the rattlesnakes and their "grandchildren" had been on good terms.

35

The Delawares preserved food by drying it in the sun or over a fire and then storing it in a bark-lined pit.

AGRICULTURE

The Delawares did not farm as intensively as the Iroquois, but nevertheless it was chiefly their crops that fed them. The fertility of the river-bottom fields they had cleared is attested by the eagerness of white men to possess them. Frequently, warrants for survey (as we read them now in the Commonwealth's Bureau of Land Records in Harrisburg) were worded "to include the Indian field."

Corn, the principal crop, was not broadcast but planted in hills about two and a half feet apart. It was cultivated by earthing-up and weeding with short-handled hoes made of deer shoulder blades or tortoise shells. There is evidence that the Delawares fertilized the ground with fish scrap. But there was no rotation of crops. Instead, there was rotation of villages. When the soil was exhausted, the whole village moved to new quarters a few miles away. That is why "Old Town" is so familiar a name on early maps of Pennsylvania: Chartier's Old Town, Conemaugh Old Town, Kickenapaulin's Old Town, and so on.

HUNTING

Before European fashions put a premium on beaver, the animals most sought by the Delawares were deer and bear, which provided essentials in food and clothing. Other creatures were eaten, too, except those protected by taboo. The hare, wildcat, ground hog, and rattlesnake have been noted already in this category. To these must be added the wolf.

The source of this interdiction against killing wolves is to be found in the primal myths of creation, birth, and death, in which the wolf played a heroic but tragic role. He was the first to taste death, after having drawn the Munsees out of the great cave in which they had been confined in the interior of the earth.[6]

The wolf taboo at a later time was to give great trouble to the Moravian missionaries. When the wolves became ravenous in the vicinity of mission villages, the only way the Christian Delawares could protect their flocks without scandalizing their non-Christian neighbors was to dig pits and let the wolves fall in and kill themselves.

The Delaware hunter sometimes worked alone, sometimes with a group. Collective hunting was thus described by Lindeström:

[6] See Heckewelder's explanation, pages 83-84.

36

When now the sachem [chief] wants to arrange his hunt, then he commands his people [to take a position] close together in a circle of ½, 1 or 2 miles [Swedish or German miles], according to the number of people at his command. In the first place each one roots up the grass in the position, [assigned to him] in the circumference, to the width of about 3 or 4 ells, so that the fire will not be able to run back, each one then beginning to set fire to the grass, which is mightily ignited, so that the fire travels away, in towards the center of the circle, which the Indians follow with great noise, and all the animals which are found within the circle, flee from the fire and the cries of the Indians, traveling away, whereby the circle through its decreasing is more and more contracted towards the center. When now the Indians have surrounded the center with a small circle, so that they mutually cannot do each other any harm, then they break loose with guns and bows on the animals which they then have been blessed with, that not one can escape and thus they get a great multitude of all kinds of animals which are found there.[7]

To attract the deer, "calls" were made of cedar wood. If a hunter could not get within range of his prey, he would follow it, if need be, for a whole day.

FISHING

The Delawares had many ways of catching fish. They used fishhooks of dried birds' claws. They used dragnets which had been knitted by the women with thread from the wild hemp. They trapped fish behind dams, catching them there with their bare hands or shooting them with bow and arrow. Sometimes they placed a "fish basket," or trap, below the sluice and collected the fish as they came through. They also speared fish by torchlight.

TRADE

From archaeological evidence it would appear that trade between distant Indian communities was brisker in ancient times than it was in the late prehistoric period. Spear points from the jasper quarries at Macungie in Lehigh County are said to have been found in New England. When the bow and arrow replaced the spear, however, the jasper trade dwindled and died. Small triangular arrowheads could be manufactured anywhere from local stone, and jasper lost its importance in the arms race.

The fur trade changed everything. With the coming of the white man, firearms became a necessity for survival, and the Indian could

[7] *Geographia Americae*, 213-14.

get them only in exchange for furs. The first permanent trading post in these northern latitudes was established by the French in 1603 at Tadoussac on the St. Lawrence River; but even before that time European goods had been reaching the Indians from trading vessels along the Atlantic coast. John Smith in 1608, the year of Champlain's founding of Quebec, observed the Susquehannocks to be already in possession of traders' goods.

The fur trade was then still in its infancy. When it reached maturity a few years later, it dominated Indian life, drawing all able-bodied men into lengthy excursions, far from the family hunting grounds, in search of deer, beaver, otter, raccoon, fox, and wildcat. The skins of these animals were exchanged for firearms and metal tools of all kinds, as well as for cloth, brass kettles, and ornaments.

Unfortunately the fur trade did more than change the native economy. It brought fierce competition between the tribes. National wars of a ferocity hitherto unknown ensued, in which whole populations were destroyed or uprooted and their territories turned into hunting grounds for the victors.

PHYSICIANS

There were two kinds of medicine men: *physicians,* who had a wide knowledge of medicinal herbs and who could set bones and cure wounds with great skill; and *conjurors,* who claimed (and usually believed themselves) to possess supernatural powers which enabled them to detect evil spirits in men's bodies and to cast them out. Both roles, that of physician and that of conjuror, were sometimes played by the same person, and most Indians had a good knowledge of herbs.

In the eighteenth century good Indian physicians were respected by all men, white and brown. Heckewelder's sciatica was relieved, as he tells us, by the application of an Indian poultice. Andreas Hesselius reports that his young son was cured of worms by an Indian remedy. Dr. Benjamin Rush made note of Indian cures. Many Indian medicines have found their way into modern medical practice.

> The *Materia Medica* of the Indians [wrote Heckewelder] consists of various roots and plants known to themselves, the properties of which they are not fond of disclosing to strangers. They make considerable use of the barks of trees, such as the white and black oak, the white walnut, of which they make pills, the cherry, dogwood, maple, birch, and several others. They prepare and compound these medicines in different ways, which they keep a profound secret.[8]

[8] *History, Manners, and Customs,* 224.

Wounds and external injuries [wrote Zeisberger] the Indians treat very successfully, knowing what applications to make. In the curing of those suffering from snake-bite, they are particularly capable. For the bite of every variety of snake they have a special *Beson*.[9]

For headache they lay a piece of white walnut bark on the temples, toothache is treated by placing the same kind of bark on the cheek over the tooth that gives trouble. The bark is very heating and burns the skin in a short time, often affording relief. . . . This bark pounded fine and boiled to the consistency of a strong lye stops the flow of blood when applied to a fresh wound, even though an artery may have been ruptured, prevents swelling and heals the wound rapidly.[10]

In gathering herbs, as Gladys Tantaquidgeon tells us in *Folk Medicine of the Delaware and Related Algonkian Indians*, the medicine man followed a certain ritual. He left untouched the first plant, placing beside it in the ground to the east a little tobacco. Then he lighted his pipe and, as the smoke ascended, addressed a prayer of intercession to the Creator and the spiritual forces that govern vegetation. That done, he looked for other plants of the same kind and gathered as many as he needed. When later he prepared the plants for use, he prayed to the Creator to bless them and make them effective.

CONJURORS AND SORCERERS

In Heckewelder's opinion, the Delawares' greatest weakness was superstitious fear, the "apprehension of an occult and unknown power." They believed in charms, "deadening substances," and all sorts of magic formulas. As a result, they were easily preyed upon by what the Munsees called *Medeu* (conjurors) who exacted ruinous fees from patients by the pretense of expelling evil spirits. In case of serious illness, the conjurors sometimes continued their visits until the patient's property was exhausted, when they declared his disease to be incurable. Heckewelder thought the death of Shingas' wife resulted from her turning from proper physicians to these conjurors.

WITCHES

The Delawares, like the rest of the world, believed in witches. Zeisberger, whose disbelief in such things was easily shaken, is our source for some of the best Indian folklore about the black art. The Delawares, he reported in 1769, had acquired this art from the Nanti-

[9] "History of the Indians," 25.
[10] *Ibid.*, 148-49.

39

cokes and, not knowing the potency of the spells the Nanticokes sold them, sometimes in their eagerness to revenge themselves upon individuals, destroyed whole towns (so it was said) by poisoning the spring water. Sometimes they took their "witchcraft" to a nearby hill, put the magical stuff in a hollow tree trunk or rock crevice, and let the wind take it to the doomed town. Everything there, it was believed, became contaminated. That is why, Zeisberger says, when plague struck a town, the Indians cleared out at once, thinking they were bewitched. The Delaware prophet Wangomen (Zeisberger's rival and enemy at Goschgoschink on the upper Allegheny) owed his great influence over the people to their belief that he possessed "witchcraft" and that their lives were in his power.

The punishment for witchcraft was death: not by burning at the stake as in Europe nor by hanging as in New England, but by one swift blow of the hatchet. (In 1806, however, three Delaware Indians, one of them a woman, were burned during a witchcraft craze among the Indians on the White River in Indiana.)

THE MEDICINE BUNDLE

The medicine bundle was sacred, so sacred that it was seldom allowed to be seen and almost never opened. It was used by physicians, conjurors, and the laity to cure diseases. For that reason it is discussed here rather than in the chapter on Delaware religion.

Nearly everyone had a medicine bundle. As the name suggests, it was a small buckskin bag containing medicinal roots and a variety of other objects—perhaps a feather, an animal tooth, a magic stone— things that had been suggested in dreams by one's Guardian Spirit.

"The medicine bundle," writes Gladys Tantaquidgeon, "is the most highly cherished material possession of a chief, warrior, or medicine man."[11] Through it the possessor could communicate with his Guardian Spirit. A medicine man might ask this Supernatural for the diagnosis of a difficult case; a hunter, for assistance in tracking the game; a warrior, for the discovery of his enemy's position; a chief, for clearer insight into his people's needs.

---

[11] *Delaware Indian Medicine Practice and Folk Beliefs* (Harrisburg, 1942), 22.

40

6

Delaware Travel

INDIAN TRAILS

EXCEPT FOR A FEW YEARS of our nineteenth-century canal boom, Pennsylvania's best transportation has always been by land. Her rivers have, on the whole, been more of an obstacle than an aid to getting about. That was certainly true during Indian days. Neither in a north-and-south nor in an east-and-west direction did they offer the canoeman an easy passage through the mountains. Canoes might descend the Susquehanna from the Iroquois country well enough during the spring flood; but at other times great stretches of it were rocky and treacherous, difficult to ascend against the current, dangerous to descend with it. The Susquehanna West Branch and the Juniata gave access to the middle ranges of the Appalachian Mountains, but the traveler, when he reached the Allegheny Front (west of Bedford and Hollidaysburg), had to leave his canoe and climb over high ridges before he found navigable water flowing into the Allegheny and Ohio.

As if to compensate for that, Pennsylvania had plenty of good trail country. Geological changes in earlier ages had left a legacy of wind gaps (old abandoned water courses) which offered low-level crossings of some otherwise formidable ranges. Except for an occasional forest of white pine and hemlock, which vied with each other to blot out the sun and earned from discouraged European travelers the name "Shades of Death," the woods for the most part were open. Some streams difficult to navigate—Pine Creek, for instance, and the Sinnemahoning—cut passageways through the mountains which could be used by early travelers, just as they are used today by our railroads.

It seems a fair inference from what we know of early Indian habitations that the Indian paths of the eighteenth century—the period from which comes our fullest knowledge of Indian travel—were much the same as those that had been in use during earlier centuries. If we are correct in this, we may say that the Indian's road map (if he had had one) would have shown almost as intricate a crisscross of travelways as are found on our road maps today.

There were paths for all weathers, wet and dry, hot and cold; and for all kinds of people, hunters, warriors, messengers (runners), diplomats, and even family parties crossing the mountains to visit friends. Most of the paths were narrow, about eighteen inches wide, just sufficient for persons moving in single file. A few paths, notably those crossing the mountains of Greene County (from the Ohio Valley to the Monongahela) were wide and well-worn buffalo traces. In the Iroquois country some trails were wide enough for two men to walk abreast.

It must be understood, of course, that Indians did not build roads, but were adept at *finding* the best ways to travel. No paving was required, nor were bridges; smaller streams could be forded, and at major crossings canoes were usually available.

It was only in the more settled regions that paths were kept clear of brush and fallen trees. In the lonelier mountain regions, windfall made necessary a constant crawling over and under tree trunks or walking round them. Sometimes in the wake of a hurricane the windfall was so bad that travelers could not get through at all and had to take another route. At such times even Indians could get lost.

Where possible, Indian paths avoided water, heavy underbrush (especially the mountain laurel), and steep ascents; but in a pinch all these obstacles were met and overcome for the sake of some compensating advantage. The Wyalusing Path, a short route between the two branches of the Susquehanna, crossed Muncy Creek more than thirty times; the well-graded Minisink, Frankstown, and Raystown paths passed through the Shades of Death; and the Conemaugh Path, by ascending the Allegheny Mountain at a place too steep for our

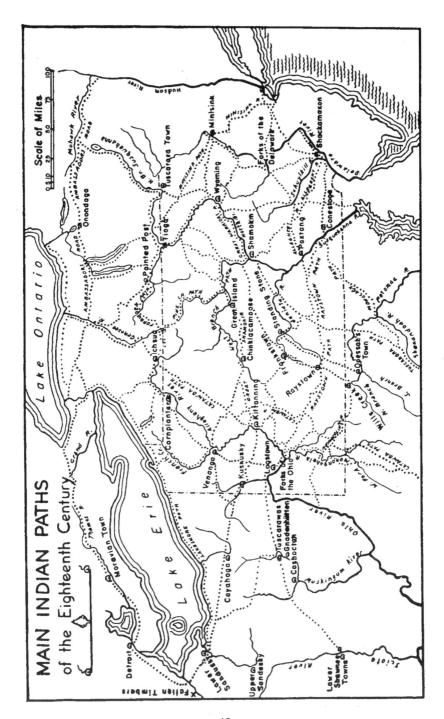

MAIN INDIAN PATHS
of the Eighteenth Century

43

modern traffic, was several miles shorter than the present highway between Bedford and Johnstown.

In some places the path ran along the summit of a ridge, but it avoided mountain spines like the Blue Mountain (the Kittatinny) in eastern Pennsylvania, where every few miles the range is cut by a deep gap which the traveler would have had to drop into and climb out of again. The famous Appalachian Trail ("from Maine to Georgia") crosses from the Delaware to the Susquehanna by a route not used by Indian travelers. It was devised for sport by modern white men.

The coming of Europeans caused the relocation of some Indian highways. The so-called Warriors Path will serve as an example. At one time the section of the trail which was known to early settlers as the Virginia Path ran southwest from Paxtang (Harrisburg) to cross the Potomac at the mouth of the Conococheague. Settlers moving into Cumberland Valley resented the Indians' crossing of their clearings. To avoid trouble, Indian war parties and embassies took a route farther west, running south from Standing Stone (Huntingdon) to cross the Potomac at Opessah's Town (Oldtown, Maryland). Later we find the Catawba Path, another version of the Warriors Path, crossing Pennsylvania on the west side of the Alleghenies and running south through Connellsville and Uniontown. When in 1767 Mason and Dixon ran their line west of the Monongahela River, the Iroquois stopped them at a branch of the Catawba Path which crossed the nearby Dunkard Creek in Greene County.

Trails led from one to another of the main fords or river crossings. The Allegheny Path, for instance, ran from any one of several fords of the Schuylkill at what is now Philadelphia to the Susquehanna ford at Paxtang (Harrisburg), and from there to fords of the Allegheny and the Monongahela at the Forks of the Ohio (Pittsburgh). Most trails "kept their level" well enough, twisting through water gaps and wind gaps to avoid too much climbing. Despite these windings, the paths were so well routed that they were shorter, take them as a whole, than the corresponding roads we use today.

The white traders' use of horses to carry goods and peltry to and from the Indian country, and the acquisition of horses by the Indians themselves, undoubtedly altered the traffic pattern on some of these paths; and the paths used by the traders are among those that are best known. Many of our modern highways follow the general course of Indian paths, but differences in travel objectives and weight of traffic (today's trucks as compared with yesterday's moccasined men and women) have made it impossible for our roads to follow the old paths for any distance.

North, east, south, and west, Pennsylvania's main paths connected with Indian highways of continental reach. Good trails sped the Iroquois warrior south toward the Cherokee country and brought Shawnee refugees from North Carolina to the Delaware Water Gap. Trails ran from the Atlantic to the Pacific. Trails connected Hudson Bay with the Gulf of Mexico. A path from Philadelphia to Conestoga (near Lancaster) and the Shenandoah Valley passed through Virginia and Tennessee to the Cumberland Gap—a distance of about eight hundred miles. The Allegheny Path from Philadelphia made connections at what is now Independence, Missouri, with predecessors of the Santa Fe Trail to New Mexico and of the Oregon Trail to the Pacific. Several Pennsylvania paths made connections with the Natchez Trace by way of the Shenandoah Valley, the Holston Valley, and Avery's Trace from Knoxville to French Lick (Nashville), where the Chickasaw Path or Natchez Trace took off.

The peacetime Indian traveler of the eighteenth century, who was probably not very different from his ancestor of the sixteenth, has been well described for us by David Zeisberger:

On their journeys they are never in haste, for they are everywhere at home and whithersoever they wander they find sustenance in the forest. Therefore, if a white man travels with them it is wisest that he be content not to hasten but accommodate himself to their movements. In the morning they do not break camp early, not until they have eaten heartily, by which time the sun has usually been above the horizon two or three hours. Thereafter, they proceed very steadily until near sundown, when they go into camp. In rainy weather they peel bast from the trees and speedily build a hut, that is, a roof supported by four posts, under which they remain comfortably dry. This they do not only in summer but also in winter, at which time they know what trees to peel.[1]

When traveling any distance on foot, the Indian often carried a pack on his back. Men wore the packstrap slung over the chest; women, over the forehead. What saved Shickellamy from death in 1737, when he slipped on the edge of a cliff above Lycoming Creek, was the catching of his packstrap on a bare tree branch.

[1] "History of the Indians," 22.

CANOES

The canoe, which could on occasion provide the Indian with swift and silent passage, was not so much used in Pennsylvania as the romantic reader would like to think. For one thing, Pennsylvania's streams were not suitable for through travel between east and west, since the Allegheny Ridge set up a gigantic river block. For another, Pennsylvania's open forests made land travel so easy in most places that canoes were less necessary than, for instance, in New England where the forests were denser. More important still was the fact that the canoe birch, from which the northern Algonkians made the lightest and (for its size) the most efficient watercraft known to man, did not grow in Pennsylvania. Our Indians, therefore, unless they bartered for the northern product, had to be content with the dugout and the elm-bark canoe.

The dugout (of cedar, poplar, sycamore, tulip, or even walnut) took days to manufacture. A good tree having been selected, a fire was built round it. When the fire had eaten well into the trunk, stone axes were used to bring the tree down. Fire and ax were again applied to cut the trunk to the required length. Stone axes shaped the vessel from the outside, while the inside was hollowed by burning the wood and chipping it out with a stone adze. The dugout was unsinkable. It took rough water and did not split open when it struck a rock; but it was awkward to navigate and almost impossible to carry.

Canoes were also made of bark from the elm, black oak, or hickory. Of these, the elm-bark canoe was the favorite. It was made by carefully stripping from the tree—some time after the sap had risen—a single sheet of bark the length of the proposed craft, bending it with the smooth side out, cutting it at the quarters to give it shape, sewing it with bast, and providing gunwales, thwarts, ribs, and stems of maple, hickory, or oak.

Elm-bark canoes were clumsy to paddle, unseaworthy in white water, and too heavy for the long portages that separated the Allegheny drainage from the Susquehanna. But they were useful for swift travel with the spring freshets and for the transportation of heavy goods. The name "Canoe Place" is often found on old maps, as at the present Port Allegany on the portage between Sinnemahoning Creek and the Allegheny River, or at Cherry Tree on the portage between the West Branch of the Susquehanna and Two Lick Creek. "Canoe Place" meant the head of canoe navigation. It also meant the place where new canoes could be built for the down-river journey.

The portage of Cherry Tree was important in the days before horse carriage, when the western Indians used water transportation to carry their peltry to market. This may well be the portage mentioned by Augustin Herrman in 1670, and it is certainly the one described in January, 1763, by a Delaware Indian, Nemacolin, to James Kenny at Pittsburgh: "he used to take skins in a canoe up Kiskiminetas and carry them . . . in a day cross to the West Branch Susquehanna, . . . from thence had a good passage down that Branch. . . ."[2]

[2]*Pennsylvania Magazine of History and Biography*, XXXVII (1913), 183.

7

Delaware Warfare

WHEN THE DELAWARES first came into view, they were not a warlike people. They could hardly be, with so little organization and discipline. They had no central "fire" or national council. The local community was supreme, as though the need of concerted military action was not thought of. In 1633 they seem to have offered little resistance to the Susquehannocks, who drove them east across the Delaware River. In later years, after European trade had sharpened economic rivalries among the Indians and set up everywhere a struggle for national survival, the Delawares tightened their organization and in the careers of Captain Jacobs, Shingas ("the Terrible"), and Captain Pipe proved that their warriors could be as good as any. But before the coming of the white man, it is doubtful if the Delawares conducted anything more extensive than locally organized family raids to avenge the deaths of kinsmen.

The tactics used in such raids were the norm of most Indian warfare: surprise, destruction, the seizure of prisoners, and retreat. These are what today are called *commando tactics*. The Delawares used them throughout the French and Indian War. The Iroquois, though they too used them, were capable also of larger strategic conceptions. They could conduct wide evolutions in the woods without losing control of their forces. In 1649 they assembled, unsuspected by their enemies, an army of a thousand warriors in the heart of the Huron country and demonstrated a power of co-ordinated attack that demoralized their enemies. In 1689 they paralyzed New France with an invasion carried out by 1,500 men who destroyed Lachine and reached the gates of Montreal.

Volunteers for Delaware expeditions were recruited at war dances. Their early weapons were the war club and spear, the latter rendered more deadly by a sling-lever device known as the spear thrower. It was not until comparatively late in their development, perhaps about two thousand years ago, that the bow and arrow replaced the spear. In this connection, it is interesting to remember that most of the projectile points found in our fields today are spearheads rather than arrowheads. Archaeologists tell us that the small triangular point, which was formerly thought to be a distinctively Iroquoian weapon, was in fact used as an arrowhead by all Indians east of the Rockies.

The sharp, high-pitched war whoop (variously called also the death halloo, death whoop, death cry, and scalp cry) was not confined to battle. Warriors returning from an expedition repeated the cry to indicate the number of scalps and prisoners they had taken.

Prisoners

The capture of prisoners was a main objective of most Indian raids. Matrons sometimes sent their young men on the warpath with instructions to bring home replacements for deceased relatives. When the warriors returned, the disposal of prisoners was left largely to the matrons to determine. But the general public had rights, too. A prisoner's running the gantlet gave the people an opportunity to test his mettle and his prospective worth as a citizen.

George Henry Loskiel has described for us the custom of running the gantlet:

> The warriors, upon their approach to the first town in their own country, repeat the death-whoop, according to the number of scalps, trophies, or prisoners in their possession. Upon this signal, men, women, and children, run out to meet them, placing themselves in two rows. The warriors step forward into the midst, with the scalp-poles and prisoners, and force the latter to dance for the amusement of the spectators. An house or post is then shown them in the village, to which they are ordered

49

to go. As soon as they set out, the people begin to strike at them with switches, clubs, hatchets, or their fists. If they gain the house or post, though ever so bruised and bloody, they are perfectly safe. Indians acquainted with this barbarous custom, escape great part of these cruelties, by running towards the mark with all their might. Female prisoners are frequently rescued by the women, who take them between their ranks, and carry them to the town.[1]

Final decision on what to do with a captive was usually made by the matron to whom he was presented. If a white prisoner was to be adopted, Zeisberger tells us that his head was "shorn in Indian fashion, only a little hair remaining on the crown," and his face was painted red. If, on the other hand, he was to be burned, his face was painted black.

Stories of Indian captivities and tortures supplied the most popular reading, next to the Bible, of most Americans during the adolescent years of this nation and so helped to draw the people of thirteen separate colonies together in recognition of a common danger.

Different peoples have different fashions in cruelty as well as in dress. It horrified white men to know that Indians in the excitement of war tortured some of their prisoners. It horrified Indians to know that white men ill-treated Indian women and sold their children into slavery. Today, as we look back upon Indian tortures, all of us— Indians and white men alike—are ashamed that humanity should have sunk so low. We are no less ashamed when we read of the tortures that were part of the normal judicial process in "civilized" countries as late as the seventeenth century—tortures used to extort the "confessions" that sent many innocent persons to the stake.

The Indian's respect for the person of woman, even in time of war, was well known. "Bad as these savages are," wrote General James Clinton in 1779, "they never violate the chastity of any woman, their prisoner."[2]

It is a mistake to suppose that the Indians put all captives to death. Most of the women and children and many of the men were adopted into Indian families, where they were treated with as much kindness as if they were of the same flesh and blood. In return, adopted prisoners often became so much attached to the Indians who adopted them that they were reluctant to return to "civilization."

Thomas Proctor [Procter] in his diary for April 9, 1791, tells of meeting a white prisoner, Nicholas "Deamhoat" (Demoot) at Venango:

[1] *History of the Mission*, I, 149.
[2] Quoted by J. N. B. Hewitt, "Status of Woman in Iroquois Polity Before 1784," Smithsonian Institution, *Report for 1932* (Washington, 1933), 483.

He was dressed in the Indian garb, and what I was grieved to see, his ears were cut around and each hung with a considerable weight of lead, designed to stretch them to a proper length. He acquainted me that his friends lived in Schenectady; his father lately dying, left him a considerable sum of money, I urged him to go around with me on my tour, and on our arrival at Philadelphia, I would give him decent apparel, and subsistance while going to his relatives, but he declined it, saying that he could not live so agreeable with the white people as with the Indians.[3]

The Delawares were less ruthless than some other Indians in the treatment of prisoners, although the burning to death of Colonel William Crawford in 1782 has been remembered against them. Colonel Crawford was captured at the Battle of Upper Sandusky. One of his officers, Colonel David Williamson (who escaped), had been responsible for the massacre of some ninety defenseless Christian Indians, most of them women and children, a few months before at Gnadenhütten, Ohio. Crawford himself had taken part in the "Squaw Campaign," when American militia attacked peaceful Delaware camps on the Shenango. On that occasion a brother of Captain Pipe, a Delaware war chief, was killed and his mother was wounded. The Delawares regarded the burning of Crawford as a judicial execution, and Captain Pipe, when appealed to, declined to intervene.

[3]*Pennsylvania Archives*, 2d Series, IV, 571 (1876 ed.).

8

Delaware Government and Social Organization

GOVERNMENT

I T IS DIFFICULT for the modern American, living under a strong federal government, and within closely defined geographical boundaries, to understand early Delaware government. The bounds of the Lenni Lenape territory were nebulous. There was no Delaware "nation" in the modern sense. There were, however, contiguous communities of Indians in what is now Pennsylvania, New Jersey, and Delaware who spoke dialects of the same Algonkian tongue, shared much the same history and culture, had the same enemies, and, in short, had a sufficient feeling of identity to call themselves *Lenni Lenape*, "Real People," as distinct from all others.

The social and political organization of the early Delawares is not fully known, but it is safe to say that the basic unit was the band and, within this, the maternal "lineage," a group of people of the same descent through the female line.

Each band or community seems to have had its own chief or sachem, who probably represented the most important lineage in the group. However, since the lineages were *exogamous* (a person had to marry outside his own lineage), every community must have included persons of other lineages as well, and these must also have been represented in the village council.

> . . . Their Government is by Kings [wrote William Penn], which they call *Sachema,* and those by Succession, but always of the Mothers side; for Instance, the Children of him that is now King, will not succeed, but his Brother by the Mother, or the Children of his Sister, whose Sons (and after them the Children of her Daughters) will reign; for no Woman inherits; the Reason they render for this way of Descent, is, that their Issue may not be spurious.
>
> . . . Every King hath his Council, and that consists of all the Old and Wise men of his Nation, which perhaps is two hundred People: nothing of Moment is undertaken, be it War, Peace, Selling of Land or Traffick, without advising with them; and which is more, with the Young Men too. 'Tis admirable to consider, how Powerful the Kings are, and yet how they move by the Breath of their People. I have had occasion to be in Council with them upon Treaties for Land, and to adjust the terms of Trade; their Order is thus: The King sits in the middle of an half Moon, and hath his Council, the Old and Wise on each hand; behind them, or at a little distance, sit the younger Fry, in the same figure.[1]

At a later date, if not in William Penn's time, the "king's council" probably would include one or more of the outstanding warriors, usually referred to by the English as "captains."

"King" was not a very apt title for an Indian, as Col. James Smith, who was captured by Indians in 1755, has reminded us:

> I have often heard of Indian Kings, but never saw any.—How any term used by the Indians in their own tongue, for the chief man of a nation, could be rendered King, I know not. The chief of a nation is neither a supreme ruler, monarch or potentate— He can neither make war or peace, leagues or treaties—He cannot impress soldiers, or dispose of magazines—He cannot adjourn, prorogue or dissolve a general assembly, nor can he refuse his assent to their conclusions, or in any manner controul them. . . . The chief of a nation has to hunt for his living, as any other citizen—[2]

[1] Myers (ed.), *Narratives of Early Pennsylvania,* 234-35.
[2] William M. Darlington (ed.), *An Account of the Remarkable Occurrences in the Life and Travels of Col. James Smith* . . . (Cincinnati, 1870), 147.

Nonetheless, the sachem (a person approved not only by his own lineage but by the rest of the community as well) had considerable influence. He presided at council meetings, which he called as needed; he acted as spokesman for his band in conferring with other groups or (after the coming of the white man) in the sale of land; and he presided at ceremonies and festivals scattered through the year. The community had no police to enforce the law. The Delawares, indeed, had no law at all in the statute-book sense. But individual Indians seldom violated the community's code. If they did violate it, they submitted to punishment without a murmur. "Their honor was their law." [3]

There is no evidence that the early Delawares had any higher regional or tribal organization. Like the ancient Greeks, they were united by language, custom, and geography rather than by political institutions. However, communities could, and undoubtedly did, band together for particular purposes, as is illustrated in the accounts of some wampum belts exchanged between the Iroquois and the Indians of the lower Delaware River—a belt from the Iroquois in 1694 and a number collected by the Delawares in 1701 and finally delivered in 1712. In both instances a group of chiefs, representing different bands, conferred with the Pennsylvania governor. In 1694 a chief named Hetcoquean was spokesman for the group, and it was he who was to have delivered the 1701 belts; he died, however, and Sassoonan replaced him.

Other groups of Delawares probably cooperated too, but the bands that Sassoonan represented became a closer association for which he was the "king" or designated spokesman. This was his role in the 1718 treaty by which the Delawares of southeastern Pennsylvania confirmed all their previous land sales. By this time they were identified as "Schuylkill Indians"; later, after they had sold all their land and Sassoonan lived at Shamokin (present Sunbury), they were called "Delawares of Shamokin"; in 1757 Teedyuscung called them "Unami" ("downriver people"), the name by which they are commonly known. By this time most of them had moved to the Ohio country, where some ten years later they developed into the Delaware Nation, of which Netawatwees was "king." This "Nation" did not include all the Delaware people, and it did include some other Indians, Munsees especially, but it was the Delawares' closest approach to an inclusive tribal organization.

Delaware tribal identities have been fluctuating ever since Penn's

* Christian Cukler to Lyman C. Draper, February 20, 1863, Draper MSS, 6E, 32 (Brady and Wetzel Papers), State Historical Society of Wisconsin (microfilm). Punctuation and spelling have been corrected.

day. There has been a constant movement of small groups leaving the parent stem and becoming known for the place at which they settled. So, as bands of Delawares moved west, the Brandywine Indians, the Schuylkill Indians, and many other groups were mistakenly treated in literature as if they were independent tribes.

"INDIAN ARCHIVES"

Having no written language, the Delaware Indians were necessarily selective in what they undertook to remember and to pass on to posterity, but the information that needed to be remembered they preserved with great care. Long-term examples were treaties with other peoples, short-term items were formal messages and the speeches to be made at treaties; for these they relied on memory and repetition, aided by strings or belts of wampum. In addition—and somewhat suggestive of modern graffiti—pictographs commemorating the exploits of war parties and other events might be carved or painted on trees (whence the name of Painted Post, New York); and pictographs painted on bark or skins were also aids to memory. An interesting example of this last usage, somewhat influenced by white people, it is true, is the "bible," described by James Kenny and others, which the Delaware preacher Neolin used in the 1760s to illustrate his teachings.[4] He displayed this as he preached and made copies for his listeners, so that they might the better remember his message.

A remarkable use of pictographs in support of the oral transmission of a long text is the *Walam Olum*, published in 1836 by C. S. Rafinesque. This text purports to preserve an ancient traditional account of the Delaware people from the time of their arrival in America. That it is in fact an intact tradition is questionable, and the text has been branded as an outright forgery or, less drastically, as a modern composition incorporating more or less native tradition.[5]

However, the use of pictographs for short-term memorials and of wampum belts for long-time records is well established. The remembrance of treaties was especially important; the wampum belts commemorating them were entrusted to specially appointed persons (we would call them state archivists), who brought them out on special occasions and repeated their messages.

[4] *Pennsylvania Magazine of History and Biography*, XXXVII (1913), 171-173.
[5] David Zeisberger, long and intimately acquainted with the Delawares, asserted that "Concerning their origin no trace of tradition is to be found among the Indians." ("History of the Indians," 132)

"Wampum" comes from an Algonkian word, *wampumpeak*, meaning "strings of white shell beads." There were two kinds of wampum: white and black, both usually made from the hard-shelled clam or the whelk. Black wampum was made from the thick, purple part of the shell; being more difficult to make, it was twice as valuable as white wampum.

It was not until after the white man had brought steel awls by which to perforate small cylindrical beads that the art of making wampum belts became highly developed and that wampum became a medium of exchange. "Before the Europeans came to North America," wrote Loskiel, "the Indians used to make their strings of wampom chiefly of small pieces of wood of equal size, stained either black or white."[6] A few natural shells were also used, shells of a kind that could, with only slight modification, be strung lengthwise. But these were too clumsy to use in making the delicate figures that are familiar to us in historic wampum.

Wampum was sacred. For a speaker in council to hold a wampum belt in his hand was like a white man's laying his hand on the Bible and taking the oath. "What Indians say with hand upon the wampum belt is true," said Chief William Dewaserage Loft (Sharenkhowane of the Mohawks).

In public debate, strings or belts of wampum served to refresh the memory. The speaker held in his hand as many belts as there were separate matters to be discussed. As he completed each division of his talk, he put a belt of wampum on a pole which had been laid across two crotched sticks before him. The speaker who replied, took up each belt in turn and dealt with the particular point it betokened. The touch and sight of the belts helped both speaker and audience to follow the argument.

White wampum was a symbol of peace; black wampum, of grief or death. In historic times wampum belts usually had designs inwoven in dark beads on a white ground to indicate the terms of a treaty or the substance of a message.

[6] *History of the Mission*, I, 26.

The most famous belt in Pennsylvania is the Penn Wampum Belt of eighteen rows containing some three thousand beads. Romantic fancy has associated it with the legendary "Great Treaty" between William Penn and the Indians beneath the Shackamaxon Elm. The actual occasion on which it was used is not known, but its symbolism is clear, and it may well serve us as a reminder of the friendship between Penn and the Indians. The Penn Wampum Belt was in the possession of the Penn family in England until 1857, when it was given to the Historical Society of Pennsylvania at Philadelphia, where it may now be seen.

KINSHIP

"Individual behavior," writes William W. Newcomb, Jr., "was controlled primarily by family and kinship groups, rather than by special institutions." [7]

The Delawares' kinship system was complicated and, because it took a viewpoint different from our own, is not easily understood. We can best approach it, perhaps, by looking at it at three different levels:

1. The single family.
2. The kinship of which the single family was a part.
3. The major lineages into which the Delaware people were divided.

The single family consisted, like our own, of husband and wife and their children; as with us, there might be some variation—the addition of a grandmother, for example. It differed from ours, however, in that the children belonged to the mother's lineage, but since that did not greatly affect relations between members of the family, it does not seem important until we turn to this family's relatives.

In these wider relationships the differences become obvious. To begin with, the Delaware system had a different purpose from ours. To a large extent, our system was shaped by the inheritance of property (money, land, titles); so one's relation to an ancestor was important. The Indian had no such property to inherit, and his concern was with the living members of his community. The Indian's closest relatives in the community were the members of his lineage—which was that of his mother; his father's relatives were more like "friends of the family." In this system, a child's "mothers" included not only his own mother but her sisters as well; and its mother's mother and *her* sisters were all "grandmothers." Thus, if a woman died and left small children, they would be cared for by one of her sisters, who also had the responsibility of a mother to them. We call such a kinship "classificatory" because it

[7] *Culture and Acculturation*, 53.

groups together the persons ("mothers," for example) who had the same responsibilities.

The largest kinship units were the major lineages. There were three of these among the Delawares, symbolized by Turtle, Turkey, and Wolf, and every Delaware belonged to one or another of them. As already noted, each one's lineage was that of his (or her) mother, and the lineages were exogamous—that is, a person married outside his own lineage. Presumably, members of all three lineages might be found in any Delaware community and it probably is fair to say that the Delaware people were united in large part by this system of intermarriages.

Old as these lineages must have been, it may seem strange that there is no specific mention of them until 1764. A plausible explanation is that in the absence of a central tribal organization the lineages functioned primarily in ceremonials, village councils, and marriage agreements, where they would attract little outside attention. However, William Penn's statement about Delaware government (quoted earlier) accurately reflects the lineage system, though he probably did not fully understand it.

The later prominence of these lineages probably was a consequence of the Delawares' emigration from their old homes to the Ohio country. The old village groups were of course broken up, but the lineages survived and in the new country the migrants found and joined others of their own kinships. When in 1758 "king" Beaver told C. F. Post, regarding peace negotiations, that "We are three tribes, which must separately agree among ourselves," his "tribes" probably were the three lineages. Six years later, when Colonel Bouquet called the Delaware chiefs to council, he found that he had to deal with three groups, Turtle Tribe, Turkey Tribe, and Wolf Tribe, functioning as tribal subdivisions. The later agreement that Newcomer, head of the Turtle lineage, should act as spokesman or "king" for the whole body of Delawares completed the organization of "The Delaware Nation," mentioned under "Government."

Kinship was so basic to the Delawares' life and thought that it was very natural for them to use kinship terms to describe their relations with other groups. Thus, David Zeisberger observed that "The Delawares call the Shawnees their grandchild, these on the other hand call them grandfather. The Munsees call the Shawnees their youngest brother and these in turn call them older brother." (The Munsees had behaved like an older brother by giving the Shawnees protection and a place to live when they were hard pressed by their enemies.)

58

THE DELAWARES AS "WOMEN"

Among Indians, national status was expressed in kinship terms. After the conclusion of the Iroquois-Mahican war in 1673, the victorious Iroquois addressed the Mahicans as "Nephews," and the Mahicans in return acknowledged their conquerors as "Uncles." The same terms of address were exchanged between Iroquois and Delawares. But there was another term, "Woman," that more exactly defined the position of the Delawares in the Iroquois federal system.

The question is often asked why the Iroquois called the Delawares "Women." It is difficult to answer the question briefly, because the term was applied by different people at different times with different meanings. We do not even know when or by what means the Delawares were first brought to accept the title. Some think the Iroquois "inherited" the Delawares from the defunct Susquehannock nation. Others think the Iroquois, after disposing of the Susquehannocks, conducted their own forays (political and military) in order to demonstrate to the Delawares who was now Uncle. There may be truth in both theories. Perhaps, too, the Delawares became tributary ("in an Indian Sense," as Conrad Weiser warned, knowing that the word in English implied greater subordination than actually existed between Delaware and Iroquois) from a somewhat vague sense of the fitness of things or a general instinct for accommodation. For we must remember that Indian political arrangements were usually less cut and dried (though not less effective) than those of today's highly codified systems.

One thing is certain. "Woman," as a national designation, was not originally a term of abuse, though it was made to appear so in the later eighteenth century. There are various words for "woman" in the Iroquois tongue. The one applied to the Delawares was an ancient ceremonial term, *Gantowisas*, which we might render "Lady," "Matron," or "Dame" (as in "Dame of the British Empire"). It was a title to be proud of, "like Queen," as Chief Joseph Montour of the Delaware Line on the Six Nations Reserve explained it. The title, *Gantowisas*, Woman, announced to the world that the Delawares held an honorable position, though not full membership, in the Iroquois Longhouse.

As "Women" the Delawares enjoyed the protection of the great League. This is what Chief Tamaqua, the Beaver, said to the Six Nations on the eve of the French and Indian War. His words were recorded at Aughwick, September 3, 1754, by Conrad Weiser.

59

Uncle: I still remember the Time when You first conquered Us and made Woman of Us, and told Us that You took Us under your Pro[t]ection, and that We must not meddle with Wars, but stay in the House and mind Council Affairs. We have hitherto followed your directions and lived very easy under your Protection, and no high Wind did blow to make Us uneasy; but now Things seem to take another turn, and a high Wind is rising. We desire You, therefore, Uncle, to have your Eyes open and be watchful over Us, your Cousins, as you have always been heretofore.[8]

Similarly, when in 1758 the Beaver said that "I have not made myself a king. My uncles [the Iroquois] have made me like a queen, that I always should mind what is good and right," he meant that he was to be the kind of "king" (spokesman) who would devote himself to making peace.[9]

In the same spirit, when Zeisberger and some of his Munsee converts were about to hold a council with the Delaware chief at Kuskusky (present New Castle) in 1769, they considered whether they should address him as "brother" or "sister," and they decided on "sister" because they were on a peaceful errand and wanted the chief to understand that they themselves did not engage in war.

Unfortunately the word *Gantowisas*, when translated into English as "woman," underwent a change of meaning and loss of dignity. White men, among whom women did not hold as high a position as they did among Indians, made sport of warriors who allowed themselves to be called "women." Some of the Delawares became ashamed of the word. "We are men," they declared in 1755, and took out their scalping knives to prove it.

[8] Pennsylvania, *Minutes of the Provincial Council of Pennsylvania* . . . , VI, 155-56. Cited hereafter by binder's title as Pennsylvania, *Colonial Records.*
[9] "Two Journals of Western Tours by Christian Frederick Post," in *Early Western Travels, 1748-1846*, 32 vols., ed. Reuben Gold Thwaites (New York, 1966), I, 273.

9

The Delaware Life Cycle

BIRTH

DELAWARE WOMEN were physically strong. They seldom
needed assistance in childbirth, although there were experienced
women ready to give them whatever advice and help they might desire.
When the event was approaching, the expectant mother got everything
ready, but did not cease her regular work until an hour or two before
the time. If the child was born while the mother was out in the woods,
she was able to look after herself and carry the baby home.

As soon as the child was born, it was wrapped in a skin and placed
on the cradleboard. This the mother carried about on her back when
away from home. Sometimes she hung it up on a peg in the house
or on a tree branch outside. More often, when the weather was warm,
she allowed the child to roll about freely on the grass. It has been
suggested that one cause of the Indian child's composure was that
its movements were less constricted than those of a white child during
infancy. Delaware boys wore no clothes in summer until they were

about six years old. Girls were given a light coat to wear as soon as they could walk.

CHILDHOOD

A child was usually six or seven years old before its parents gave it a name. There was no need to hurry. Personal names were not used at home, kinship terms taking their place. It was only when a person came in contact with the outside world that need arose for an independent name.

When the time came to name a boy or a girl, a ceremony known as "Praying over the Child" was held. Later in life at a similar ceremony the adult might receive another name more descriptive of his career. For a long time after a man's death, it was bad form to refer to him by his personal name.

Indian home life was quiet, free from the noise and anxiety which, according to some psychiatrists, endanger the nervous system of the white child and predispose him to nervous explosions for the rest of his life. From whatever cause—the example of parents, the freedoms enjoyed in infancy, long generations of social conditioning—the Indian child was less given to tantrums than the white child and made a less quarrelsome playmate. He led an active, happy life, assured of his parents' love and warmly responsive to it.

EDUCATION

Children were not weaned until they were two, three, or even four years old, but they were taught to walk at nine months. At the age of four or five, they began their initiation into adult life. The boys were taught woodcraft and hunting; the girls, housekeeping and gardening.

For the boys especially, this training was exciting. They were taken into the hunting woods and given tasks of increasing difficulty to harden them. A religious occasion was made of a boy's first killing of a deer. The boy gave the venison to the oldest man or woman of the village, who thereupon held a feast at which the deer was offered as a sacrifice to the twelve gods: the Great Spirit and His eleven chief agents. At this Burnt Offering or First Fruits, the boy's elders offered prayers for him and gave him advice concerning his duty to his fellow men, especially to the old people upon whose memories depended the continuance of the tribe's way of life.

Physical punishment was not often inflicted on a child, though a slap given in anger was not unheard of. More common was a dash of cold water in the face, a ducking in the stream, or a rubbing of the tongue with a bitter root. Sometimes the bad child was warned that the Naked Bear might get him or the Mask Being poke him with a stick. But it was not often necessary to discipline children, the tasks to which they were assigned being out in the open air, active, and interesting.

Learning the tribal legends and committing the records of events to memory was part of a child's education. The Delawares had no written language, yet they believed a knowledge of the past to be the necessary foundation of a stable society. To safeguard the tribal memory, not only were the old people given special reverence, but every boy's mind was filled with the tribe's traditions. In story and song, in religious ritual and its interpretation, the past was kept constantly before him. For more exact training of this kind, boys from chiefly families were expected to attend certain council meetings at which old belts of wampum were brought out while sages explained their meaning. Young men memorized these historical interpretations word for word, so that the past should not fade with the death of their elders.

INITIATION

A boy at the age of puberty or a little later entered manhood through an initiation or ordeal sometimes known as Youth's Vigil, by which he linked himself with the spiritual world and obtained a guardian *Manito.* The duration of this vigil and the preparations for it varied from place to place, but the essentials were the same everywhere. The boy retired to some hidden place in the forest and remained there for days, fasting and alone. Sometimes his parents, in order to humble him and thus prepare him emotionally for a redemptive vision, drove him away from home in pretended anger. If, after some days of solitary fasting, there came to him a dream or waking trance in which, at sight of some animal or natural object, he was swept by a feeling of security and peace, it was believed that he had found his link with the world beyond. The Creator had sent him a Manito, a spiritual power, on which he might rely for strength and protection throughout his life.

In maturity some men had further visions, which they recounted at sacred ceremonies. Sometimes the visionary found himself in touch with departed friends, as when a Delaware in Ontario some years ago found himself standing on the bank of "a great water," and heard from the other side the voices of friends who had "gone beyond." They were singing over and over syllables which were unintelligible to him but which by their cadence conveyed to his ear something of the sad but not bitter mystery of death.

MARRIAGE

Marriage was usually arranged by the parents, but no compulsion was laid upon the children. Their wishes were respected, and were final. Indians married early, the men often at seventeen or eighteen, the girls at thirteen or fourteen—the age of Shakespeare's Juliet.

It was against Delaware propriety that young couples before marriage should talk together unchaperoned. Courtship was a matter of gift giving.

> If an Indian man wishes to marry [wrote Loskiel], he first sends a present of blankets, cloth, linen, and perhaps a few belts of wampom, to the nearest relations of the person he has fixed upon. If they happen to be pleased, both with the present and the character and conduct of the suitor, they propose the matter to the girl, who generally decides agreeably to the wish of her parents and relations. . . . But if the other party chuses to decline the proposal, they return the present, by way of a friendly negative.[1]

The love of husband and wife was not publicly demonstrated, but it was strong and usually enduring. While it might be only convention that led a Delaware husband to see that his wife was well-dressed— better dressed than he was—it was deep affection that led him to many acts of devotion. He would do almost anything to meet his wife's wishes. Heckewelder tells of a man who, in a time of famine, traveled a hundred miles and back (between Tuscarawas and Lower Sandusky) to get his sick wife a little corn. He traded his horse for "as much corn as filled the crown of his hat," and came back on foot, carrying his saddle.[2] The suicide of man or woman because of some fancied slight received from the other was not uncommon.

Polygamy was not prohibited, but it was infrequent. Divorce was easy, depending merely upon the expressed wish of one or both parties. In cases of separation the children went with the mother, since they were of her lineage. Subsequent remarriage apparently involved little if any ceremony.

OLD AGE

Old age was universally respected. Youth had no quarrel with age. Perhaps that was because the old men in council gave full attention to the opinions of youth. It was bad form for a younger man to break off conversation with an elder, or to overtake and pass him on the road without the latter's express permission. Deference was carried sometimes to an extreme. On the trail, if the leader of a party hap-

[1] *History of the Mission,* I, 57.
[2] *History, Manners, and Customs,* 159.

64

pened to be an older man and took a wrong turning, no one in the party would correct him unless his advice was asked.

DEATH AND BURIAL

The warmhearted Delawares were subject to deep and overwhelming grief. Their burial ceremonies dramatized the emotion without compromising its sincerity. Heckewelder, in describing the funeral in 1762 of the wife of Shingas, pictured on the one hand the professional mourners in loud, conventional lamentation, and on the other the chief at a distance weeping silently by himself.

The last service performed for a woman about to start on her journey to the Sky World was to attire her in her best clothes and to place beside her body whatever she might need on the way: deerskin for fresh moccasins, needles and thread for sewing, food, a wooden bowl and spoon, and some of the little things that had pleased her while she lived. A man's necessities and desires were attended to in the same way.

The funeral ceremonies, known as "Mourning over the Corpse," consisted mainly of a long period of silence (two hours, according to Heckewelder's observation), followed by the cries of the mourners while the body was being lowered into the grave, and the erection of a painted post covered with designs representing the deceased's situation in life. A meal was served and gifts were presented to all present.

At dusk [wrote Heckewelder] a kettle of victuals was carried to the grave and placed upon it, and the same was done every evening for the space of three weeks [more usually eleven days]. . . . During that time the lamentations of the women mourners were heard on the evenings of each day, though not so loud nor so violent as before.[3]

It was believed that, unless food were placed on the grave, the soul would have to enter some private house to refresh itself. Not that it devoured any material substance. It was nourished by the food's spirit-essence.

Every person, they believed, had two souls: one in the heart and one in the blood. It was the former that made the Sky Journey. The heart soul remained near the body for eleven days. Then, on the twelfth, after being offered food by its living friends in a Feast of the Dead, it started on its way to the Spirit World. The soul in the blood, on the other hand, remained on earth. This was the ghost that ap-

[3] Paul A. W. Wallace (ed.), *Thirty Thousand Miles with John Heckewelder* (Pittsburgh, 1958), 62.

peared at night to friends, sometimes causing paralysis and lameness, especially if they had neglected to provide the Feast of the Dead.

"For fear of this soul," writes Dr. Newcomb, "nobody ever eats in the dark or allows a sick person to be in a dark room."[4]

[4] *Culture and Acculturation*, 64.

10

Delaware Religion

If the word religion means a formal belief in certain written
Articles of Faith . . . then we can truly say: the Indians . . .
have no religion. . . . But if by the word religion we under-
stand the knitting of the soul to God, and the intimate
relation to, and hunger after the highest Being arising there-
from, then we must certainly allow this apparently barba-
rous people a religion.—Conrad Weiser[1]

THE GREAT SPIRIT AND HIS AGENTS

THE BASIC PRINCIPLE of Delaware religion was that spirit was
the prime reality. All things had souls: not only man, but also
animals, the air, water, trees, even rocks and stones.

In control of nature—usually for man's benefit—were three orders
of supernatural beings: (1) certain spirit forces on earth; (2) eleven
appointed spirits, demigods, who from eleven heavens controlled

[1] Paul A. W. Wallace, *Conrad Weiser, Friend of Colonist and Mohawk* (Philadelphia, 1945), 21.

natural phenomena on the earth below; (3) the Great Spirit or Creator, dwelling in the Twelfth or Highest Heaven.

The Delawares had no strict creed, and they enforced no orthodoxy. There was considerable latitude in the detail of their beliefs. All gave thanks to the Great (and good) Spirit, the Creator, described by a Delaware who claimed to have seen him as a great man "clothed with the day; yea, with the brightest day he ever saw . . . this whole world . . . was drawn upon him, so that *in* him, the earth, and all things on it, might be seen."[2] All Delawares gave thanks also to eleven demigods for the gifts of nature. But they were not all agreed on the identity of these eleven.

The Reverend John Jacob Schmick, a Moravian missionary at Wyalusing, listed the following demigods in his description of the "Burnt Offering": Sun, Moon, Earth, Fire, Water, House, Corn, and the Four Quarters—East, West, North, and South. M. R. Harrington, from observations of the Delawares in Oklahoma, listed the two Thunders and the Mask Being in place of Fire, Water, and House:

> This Great Spirit gave the four quarters of the earth and the winds that came from them to four powerful beings, or *manitowuk*, namely, Our Grandfather where daylight begins, Our Grandmother where it is warm, Our Grandfather where the sun goes down, and Our Grandfather where it is winter. To the Sun and the Moon, regarded as persons and addressed as Elder Brothers by the Indians, he gave the duty of providing light, and to our Elder Brothers the Thunders, man-like beings with wings, the task of watering the crops, and of protecting the people against the Great Horned Serpents and other water monsters. To the Living Solid Face, or Mask Being, was given charge of all the wild animals; to the Corn Spirit, control over all vegetation, while Our Mother, the Earth, received the task of carrying and feeding the people.[3]

It has been suggested that the concept of the Great Spirit may have been derived from the teaching of Christian missionaries, but the evidence points the other way. David Zeisberger wrote: "They believe and have from time immemorial believed that there is an Almighty Being who has created heaven and earth and man and all things else."[4] M. R. Harrington, after running over some of the evidence, makes this summary: "Thus we have a practically unbroken chain of authorities, including most of the best ones since 1679, all speaking of the 'Great Spirit' as a well-developed concept."[5]

[2] M. R. Harrington, *Religion and Ceremonies of the Lenape* (New York, 1921), 23.
[3] *Ibid.*, 193.
[4] "History of the Indians," 128.
[5] *Religion and Ceremonies of the Lenape*, 22.

John Heckewelder commented:

It is a part of their religious belief, that there are inferior *Mannittos*, to whom the great and good Being has given the rule and command over the elements; that being so great, he, like their chiefs, must have his attendants to execute his supreme behests; these subordinate spirits (something in their nature between God and man) see and report to him what is doing upon earth; they look down particularly upon the Indians, to see whether they are in need of assistance, and are ready at their call to assist and protect them against danger. . . .
. . . .
But, amidst all these superstitious notions, the supreme Mannitto, the creator and preserver of heaven and earth, is the great object of their adoration. On him they rest their hopes, to him they address their prayers and make their solemn sacrifices.[6]

Dr. Vernon Kinietz, after making a thorough study of the documentary material and undertaking field work among the Delawares now living in Oklahoma, makes this report:

Religion among the Delaware appears to have been very insusceptible to change. From the records available, over three hundred years of white contact and more or less continuous missionary efforts have produced only one significant change [the idea of hell].
The concept of a Supreme Being, superior to subordinate good and evil deities, who has moral superintendence over worshipers that pray to Him for favors and assistance, is reported from 1643 to the present day, with only occasional dissent and never denial from all sources for any one period. On the belief in a future state of punishments and rewards for which judgment is given immediately after death, there is again complete agreement.[7]

Delaware, Iroquois, and other Indian peoples, after the Christian missionaries began to spread their doctrines, found much to attract them in the new religion, but were repelled by many of those who professed it. The men whom the Indians met in the border country were—with some honorable exceptions—far from the best representatives of Christian civilization. Contact with them inevitably colored the Indians' attitude toward the whole white race. The Shawnee chief Kakowatchiky explained this to Count Zinzendorf in 1742 when he said that the difference between the Indian's religion and the white man's was that the Indian had it in his heart while the white man had it on his lips. Devoted missionaries like the Jesuits in Canada and the Moravians in Pennsylvania showed what Christianity could be,

[6] *History, Manners, and Customs*, 212-13.
[7] *Delaware Culture Chronology* (Indianapolis, 1946), 21.

and many Indians were drawn to it. Yet most of them clung to the faith of their fathers, saying, as the Delaware preacher did to Zeisberger at Goschgoschink, that there were two paths to the Sky, the white man's and the Indian's, or four paths (one for each of the four great races) as Handsome Lake believed.

Religion permeated all life. To the Delawares, the spirit world was alive and visible in every aspect of nature. When the storm cloud approached and the lightning flashed, it was no electrical phenomenon they saw but man's spirit friends, the Thunderers, come to do battle with the Horned Serpent and to bring water for the crops. The fact that the Delawares have not handed down to us any clear body of religious doctrine does not mean that they had no mental universe. It means only that their best thought has been handed down, not in creeds and formulas, but (to borrow words from Mircea Eliade) "in myths, symbols, and customs which still, in spite of every sort of corruption, show clearly what they meant when they began."

THE BIG HOUSE CEREMONY

At the heart of all religions lies the belief that power, *mana*, resides in certain things, material or immaterial. These are objects of awe and adoration. Anything associated in the believer's mind with these objects and this divine power is sacred, be it song, ritual, or image. It is a mistake to confuse the object of awe with the poetic symbols that call it to mind. Nevertheless, one of the surest ways to get at the essence of a particular faith is to note its chief symbols and look through them to see what they meant to the believer.

To understand the ancient religion of the Delaware Indians, it is necessary to look first at the symbols contained in their most important annual event, the Big House Ceremony. It is, of course, probably true that the precise form in which its twelve-day ritual has come down to us does not antedate the year 1805, when the revelations of a Munsee prophetess gave it final shape; but its central symbol, the World Tree (imaged in the Center Post), is very old.

If some of its symbols seem strange today—too strange to satisfy our sense of the sacred—we should remember that they come from a very distant past. They were the natural forms by which great ideas were brought home to hunters of the early Stone Age, just as the religious thought of the Old Testament was brought home to a pastoral people by metaphors taken from the life of the shepherd. If we look through these Delaware metaphors to the vision beyond them, we shall find ourselves in company with ideas that are quite modern, although the garb in which they are dressed is ancient.

70

The prime purpose of the ceremony was to give thanks to the Great Spirit in the Twelfth Heaven and to His principal agents below: Mother Earth, the Sun, the Moon, the Four Winds, and all the others. A second purpose was to remind the devout Delawares that the spirit powers were the realities.

The origin of that part of the Big House Ceremony known as the Bear Sacrifice is explained in a narrative given to Dr. Speck (from whom our best knowledge of the ceremony comes) by the late Nicodemus Peters (Nekatcit) of the Grand River Reserve in Ontario. The constellation known as the Great Bear or the Big Dipper represented to the Indian imagination a bear hunt. The four stars making the quadrangular figure were the body of the bear; the three stars in the handle of the Dipper were three hunters (the often-heard interpretation that these were the bear's tail is absurd, because bears have short tails) ; and the little star, Alcor, behind the second hunter, was his dog. Every year in October the bear was overtaken and killed. It was his blood that reddened the forest leaves.

That this was an exceedingly old myth is suggested by the fact that the ritual in which it is preserved contains no plant symbols. Dr. Speck believed it to be a survival from a time before the cultivation of plants began, when men lived by hunting.

The late Chief Joseph Frederick Montour (1853-1938) thought the origin of the Big House Ceremony was to be found in a story that is widespread among Algonkian peoples, especially in New England, where Nathaniel Hawthorne found it and gave it fresh currency: the story of the Great Stone Face. In Dr. Speck's recording of Montour's version, the Delawares were once traveling among the mountains in their home country, somewhere in the Delaware-Hudson region.

"They were under a spiritual ban [said Montour] caused by their wickedness and failure to heed the worship of the Creator. Misery and unhappiness oppressed them. In passing through a bristling defile between mountains they suddenly saw a stone face outlined in the crags above them. The sight impressed them so deeply that their leaders took it as a sign placed in the path by the Creator as an admonition to them for their remissness. They realized that it was meant as a reminder of the Father-Creator—it was his image."

"Impressed accordingly by this revelation," concludes Dr. Speck, "they carved the images of the Creator's face in wood and placed them thereafter on the east and west sides of the center-post of the Big House."[8]

[8] Frank G. Speck, *The Celestial Bear Comes Down to Earth* (Reading, 1945), 41-42.

The symbolism of the Big House itself—a simple wooden structure of perhaps fifty by thirty feet in size—is thus explained:

. . . the Big House stands for the universe; its floor, the earth; its four walls, the four quarters; its vault, the sky dome, atop which resides the Creator in his indefinable supremacy. To use Delaware expressions, the Big House being the universe, the center post is the staff of the Great Spirit with its foot upon the earth, its pinnacle reaching to the hand of the Supreme Deity. The floor of the Big House is the flatness of the earth upon which sit the three grouped divisions of mankind, the human social groupings [Turtle, Turkey, Wolf] . . . in their appropriate places; the eastern door is the point of sunrise where day begins and at the same time the symbol of the beginning of things; the western door the point of sunset and symbol of termination; the north and south walls assume the meaning of respective horizons; the roof of the temple is the visible sky vault. The ground beneath the Big House is the realm of the underworld while above the roof lie the extended planes or levels, twelve in number, stretched upward to the abode of the "Great Spirit, even the Creator" as Delaware form puts it. . . .
But the most engrossing allegory of all stands forth in the concept of the White Path, the symbol of the transit of life, which is met with in the oval, hard-trodden dancing path outlined on the floor of the Big House. . . . This is the path of life down which man wends his way to the western door where all ends. Its correspondent exists I assume in the Milky Way, where the passage of the soul after death continues in the spirit realm. As the dancers in the Big House ceremony wend their stately passage following the course of the White Path they "push something along," meaning existence, with their rhythmic tread. Not only the passage of life, but the journey of the soul after death is symbolically figured in the ceremony. . . .[9]

The most conspicuous object inside the Big House was the Center Post, which symbolized the World Tree, extending from the earth to the Creator in the sky.

THE AFTERLIFE

Delaware beliefs concerning the afterlife have been summarized by M. R. Harrington:

The doctrine of the survival of the soul or spirit after the death of the body, forms an integral part of the Lenape belief. The spirit is supposed to leave the body at the moment of dissolution, but remains in the vicinity eleven days, during which time it subsists on food found in the houses of the living, if none has been placed at the grave. . . .

[9] Speck, *Big House Ceremony*, 22-23.

On the twelfth day the spirit leaves the earth and makes its way to the twelfth or highest heaven, the home of the Creator, where it lives indefinitely in a veritable "Happy Hunting Ground," a beautiful country where life goes on much as it does on earth, except that pain, sickness, and sorrow are unknown, and distasteful work and worry have no place; where children shall meet their parents who have gone before, and parents their children; where everything always looks new and bright. There is no sun in the Land of Spirits, but a brighter light which the Creator has provided. All people who die here, be they young or old, will look the same age there, and the blind, cripples,—anyone who has been maimed or injured,—will be perfect and as good as any there. This is because the flesh only was injured, not the spirit.

This paradise, however, is only for the good, for those who have been kind to their fellows and have done their duty by their people.[10]

THE WORLD ON THE TURTLE'S BACK

The Delaware story of the Creation has little to do with religion, and certainly nothing to do with science. Yet it is an honest attempt to explain the origin of things. It may not be good metaphysics, but it has social significance, for it explains the respect paid by the Indians to those lineages which claim the turtle as their ancestor.

The story is told in one form or another in most parts of the earth. The Iroquoian and Algonkian versions are very much alike. The particular variant accepted by the Delawares has never been recorded in full. What we know of it comes chiefly from reports made by the Moravian missionaries Zeisberger and Heckewelder.

In the beginning, we are told, there were people in Heaven. It might be observed here that, just as modern Americans find it difficult to think of infinity and eternity ("out of space, out of time"), so the early Indians found it difficult to conceive of existence without people to "take it in." The sky people were much like the people now on earth, but they possessed powers which men have since lost. One day a pregnant woman fell through a hole in the sky. She landed on the back of a great turtle in the midst of a wide sea. There she gave birth to a daughter, who in time gave birth to two boys, twins (some versions make it four sons). One of these grew up to become the life-giving principle of the universe, the Creator—continuously creative, as we see in the renewing life of plants, animals, and man. The other was barren and destructive. A struggle between them ensued, in the course of which the Creative Spirit was conqueror.

[10] *Religion and Ceremonies of the Lenape*, 52.

73

As for the origin of the earth, the creation of the land, a diver bird (in Zeisberger's version) brought up a bit of mud from the bottom of the sea and deposited it on the turtle's back. According to Hecke-welder, the turtle itself brought up some earth. Other versions give the honor to the muskrat, which dived, scooped up some mud, but failed to get back to the surface alive. From a speck of earth, however, clutched in its dead paws, the world miraculously took its birth.

Among the Blacksnake papers in the Draper Manuscripts in Wisconsin is found an early nineteenth-century Iroquois version of the creation legend, which is here briefly summarized:[11]

Before the creation of our earth, there was a land of happy people above the sky. The lord of that land provided everything for his people's comfort and happiness. There was neither sickness nor pain. The fruits of the earth were always ripe. No sun shone there, but a Living Tree with white blossoms gave light.

One night a man-being, sometimes known as the Chieftain of the Skies, had a dream, and he knew he must die if the dream were not fulfilled. He dreamed that the Tree of Light was plucked up by the roots. His four brothers worked hard to fulfill the dream and save his life. When at last they brought the tree down, it fell with such force that it knocked a hole through the ground, so that the sky could be seen below.

Then the man-being rose and called to his wife to come and see. Together they sat on the edge and as they looked down they saw the light coming upward from the Tree of Light as it fell. (In the soil beside them, there were shoots from the Tree which were already strong enough to illuminate the above-sky world.) They felt a tender air coming up from below, and they heard the sound of the South Wind bringing "the air of life."

The man said to his wife, who was with child, "Do you see the light below?" She answered, "Yes." He said: "You shall create a new world down there. You shall be the mother of all generations on the Earth." And he pushed her through the opening and she went down towards the great light below.

As she fell, she looked up, and there was nothing but blue above her as far as the eye could reach. Birds flew by. They asked her if she were afraid, and told her not to fear; there were ten thousand below who would take care of her. As she approached a great expanse of water, birds gathered under her and bore her safely up. Looking about for someone strong enough to hold her forever above the water they

[11] Draper MSS, 22 F, 23 ff. (Joseph Brant Papers), State Historical Society of Wisconsin (microfilm).

chose the mud turtle, for, they said, "He never tires, nor dies without his father's consent."

So the mud turtle swam up to the surface of the water, and the birds let the woman down gently on his back. While she rested there, the water fowls and the water animals dived into the water to find a little bit of earth. When they found it, they put it on the turtle's back. The soil and the turtle together began to grow in size, and soon there was enough land for the woman to walk about on.

The mud turtle then said to the woman, "I will remain forever to support you and all the generations that are to come. These commands I have received from above."

So the turtle continued to grow and the land on his back became covered with grass. After a time the woman gave birth to a girl child. When the child grew to be a woman, she walked into the sea, and from that union she gave birth to twin boys. One, the Good Twin, was born like a normal child. The other, the Bad Twin, came out from under his mother's armpit and killed her. The grandmother buried her daughter, with her feet toward the sunrise. Corn grew from her body in the earth.

The Good Twin, usually known as Sapling (who represents the creative principle), smiled on the earth, but the Bad Twin, Flint, only mocked at everything. The Good Twin created the sun to give light by day and the moon to give light by night. He created the plants and animals and man. The Bad Twin hid the animals in a cave (until his brother released them) and created misshapen things like bats and snakes.

There was as yet no woman to till the ground and make the plants multiply. Sapling, the Creator, made woman; and he told man and woman to live together and enjoy the fruits of the earth.

John Fadden (Ka-hon-hes), a Mohawk of the Turtle Clan, has painted his concept of the Creation legend on the side of an Indian drum. His version is reproduced as the frontispiece of this book.

TOBACCO

Tobacco held a unique place in Indian life, offering solace to mind as well as body. It may very likely have first come into use as medicine, for which it is still used; but its primary, its essential, meaning is religious. The fume that goes forth, as Dr. Hartley Burr Alexander observes in *The World's Rim,* is both a gift of incense to the Great Spirit and a breath of prayer.

Its fullest meaning is found in the rite of the calumet. By means of the ceremonial smoke rising from the pipe's bowl, the Indian sought to bring himself into harmony with the life of all nature.

That the instrument employed [writes Dr. Alexander] has been called "the Pipe of Peace" is due, no doubt, to the fact that every Indian council in which men sought to resolve their differences and every rite in which they endeavored to put themselves into tranquil accord with the powers which participate with man in the life of nature, was inaugurated with the ceremonial smoking. The whole meaning of human existence is bound up with the ritual of the calumet.[12]

John Jacob Schmick tells how, at the Burnt Offering Ceremony, tobacco was placed on twelve heated stones, that the smoke as it rose might carry prayers to the Twelve Heavens.[13]

The Medicine Bundle, which also was sacred and had a profound influence on Indian life, has been discussed in Chapter 5.

TWELVE—THE SACRED NUMBER

To the Delawares, the number twelve was sacred. It is not certain how this had come about. Dr. Frank Speck[14] thought it might be because of the arrangement in twelves of the scales on the shell of the turtle, an animal revered for its role in the creation and because it bears the earth-island on its back. There are twelve marginal scales on each side of the turtle's back, twelve plus one scales on top (corresponding with the twelve or thirteen moons in the Indian year), and twelve scales underneath. Some Delawares explained the sacredness of twelve in this way: The Great Manito, they said, at one time came down to earth to show men how to worship. When he returned

to heaven, he took with him twelve sumac sticks, which they could see shining far up in the air. "Every now and then he dropped one, and when he dropped the twelfth he disappeared, while they heard the heavens crack like thunder behind him as he went in."[15]

For whatever reason, the Delawares used the number twelve repeatedly in their religious observances. As we have seen, there were twelve heavens, in the highest of which lived the Great Spirit, while each of the eleven lower heavens was presided over by a manito or spirit who was a benefactor to man. These lesser manitos repeated

[12] The World's Rim, 4.
[13] Friedenshütten Diary, September 23, 1770, Archives of the Moravian Church, Bethlehem.
[14] The Celestial Bear, 46.
[15] Harrington, Religion and Ceremonies of the Lenape, 127-28.

man's prayers from one heaven to another until they reached the Great Spirit in the Twelfth Heaven.

In the First Fruits Ceremony, twelve deer were sacrificed. There were twelve heated stones in the Sacred Sweat Lodge Ceremony. The great annual festival of worship, the Big House Ceremony, lasted for twelve nights. In the Big House, twelve carved faces adorned the posts, twelve prayer sticks were used in the ritual, and tobacco was thrown twelve times into the fire. The ceremony was concluded on the twelfth night with twelve songs and twelve prayers, after which the chief said: "We have heard our old parents say that, if you sweep this Meeting House twelve different times, you will sweep up to where our great Father is, as he is up in the twelfth Heaven above the earth."[16]

A Delaware community had twelve "Selected Men," persons of good physique who were specially gifted in the spiritual way. They took a leading part in the religious rites and were allowed a good deal of authority in the civil life of the people. It was believed they had power to detect untruthfulness and also to prophesy. They were, in consequence, advisers to the chiefs, and they undertook important missions. When a criminal was condemned to death by the chief and his council, one of the Selected Men delivered the deathblow with a club.

To rid themselves of evil, some men caused themselves to be beaten with twelve sticks, one after another; others cleansed themselves with a medicine compounded of twelve different herbs. Boys who, during their ordeal, managed to fast for twelve days, were believed to attain magic powers, such as the ability to rise above the ground, to sink into the earth, and to foretell the future.

When a man died, his soul, though it immediately left the body, remained in the neighborhood for eleven days. On the twelfth, it set out on its twelve-year journey, as some said, to the Twelfth Heaven.

Nowhere is the persistence of the number twelve better shown than in David Zeisberger's description of the Sweating Rite in his "Diary of a Journey to Goschgoschink":

> If one would arrange a feast of this kind, he goes hunting and shoots one or two bears. Then he invites his guests. In the house where the feast is to be celebrated, a sweating-oven is built of twelve pieces of twelve different kinds of wood, not more and not less, which are covered closely with blankets. Then twelve stones of medium size, heated to their greatest intensity, are put in. Thereupon, the host and eleven others of his choosing creep into the oven and remain there until they are unconscious and have to be dragged out. The occupants may

[16] *Ibid.,* 107.

not come out sooner, else the sacrifice is of no value. While the twelve are in the oven, tobacco is strewed upon the stones by the one who has instituted the feast, and prayer is offered by him to his god. To another Indian he gives from ten to twelve fathoms of wampum as a present, in return for which the recipient must go out and with loud voice pray to the god, toward the rising sun. Then the bear's flesh is consumed. Whoever has repeated this sacrifice twelve times is sure of his salvation.[17]

The Good Life

How did the Delaware's religion affect his daily life?

His assurance of contact with the spiritual world, reinforced as it was by the sights and sounds of the natural world around him, helped to give him a certain poise, a feeling that he "belonged." He "trod lightly through his natural environment," writes Dr. William A. Ritchie, "merging himself sympathetically into the world of living and non-living things."

He felt joy and pain, both intensely, but he seldom gave way to disillusionment. He was early taught to believe that life, like Youth's Vigil, was an ordeal, and he adjusted himself to it. He did not, however, believe that the governance of life on this earth was in hostile hands.

Belief in future rewards and punishments encouraged self-control. The Indian showed remarkable courage and endurance. He was honest in his dealings, observant of community customs. In the Land of Happy Spirits beyond the Sky Path, good men and women were assured of a home among their kin, while evil persons wandered, perpetually restless and dissatisfied.

Like all religious people in greater or less degree, the Indian was able to identify himself, through the imagination, with things and purposes beyond the range of his immediate interest. We see this, for example, in his practice of conservation. John Witthoft in "The American Indian as Hunter" has expressed this well:

The white man saw nature as a source of property, to be mastered by his efforts, while the Indian saw himself as a part of nature, who survived only because he kept his place in the scheme of things and was therefore aided and protected by the deities who controlled his natural environment.[18]

[17] David Zeisberger and Gottlob Senseman, Diary of a Journey to Goschgoschink, January 27, 1769, Box 135, Folders 1-2, Archives of the Moravian Church.
[18] Pennsylvania Game News, XXIV, No. 2 (February, 1953), 12.

It is true that the Indian hunted, but it was for food and not mainly for sport. In the words of Dr. Hartley Burr Alexander, he felt even the humblest animals

to be participant with man in nature's rights. He will not rob the bee of all its honey; with the field mouse he traffics maize for the rodent's store of beans, being careful to leave the kernels in the nest whence the store of prized wild beans has been accumulated; and he erects tabus against the slaughter of animals with young, or the needless diminution of the herd. The white hunter, to the Indian, who slays for sport and beyond any food need, is a criminal against nature, and blasphemous of the meaning of life.[19]

The Indian thus expressed in action what one of Europe's best minds has counseled. Wrote Montaigne in sixteenth-century France: "We owe justice to men and kindliness to other creatures; there is an intercourse and mutual obligation between them and us."

The Indian's attitude to the land (always difficult for the eighteenth-century land speculator to understand) stemmed from his religion. He believed that both the land and the animals that roamed the forest had been given by the Creator for the common use, and were not to be regarded as anyone's private property.

"What," said Tecumseh. "Sell land! As well sell air and water. The Great Spirit gave them in common to all."[20]

The Indian's proverbial hospitality, which distinguishes him to this day, was religious in origin.

They give and are hospitable to all, without exception [wrote John Heckewelder], and will always share with each other and often with the stranger, even to their last morsel. They rather would lie down themselves on an empty stomach, than have it laid to their charge that they had neglected their duty, by not satisfying the wants of the stranger, the sick or the needy. . . . Besides, on the principle, that all are descended from one parent, they look upon themselves as but one great family, who therefore ought at all times and on all occasions, to be serviceable and kind to each other, and by that means make themselves acceptable to the head of the universal family, the great and good Manitto.[21]

Sex crimes were unknown; crimes of violence, rare. Theft was almost unheard of. They did not fasten their houses when they went out. They left a stick leaning against the doorway to signify that they were not at home; nobody would then enter. Hunters often left their

[19] *The World's Rim*, 183-84.
[20] Quoted by John Collier, *The Indians of the Americas* (New York, 1947), 214-15.
[21] *History, Manners, and Customs*, 101-102.

79

utensils by the trail, unconcealed, knowing that no one would touch them.

Conrad Weiser in the early eighteenth century summed up what "the good life" meant to the Indian:

The teachings of Christ and his apostles are more congenial to them than to [many so-called Christians]: for when it is said Owe no man anything save to love one another Rom. 13:8 Be not anxious for the morrow Matth 6:34 He that is greatest among you shall be your servant Matth 23:11. . . . That is what they actually practice without calling themselves Christian, while many who bear the name never give such things a thought.[22]

[22] Wallace, Conrad Weiser, 20-21.

11

Delaware Amusements

STORYTELLING

THE DELAWARES were great entertainers, and they had a large repertory of myths, legends, folk tales, tall stories, and amusing "situations" with which to enliven winter evenings by the fireside.

They looked on storytelling as a community art, and they bound it by strict rules. The time and place for telling a story had to be right, and conditions varied with different kinds of narrative. The time for folk tales was in the winter. If you told them in the summer, the snakes would come out and listen. The place for such tales was indoors. Telling them out-of-doors was likely to cause trouble in the animal kingdom, for many of these adventures involved tricks whereby gods and men outwitted and subdued the woodland creatures.

Storytelling was almost a ritual. Except for hunters and warriors recounting their personal adventures, the story had to be "straight," that is, word perfect. Otherwise members of the audience, who had good memories, would be offended.

Few Delaware stories in the lighter vein have come down to us, but the following traditional account of the first meeting between Indians and white men may serve as an example of the type. It came from Captain Pipe of Sandusky and was written down in 1824 by C. C. Trowbridge.

> . . . Captain Pipe says that in those days [before the white man came] the Indians were accustomed to worship annually as they now do, in a large building prepared & kept for that purpose [the Big House Ceremony]. At one of these meetings an old man prophecied the coming of some important and extraordinary event, and a few days after a ship hove in sight and a boat with some of the officers came on shore. The Indians, supposing the crew to be inferior deities sent by the great Spirit, spread beaver skins upon the ground for them to walk upon. . . .
>
> After becoming familiar with them the whites solicited them to give a small piece of land upon which they might build a fire to prepare their food. They demanded only a piece as large as a Bullocks hide and the request was readily granted, when to their great astonishment the bullocks hide was soaked in water and cut into a small cord with which the land was surrounded. However, they determined to overlook the deception and be more wary in future. They [sic] whites presented them with Axes, hoes &c and departed, promising to revisit them the next year. Upon their return they were not a little amused to see the Indians walking about with these things suspended from their necks as ornaments. They taught them their use, trafficked a little with them, and at length told them that they wanted more lands, because it was impossible from the smallness of the size of the first grant, to build a fire upon it without being incommoded with the smoke. It was therefore resolved to add to the first piece a quantity large enough to hold the chair of the whites, without the influence of the smoke. Upon this the bottom of the chair, which was composed of small cords, was taken out and like the hide, stretched around the lands. This second deception determined them never to give more lands without fixing some boundary understood by both parties distinctly.[1]

The origin of the Pleiades is explained by Oklahoma Delawares in the delightful tale of the Seven Wise Men. Gladys Tantaquidgeon records it as it was told to her by Witapanoxwe, "Walks with Daylight." A long time ago (the Indian equivalent to our "once upon a time") there were seven wise men, prophets, who were so much bothered by curiosity seekers that they turned themselves into rocks on the hillside in order to be free. At length a young man who had supernatural insight found them. He agreed not to betray their dis-

[1] C. C. Trowbridge, "Account of Some of the Traditions, Manners and Customs of the Lenee Lenaupee or Delaware Indians," Michigan Historical Collections, University of Michigan, Ann Arbor, Michigan (microfilm).

guise, but he continued his visits, for he enjoyed their conversation. One day some people, following the young man without his knowledge, discovered the secret of the talking rocks. The news was soon spread, crowds trampled the hillside, and the philosophers had to find another way to escape notice. This time they turned themselves into seven stately cedars in the forest. But again they were discovered, and again and again, changing into fresh forms but never long escaping curious eyes. At last the Great Spirit took pity on them. Walks with Daylight concluded: "The Creator thought that it was of no use to place them on earth as they were being constantly bothered by earthly things so he placed them in the heavens. There we see the seven stars as they were placed there so long ago by the Creator."[2]

We are indebted to John Heckewelder and David Zeisberger for preserving fragments of Delaware mythology.

> Of the spherical form of the earth [writes Zeisberger] they have no conception. . . . The sky, they say, rests upon the water probably because it appears so to do when they look out upon the sea. Others declare that there is a place where the sky strikes the earth, rises again and continues moving up and down, smiting a rock, which causes such a report that it may be heard many days' journey. Two great captains once visited that place, and one of them risked going through the opening when the sky rose. He succeeded in getting into heaven and coming back. Yet where this place is they know as little as they do the location of Tschipey Hacki, the land of spirits. The sun, they think, sinks into the water when it sets. . . . The milky way is the road to Tschipey Hacki. . . . In case of an eclipse of sun or moon, they say that these bodies have fallen into a swoon.[3]

Heckewelder tells us why the Delawares were proud of their lineage symbols:

> The Tortoise, or as it is commonly called, the *Turtle* tribe, among the Lenape, claims a superiority and ascendency over the others, because their *relation,* the great Tortoise, a fabled monster, the Atlas of their mythology, bears according to their traditions this great *island* on his back, and also because he is amphibious, and can live both on land and in the water, which neither of the heads of the other tribes can do. The merits of the *Turkey,* which gives its name to the second tribe, are that he is stationary, and always remains with or about them. As to the *Wolf,* after whom the third tribe is named, he is a rambler by nature, running from one place to another in quest of his prey; yet they consider him as their benefactor, as it was by

[2] Tantaquidgeon, *Delaware Indian Medicine,* 69.
[3] "History of the Indians," 147-48.

83

his means that the Indians got out of the interior of the earth. It was he, they believe, who by the appointment of the Great Spirit, killed the deer whom the Monsey found who first discovered the way to the surface of the earth, and which allured them to come out of their damp and dark residence. For that reason, the wolf is to be honoured, and his name preserved for ever among them.[4]

MUSIC

The Delawares were fond of music, especially singing. Benjamin Mortimer, a Moravian missionary, found they had good voices and a good ear. Songs accompanied all their public ceremonies. There were special songs with appropriate rhythms for particular occasions: prayer, the dance, hunting, games, courtship, battle, death.

Our eastern Indians did not, however, at first have many musical instruments. The flute, about which we hear from early travelers, may have been introduced by white men. The Indians' chief instruments were the drum, made of deerskin tightened over a frame, and the "turtle rattle," a dried tortoise shell in which had been inserted a few pebbles or some corn. These gave rhythm for dancing feet, while the human voice, solo or in chorus, provided accompaniment.

Indian melodies, though strange to our ears, had a definite musical structure. There were rhythmic patterns and well-defined melodic phrases. But, instead of the mechanical regularity of our classical music, Indian songs had measures of unequal length balancing each other and pleasing the ear with the effect of recurrence. Indians took, moreover, what at first seem liberties with the scale (actually they used at least four different scales) which remind one of European folk music.

In compass they ranged from one to three octaves. Some songs had no words but were sung to meaningless syllables: vocables, such as *ho ho*, being set to a melody. There were some songs that belonged exclusively to particular individuals or societies. Ceremonial songs, prayers to Heaven, were guarded with extreme care against error. If the words were not "straight" they might not reach the right Powers and harm might result.

GAMES

The Delawares were fond of sports: foot races, lacrosse, shinny, wrestling, jumping, hopping, lifting or throwing stones, shooting or throwing arrows. They had a game of dice in which they gambled on

[4] *History, Manners, and Customs*, 253.

84

the throw of a certain number of flat bones or oval cherry stones painted black on one side and yellow on the other. They had also something like a modern card game, played with pieces of reed.

The famous moccasin game was played on the night before a funeral. A ball was hidden under one of four moccasins lying on a deerskin. If the ball was found under the first or the fourth moccasin turned up, it counted in the tally for the finder, who then had the ball to hide. If, however, it was turned up at the second or third try, it counted for the side that had hidden it, which then had the right to hide it again. The side that won three times in a row won a game. The number of games to constitute a match was determined in advance by agreement between the players. Sometimes whole villages played, one against the other, gambling large quantities of goods on the outcome. The Indians were good losers. It was a saying among the Iroquois in such contests that the loser won a moral victory because his failure helped him to cultivate humility.

THE DANCE

The Delawares' greatest pleasure was in the dance. It provided their richest form of self-expression. In the Big House they "danced before the Lord." At harvest time they danced their thanksgiving, and they danced their patriotism in time of war. Nearly every night they gave themselves up to "social dances," in which the whole community joined.

The form of the dance, whether in religious ritual or on social occasions, was always the same. They danced in a circle, counterclockwise, each dancer by himself, the men leading off and the women closing in behind. Where the gathering was large and concentric circles had to be formed, the innermost circle was composed of men, the next of women, the third of men, the fourth of women.

The dances were decorous. The women moved smoothly as a stream. Their feet patted rapidly to the rhythm of the turtle rattle or drum, but they did not bob about. Their bodies were straight, their arms hung relaxed but still. They seemed to glide on air. The older men also, though "stomping" with their feet, moved quietly and gravely. But the younger men were permitted a little clowning. They made fantastic leaps and turns and twirls, punctuating every movement with a shrill cry; but they were careful to observe the rhythm and keep their places in the wheeling circle.

Loskiel, writing in the eighteenth century, has left us a picture of Delaware dancing, noting some variations from the norm just described.

. . . The common dance is held either in a large house, or in an open field around a fire. In dancing they form a circle, and always have a leader, whom the whole company attend to. The men go before, and the women close the circle. The latter dance with great decency, as if engaged in the most serious business; they never speak a word to the men, much less joke with them, which would injure their character. They neither jump nor skip, but move one foot lightly forward, and then backward, yet so as to advance gradually, till they reach a certain spot, and then retire in the same manner. They keep their bodies strait, and their arms hanging down close to their bodies. But the men shout, leap, and stamp with such violence that the ground trembles under their feet. Their extreme agility and lightness of foot is never displayed to more advantage than in dancing. Their whole music consists in a single drum. This is made of an old barrel or kettle, or the lower end of a hollow tree, covered with a thin deer-skin, and beat with one stick. Its sound is disagreeable, and serves only to mark the time, which the Indians, when dancing even in the greatest numbers, keep with due exactness. When one round is finished, they take some rest, during which the drummer continues to sing, till another dance commences. These dances last commonly till midnight.

Another kind of dance is only attended by the men. Each rises in his turn, and dances with great agility and boldness, extolling his own or his forefathers' great deeds in a song, to which the whole company beat time, by a monotonous rough note, given out with great vehemence at the commencement of each bar.

Some dances held upon particular occasions differ much from the above. Of these the chief is the dance of peace, called also *calumet* or pipe-dance, because the *calumet* or pipe of peace is handed about during the dance. This is the most pleasing to strangers, who attend as spectators, its appearance being peaceable, and not so dreadful as the former. The dancers join hands, and leap in a ring for some time. Suddenly the leader lets the hand of one of his partners go, keeping hold of the other. He then springs forward, and turns round several times, by which he draws the whole company round so as to be enclosed by them, when they stand close together. They disengage themselves as suddenly, yet keeping their hold of each others' hands during all the different revolutions and changes in the dance: which, as they explain it, represents the chain of friendship. A song, made purposely for this solemnity, is sung by all.

The war-dance, held either before or after a campaign, is dreadful to behold. No one takes share in it, but the warriors themselves. They appear armed as if going to battle. One carries his gun, or an hatchet, another a long knife, the third a tomahawk, the fourth a large club; or they all appear armed with tomahawks. These they brandish in the air, to signify how they intend to treat or have treated their enemies. They affect such an air of anger and fury on this occasion, that it makes a spectator shudder to behold them. A Chief leads the dance, and sings the warlike deeds of himself or his ancestors. At the end of every celebrated feat of valor, he wields his tomahawk with all his might against a post fixed in the ground. He is then followed by the rest, each finishing his round by a blow against the post. Then they dance all together, and this is the most frightful scene. They affect the most horrible and dreadful gestures, threatening to beat, cut, and stab each other. They are however amazingly dextrous in avoiding the threatened danger. To complete the horror of the scene, they howl as dreadfully as in actual fight, so that they appear as raving mad-men.[5]

The Delawares had two religious dances. One was the Worshipping Dance, performed on the White Path in the Big House around the center post. It was a symbol of man's passage through life in the presence of the Creator. The other was the Doll Dance, in which was carried a wooden replica of the Doll Being, a minor deity. Men and women of the community performed this dance in twelve sets in order to please the Doll Being, who had power to bring them health. It was thought that, if the dance were neglected, someone would surely die.

War brought the Begging Dance for the purpose of outfitting a war party. The War Dance followed a declaration of war. A dance of thanksgiving marked the return of a successful war party.

[5] *History of the Mission*, I, 104-106.

12

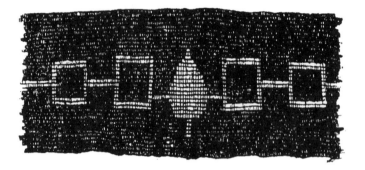

The Iroquois Confederacy

"A mighty thing, this our Great Peace. Have you, of across the water, had a greater vision?"

—*William E.* Yager, Orite of Adequentaga[1]

WHEN WILLIAM PENN first came to America in 1682, the Delawares occupied the soil of southeastern Pennsylvania, but their political overlords were the Five Nations, the Iroquois Confederacy, whose homeland was in upstate New York. The Iroquois, as a result of conquests made during their long war for survival, which culminated in the dispersal of the Susquehannocks in 1675, laid claim to extensive territories of which the lands in Pennsylvania were a part. Since it was the political and military genius of the Iroquois that gave them their principal influence upon our history, this chapter will concern itself chiefly with that part of their culture.

The Iroquois and the Delawares were both superior examples of Stone Age man, but there were great differences between them. The Delawares had what is called an "atomistic" society, that is, one in which local communities were completely independent, each being subject to its own laws only. The Iroquois, on the other hand, had

[1] (Oneonta, N. Y., 1953), 90.

in their confederacy a political organization of the highest maturity. It was a federal union of five distinct Indian nations, each of which retained its sovereignty almost intact, without, however, weakening the integrity of the whole. In spite of individual differences in outlook and interest, and frequent disagreements in policy, the five nations as a whole possessed a strong sense of national identity.

When Champlain in 1609 first met the Iroquois in battle (in this instance a body of Mohawk warriors protected with wooden armor), he praised them in a soldierly way: "I saw the enemy come out of their barricade, nearly 200 men, strong and robust to look at, coming slowly toward us with a dignity and assurance that pleased me very much."[2]

The Iroquois at that time were by no means the dominant Indian power that Pennsylvania found them to be three quarters of a century later, yet the "dignity and assurance" which Champlain saw in them was not military bluff. Many early writers commented on this Iroquois trait. It did not come from any difference in blood strain. The Iroquois practice of adopting prisoners precluded any specialization of inherited characteristics. Nor was it the result of a marked superiority in culture, except in the field of government. They had no secret weapon. Technologically, they were Stone Age people like their neighbors.

What set them apart and gave them assurance was, above everything else, their superior political organization. They had also the advantage of a sound military position resting on the mountains flanking Lake Ontario and the St. Lawrence River. In addition, they had a religion that taught them they were a people chosen by the Great Spirit to lead all men (by the scruff of the neck if necessary) into a world-wide league of peace.

> As the Five Nations are the most potent among our Western Indians [wrote Christian Frederick Post], they are also the wisest among all the rest. They have their settled Maxims of Government as well as other Nations; & their Political School is at Onondago. Their first Principles are to bring all the other Nations, if not under an absolute Dependency, at least under a certain Submission. The means they make use of to come to these Ends are sometimes Overt Force sometimes Treaties and Alliances. Prudence & Circumspection are their Guides.[3]

[2] Annie Nettleton Bourne (trans.), *The Voyages and Explorations of Samuel de Champlain*, 2 vols. (Toronto, 1911), I, 211.
[3] Post, Observations Accompanying Journal, January 19, 1759, Division of Archives and Manuscripts, Pennsylvania Historical and Museum Commission, Harrisburg.

THE LONGHOUSE

The Iroquois called themselves *Kanonsionni,* "People of the Longhouse," using a familiar figure taken from their housekeeping. They, like the Susquehannocks, lived in long, rectangular, bark-covered houses, each with its central corridor, its hearths, and its several families under the general superintendence of an elder matron of the lineage.

The longhouse was a good symbol, calling to mind as it did both the geography and the government of the Confederacy. The five independent peoples of which it was composed, each speaking a dialect of a common Iroquoian tongue, were seated in a string of villages along a trail—at one time a warpath but after confederation known as the Ambassadors' Road—which crossed northern New York from near Schenectady to the Genesee River. From east to west—as the names of rivers and lakes in that region remind us—they were the Mohawk, Oneida, Onondaga, Cayuga, and Seneca nations.

Each nation was virtually independent, having its own council, just as each family in the longhouse had its separate fire. The homely image of the longhouse brought to mind also their highly advanced (and to us surprisingly modern) concept of democratic rule. The authority of the Great Council (the central government) came from the homes of the people. On the death of a chief, the head matron of his lineage consulted the matrons of other longhouses before appointing his successor to the clan council. The chiefs of the several clans made up each nation's council, and these same chiefs represented their nation on the Great Council of the Confederacy.

The federal congress or Great Council was often known as the Onondaga Council because it met at Onondaga (Syracuse, New York), the principal seat of the Onondaga nation whose territory lay in the geographical center of the League. Meetings were held at least once a year, and oftener if pressing business (matters of peace and war) arose. When Conrad Weiser, Pennsylvania's representative, carried peace messages to the Iroquois, he sent advance notice to Onondaga; and from that place runners were dispatched to both ends of the Longhouse to summon the council chiefs to meet him when he arrived.

In the Onondaga Council, each member nation had certain privileges and responsibilities. The Mohawks, for instance, had a council veto. The Onondagas provided the presiding officer, Atotarho (Wathatotarho, Thadodaho), who was also the Head Chief of the Confederacy; and their chiefs as a body were the steering committee, "tending the fire," which meant preparing the agenda and, in the absence of the Council, attending to necessary business. The Senecas appointed the two war chiefs of the Confederacy.

90

The role of the federal council was to harmonize, if that were possible, the often conflicting interests of the different nations in the Confederacy. Each nation had its own customs, language (a dialect of the common tongue), and international problems. The Mohawks faced east, the Senecas west, and their friends as well as their enemies were not always the same. In time of great crisis, if feelings ran high and unanimity in the council was impossible (as happened during the American Revolution, when both the Americans and the British solicited Iroquois aid), each member nation was permitted to go its own way, even though it meant that different parts of the Confederacy for a time might be indirectly at war with one another.

In the Great Council, each national delegation voted as a unit. It was a council rule that no important matter should be debated on the day it was first brought up. This was intended not only to prevent snap judgments, but also to give the chiefs in each delegation time to come to agreement among themselves and appoint a speaker to present their united views before the assembly.

The government, though democratic in spirit, was not a pure democracy in form. The chiefs held office by hereditary right. On the death of a chief, the matrons of his line selected his successor from the same lineage, usually a brother or nephew (a sister's son) of the deceased but not his own son. Certain lineages (and they alone) had title to chiefships; others were without direct representation on the council. But, the population being small and the sense of social responsibility high, the selection of a chief was thoroughly talked over before any appointment was made, and it usually represented the general will.

The chiefs' council (whether on the national or confederate level) was much like a modern cabinet. It had responsibility for co-ordinating the affairs of the nation or the League and for making recommendations, but it had no authority beyond what came by concurrence with the council of warriors and women, in other words, with the general public.

The political position of women among the Iroquois has always astonished white men. The matrons did not, after appointing the chiefs, retire modestly into the political shadows. Scaroyady, the Half King, in 1756 asserted that "women have a great influence on our young Warriors. . . . It is no new thing to take women into our councils particularly amongst the Senecas." Cornplanter in 1790 said that "in the Seneca nation the women have as much to say in council

91

as the men have, and in all important business have equal authority. . . ."[4]

Iroquois women did not occupy titled positions on the League Council, but their political influence was profound. For one thing, they had their own councils, choosing representatives and spokesmen as circumstances required. For another, important women—"the Ladies of the Council," as the French called them—sat with the chiefs in council. They listened to the discussions and sometimes took part in them. Often their wishes prevailed, as when the Seneca women, during the crisis of 1794, pressed for peace with the United States and constrained Cornplanter to speak their will.[5] From the chiefs' councils they carried discussion to women's councils or the council of warriors and women. Finally they went into action, exerting their immense prestige among their kin to see that the national will was carried out.

These civil chiefs (as distinct from the war chiefs) were known as *royaneh*, "lords," and were treated with high respect, but they put on no airs. *Noblesse oblige*. They were often poorer than the people about them. It was a point of honor for them to share, or give away, whatever they possessed.

The Onondaga Council had no police to enforce its wishes. It ruled by consent, the chiefs relying on the matrons who had appointed them to move public opinion. There were other channels of pressure, but this was the main one. For example, if the Onondaga Council decided to enter peace negotiations with a former enemy, such as the Catawbas, it was necessary to hold the young men back from their scheduled war raids. The chiefs consulted the matrons, and the matrons broadcast the news through the longhouses, using their personal influence to keep the young men at home. Thus we see that, as John Collier writes in *The Indians of the Americas*, "authority flowed upward, from the smallest and most organic units. . . ."[6] Through the same channels that had put the chiefs in power, their combined wisdom was filtered back to the people.

Between the chiefs' council and the populace there were many channels of communication. There were councils at all levels, in all places, both men's councils and women's councils, family councils, councils of warriors, councils of elders. Frequently these subsidiary councils chose spokesmen to represent them before the Great Council.

[4] Edmund B. O'Callaghan and Berthold Fernow (eds.), *Documents Relative to the Colonial History of the State of New-York*, 15 vols. (Albany, 1853-1887), VII, 103; Pennsylvania, *House Journal, 1815-1816*, Appendix, 37.
[5] See Donald H. Kent and Merle H. Deardorff (eds.), "John Adlum on the Allegheny: Memoirs for the Year 1794," *Pennsylvania Magazine of History and Biography*, LXXXIV (1960), 456.
[6] *Indians of the Americas*, 201.

And the chiefs of the Great Council influenced public opinion by reversing the process and letting their advice percolate through these lesser councils to the level of the family and the individual.

"From family council to town, to tribe, to confederacy and down again there were regular steps in a chain of administration. . . . ," writes Dr. William N. Fenton. "Their confederacy was but a League of ragged villages, as Franklin said of it, but it worked better than any other in the colonies."[7]

The member nations of the Confederacy, in their official relations with one another, adopted the familiar terms of a matrilineal society founded on ties of kinship. There were three Elder Brothers: the Mohawks, Senecas, and Onondagas. The Mohawks were known as Keepers of the Eastern Door, the Senecas as Keepers of the Western Door, and the Onondagas tended the council fire in the middle, the Fire That Never Dies. The Younger Brothers were the Oneidas, affiliated with the Mohawks, and the Cayugas, affiliated with the Senecas. Two more Younger Brothers were added later, the Tuscaroras and the Delawares, who were adopted "on the cradleboard."

THE FOUNDING LEGEND

The Five Nations were united in reverence for two culture heroes, Deganawidah and Hiawatha, the traditional founders of the Confederacy, whose words were treasured as revelations from the Creator.

There is no explicit record of the founding of the Confederacy. The "Hiawatha Belt," now in the custody of the New York State Museum at Albany, has been traditionally regarded as a contemporary record of the founding. Scientific examination has shown, however, that its beads were strung together in their present form, probably in the eighteenth century, from several earlier wampum belts. The design is interesting as an ancient symbol of the League, but the belt itself is not so old.

The coming together of these five nations in the Iroquois Confederacy was not a single act of creation at a determinable moment in time. The "completed cabin" (the Longhouse) was probably the culmination of a long process of development during which smaller leagues had been formed. A committee of Iroquois chiefs in 1900 set the date of the final act of union as 1390. Horatio Hale, who worked for years among the Iroquois, thought the League had been founded about the middle of the fifteenth century. Some recent scholars have set the date as late as 1570 or even 1630. Such dating seems untenable,

[7] "Long-Term Trends of Change Among the Iroquois," in Verne F. Ray (ed.), *Cultural Stability and Cultural Change* (Seattle, 1957), 32.

for the *Jesuit Relations* of the seventeenth century refer repeatedly to the "completed cabin" as something not only beyond the memory of man, but as "of the greatest antiquity." The Relation of 1654 quotes a Mohawk Indian as saying, "We, the five Iroquois Nations, compose but one cabin; we maintain but one fire; and we have, from time immemorial [*de tout temps*], dwelt under one and the same roof."[8]

The founding of the Confederacy was described in a powerful and beautiful legend which they held sacred. It was their Bible. Although it is in part a product of the popular imagination, it is important historically both for the core of truth contained in it and for the influence it exerted on later Iroquois history. The ideal it contained of a peaceful world and the practical means it proposed to attain that end inspired men with a depth of devotion that, even in these days of fervid nationalism, can hardly be equaled. It gave to their wars something of the complexion of religious crusades. "The Master of Life fights for us," they said to the Eries.

The Iroquois believed in the divine origin of their League. As the legend runs, Deganawidah's mother was a virgin through whom the Great Spirit, in compassion for mankind, became incarnate, bringing to earth a message of "Peace and Power": peace, that is, based on law and justice, and backed by sufficient military power to make such a peace prevail.

In the beginning, it is said, Deganawidah won Hiawatha (from whom Longfellow got the name, though not the adventures, of his hero) as his first disciple and sent him out to announce the Good News of Peace and Power among the neighboring Iroquois. There followed a long political campaign. The principal obstacle was Atotarho, according to legend a tyrant whose body had seven crooks in it and whose head was covered with snakes instead of hair. In the end, Hiawatha (whose name means "He Who Combs") combed the snakes out of Atotarho's hair, and the union was completed on the shore of Onondaga Lake. Deganawidah there planted the Tree of Peace and presented to his people (according to the legend) a body of laws, which are sometimes known as the "Constitution of the Five Nations." In its legal aspect, the Confederacy became known as *Kayenerenkhowa*, the Great Peace.

The legend is full of familiar but unforgettable images, symbols of man's hope for a world in which, as a later Iroquois expressed it, "The land shall be beautiful, the river shall have no more waves, one may go everywhere without fear." The Tree of Peace was seen as a great white pine "rising to meet the sun" (the Eye of the Creator),

* Thwaites (ed.), *Jesuit Relations*, XLI, 87.

with branches representing the law and white (i. e., living) roots extending to the Four Quarters of the earth so that men everywhere might be able to trace peace to its source. Above the tree was the Eagle That Sees Afar, symbol of "preparedness," watching the horizon to warn peace-loving people of approaching danger.

The population of the Five Nations was small. According to a recent estimate, it was never more than twelve or fifteen thousand men, women, and children. How can their influence over such vast areas and such large populations as acknowledged their authority be explained? The answer is to be found in a combination of circumstances, these among others:

1. They had a driving economic motive to expand, as George T. Hunt has shown in *The Wars of the Iroquois,* once the fur trade had made their survival dependent on gaining access to territories not yet denuded of beaver.

2. They held a strategic military position among the mountains flanking the St. Lawrence River and Lake Ontario.

3. They had the advantage of a strong political organization, which enabled them to act together when necessary and to take the long view in their plans.

4. They had a highly-developed agriculture, with large corn surpluses which they stored to carry them over emergencies.

5. They were wise enough to know when to bury the hatchet and turn to negotiations.

6. Holding the balance of power in America between the English and the French, they made good use of their bargaining power.

7. Their religion gave them unity and a purpose: to make the Great Peace prevail.

Whether there was an element of self-deception in their warring for peace is not the question here. We note merely that the Iroquois had a sense of mission which nerved them—as it nerved Cromwell's Ironsides and those who sang "John Brown's Body"—to win victories.

It is easy to see that not all the actions of the Five Nations were in harmony with Deganawidah's ideal. But the ideal was nevertheless there, and the course of early American history bears frequent witness to it.

They proclaim [wrote one of the Jesuit missionaries] that they wish to unite all the nations of the earth and to hurl the hatchet so far into the depths of the earth that it shall never again be seen in the future; that they wish to place an entirely new Sun in the Heavens, which shall never again be obscured by a single cloud; that they wish to level all the mountains, and remove all the falls from the rivers—in a word, that they wish peace. Moreover, as an evidence of the sincerity of their intentions, they declare that they are coming—women, and children, and old men—to deliver themselves into the hands of the French,—not so much in the way of hostages for their good faith as to begin to make only one Earth and one Nation of themselves and us.[9]

The French chronicler went on to tell how the Iroquois followed up their peace proposals by sending a large delegation, to the number of thirty, bearing gifts of no less than a hundred belts of wampum, some of them more than a foot wide. But while on their journey they were ambushed by France's Algonkin Indian allies. Some of the peace party were killed, others were captured, and the rest fled.

"Thus the grand project of this Embassy has vanished in smoke," concluded the missionary, "and instead of the peace which it was bringing us, we have on our hands a more cruel war than before. . . ."[10]

DREAMS

One of the best known Indian stories in Pennsylvania is that of the dreams exchanged by Shickellamy, the Iroquois representative at the Forks of the Susquehanna, and Conrad Weiser, Pennsylvania's interpreter. The tradition is that one day, as the two were traveling together over the Susquehanna Indian Path opposite the Isle of Que (Selinsgrove), Shickellamy said: "I have had a dream. I dreamed that you gave me a new rifle."

Conrad Weiser, who owed much of his success in Indian negotiations to a strict observance of Indian custom, now did what religion and etiquette demanded. He gave the rifle. But he added expectantly, "I, too, have had a dream. I dreamt that you gave me that island in the river."

We are told that Shickellamy, the perfect diplomat, fulfilled Weiser's dream. But he said, "I will never dream with you again."

Stories of such dreams were popular among white men in the woods two hundred years ago, and they were told in various localities about many different people. One comes from upstate New York, with Chief Hendrick of the Mohawks and Sir William Johnson dreaming a scarlet uniform against a large grant of Indian lands. Whatever liberties with the truth may have been in these particular tales, they

[9] Ibid., XLIX, 137.
[10] Ibid., 147.

96

were a natural outgrowth of an old Iroquois custom, one which we see reflected in a curious memorandum appended to one of Conrad Weiser's Indian journals: "PS to buy a wooden pipe with a Civerin [covering?] over it and the best I Can. to answer Saghsidowas dream."[11]

Such items as these, amusing when taken out of their social and religious context, are survivals of what was at one time an important (and surprisingly modern) Iroquois belief, namely, that the health of the mind—and the body as well, since the one is dependent on the other—is achieved through the fulfillment of desires revealed in dreams. The cure of the sick was believed in many cases to depend on the satisfaction of dream wishes. Father Jerome Lalemant wrote in 1647: "The Savages know not what it is to refuse what another has dreamed ought to be done for his health. This law is common throughout the countries of America of which we have knowledge."[12]

The belief in dreams was most dramatically expressed in what the Jesuits, who had frequent opportunity to observe it, called the annual "Festival of the Demon of Dreams." The Iroquois themselves called it *Ononharoia,* the "Feast of Fools" or "Turning the Brain Upside Down." During the three days and nights of the festival, people went from cabin to cabin guessing and fulfilling one another's dreams, a thing that was not always easy to do, for the dreamers were forbidden to tell their dreams outright. They could only give a hint or act out the dream in charades.

We read in the *Jesuit Relations* for 1656:

> It would be cruelty, nay, murder, not to give a man the subject of his dream; for such a refusal might cause his death. Hence, some see themselves stripped of their all, without any hope of retribution; for, whatever they thus give away will never be restored to them, unless they themselves dream, or pretend to dream, of the same thing. But they are, in general, too scrupulous to employ simulation, which would, in their opinion, cause all sorts of misfortunes. Yet there are some who overcome their scruples, and enrich themselves by a shrewd piece of deception.[13]

Quaker missionaries to the Senecas 160 years ago thought the Iroquois respect for dreams was nothing but a primitive superstition. Today they would be less contemptuous. It is now recognized that the Iroquois theory of dreams was, as a modern psychologist has called it, "basically psychoanalytic," and that it anticipated Sigmund Freud. Father Paul Rageneau in 1648 described the theory in language which might have been used by Freud himself:

[11] Wallace, *Conrad Weiser,* 151.
[12] Thwaites (ed.), *Jesuit Relations,* XXXI, 133.
[13] *Ibid.,* XLII, 165, 167.

97

In addition to the desires that we generally have that are free,—or, at least, voluntary in us,—[and] which arise from a previous knowledge of some goodness that we imagine to exist in the thing desired, the Hurons [and, he might have added, the Iroquois] believe that our souls have other desires, which are, as it were, inborn and concealed. . . .

Now they believe that our soul makes these natural desires known by means of dreams, which are its language. Accordingly, when these desires are accomplished, it is satisfied; but, on the contrary, if it be not granted what it desires, it becomes angry, and not only does not give its body the good and the happiness that it wished to procure for it, but often it also revolts against the body, causing various diseases, and even death.[14]

Applying the psychoanalyst's technique to Iroquois dreams, Dr. A. F. C. Wallace, in "Dreams and Wishes of the Soul," comes to some interesting conclusions about Iroquois character. He finds that Iroquois dreams, as reported by early writers,

held a prevailingly anxious tone, ranging from nightmare fantasies of torture to the nagging need to define the unconscious wish and satisfy it before some disaster occurs. . . .

. . . .

. . . The community rallies round the dreamer with gifts and ritual. The dreamer is fed; he is danced over; he is rubbed with ashes; he is sung to; he is given valuable presents; he is accepted as a member of a medicine society. . . .

This observation suggests that the typical Iroquois male, who in his daily life was a brave, generous, active, and independent spirit, nevertheless cherished some strong, if unconscious, wishes to be passive, to beg, to be cared for. . . .

The culture of dreams may be regarded as a useful escape-valve in Iroquois life. In their daily affairs, Iroquois men were brave, active, self-reliant, and autonomous; they cringed to no one and begged for nothing. But no man can balance forever on such a pinnacle of masculinity, where asking and being given are unknown. Iroquois men dreamt; and, without shame, they received the fruits of their dreams and their souls were satisfied.[15]

[14] *Ibid.*, XXXIII, 189.

[15] "Dreams and Wishes of the Soul: A Type of Psychoanalytic Theory Among the Seventeenth Century Iroquois," *American Anthropologist*, LX (1958), 247.

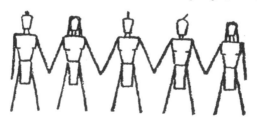

98

13

The Beaver Wars

THE FUR TRADE

WHAT THE IROQUOIS might have made of themselves if they had been given time to develop naturally under their own laws, it is impossible to say.[1] As it turned out, the coming of the Europeans changed their mode of life and put them—as it did all other Indians—on the defensive. At first contact, the Indians recognized the superiority of the white man's tools: axes and hoes, needles and kettles, and, above all, firearms. A brisk trade sprang up between the two races, much earlier than is usually supposed. It has been calculated that before the arrival of the *Mayflower* in 1620 not less than five hundred and possibly more than six hundred voyages had been made to New England alone.[2] Quite early the Indian found himself dependent on the white man's goods not only for comfort but also for survival.

[1] In this chapter the author has incorporated passages from his article, "The Iroquois: A Brief Outline of Their History," printed as an introduction to Lawrence H. Leder (ed.), *The Livingston Indian Records* (Gettysburg, 1956), 15-28.
[2] Donald F. X. Connolly, "A Chronology of New England Catholicism Before the Mayflower Landing," American Catholic Historical Society of Philadelphia, *Records*, LXX (1959), 3.

The Iroquois were an agricultural people and good farmers. Their cornfields were rich. But the white trader would not accept corn in exchange for guns, powder, and broadcloth. He demanded furs for the European market.

The monstrous effects of the white man's lust for peltries can hardly be exaggerated. Writing of the Dutch at Albany, Allen W. Trelease has this to say: "In almost every context the fur trade reigned supreme at Fort Orange. From the company directors down to the lowliest Beverwyck trader the primary object of Indian policy, foreign policy, land policy, and trade policy was to facilitate the flow of peltry toward the Hudson."[3] The Indian, in order to buy what he needed, had to devote his best energies to hunting. When his own territory was exhausted, he went farther afield, coming into conflict with hunters of other tribes, and there ensued the catastrophe of national wars.

The change in mode of living affected all Indians adversely. To the Iroquois it brought almost immediate disaster. Though their population was not large, intensive hunting on a national scale soon depleted their hunting grounds. By 1640 scarcely a beaver was to be found between the Hudson River and the Genesee. The Iroquois, to save themselves, had either to find new hunting grounds or to capture a position as middlemen in the trade between the white men and the Indians of the far north and west where the best hunting lay.

The Iroquois War for Survival

The Susquehanna Valley and the rich hunting territories extending westward to the valleys of the Allegheny and Ohio rivers, with which the name of the Iroquois was later to be associated, were in 1640 not accessible to them. The Longhouse was surrounded by powerful and jealous neighbors. The Mahicans were pressing hard from the east. To the south were the Susquehannocks, intent on protecting their trade with the Dutch and Swedes at the mouth of the Schuylkill and with the English on Chesapeake Bay. The Wenro, a small people west of the Iroquois, had in 1638 been pushed out, most of them taking refuge with the Hurons; but their removal had brought the Iroquois into direct contact with more powerful enemies, the Neutrals and the Eries, the latter of whom alone could muster more warriors than the Iroquois. To the north were the Petuns (or Tobacco Nation) and the Hurons, the latter a large and powerful people, the greatest Indian merchants on the continent, through whose activities as middlemen the French at Montreal held a monopoly of the trade with the Indians beyond the Great Lakes.

[3] *Indian Affairs in Colonial New York* (Ithaca, 1960), 137.

100

That was the tough market the Iroquois had to break into or perish. The greatest obstacle was New France. The French were determined to suffer no breach in their monopoly of the northern fur trade. It brought wealth to the colony and at the same time kept France's Indian allies dependent on her. As long as she held that monopoly, she could control her allies by threatening to deny them trade goods. Repeatedly the Iroquois sought to make a commercial treaty with the Hurons. The Hurons themselves were not averse to it, but the French found ways to block it.

Desperate, the Iroquois took to piracy, as the English had done on the Spanish Main. They raided French trade routes on the St. Lawrence and Ottawa rivers, ambushing Huron fur fleets bound for Montreal. French Canadian history and folklore are full of such incidents. So successful were these raids that the French in alarm reconsidered their policy. In 1645 they, with their Huron allies, made peace with the Iroquois. It was just such a treaty as the Iroquois had hoped for, containing the right commercial terms. Deganawidah had said that friends should "eat out of the same bowl." Kiotsaeton, Mohawk spokesman at the treaty, made this explicit. The Hurons were to trade with the Iroquois.

The treaty was soon put to the test. Out of the northwest there came next summer a Huron fur fleet of more than eighty canoes—"the greatest fur fleet in the history of New France,"[4] as George T. Hunt describes it. Unmolested by the Iroquois, the fleet descended to Montreal. Strangely, the Iroquois were allowed no part in the trade, though the high price of furs at Albany might have made it worth the Hurons' while to give Iroquois traders a middleman's cut. The Mohawks, enraged at this plain breach of the commercial terms of the treaty, sent war belts to their Brothers, the Senecas and Onondagas.

The Five Nations were in a strong military position in relation to the French. The Longhouse flanked French trade routes to the west, and, in case of French attack, the Iroquois had at their backs a range of wooded mountains into which they could retire by secret paths. Within easy reach of them, too, were the Dutch, and later the English, to supply them with guns and powder. But the French made up in diplomacy whatever disadvantage they suffered in terrain. They tightened their hold on the nations surrounding the Iroquois, and, by appealing to divergent interests among the different nations in the Longhouse itself, attempted to tear the Confederacy apart.

[4] *The Wars of the Iroquois: A Study in Intertribal Trade Relations* (Madison, Wisconsin, 1960), 83.

101

The Hurons in 1647 made an aggressive alliance with the Susque-hannocks, who agreed to lift the hatchet when the Hurons gave the word. To the Iroquois, that sounded like the closing of a deathtrap. The Hurons did more. Taking advantage of the looseness of the tie that held the Five Nations together, they sent an embassy to negotiate a separate peace with the Onondagas and the Cayugas. Such a peace, if concluded, would have broken the Confederacy in two, leaving the Mohawks and Oneidas at one end of the Longhouse and the Senecas at the other to shift for themselves. Thoroughly alarmed, the Mohawks and Senecas dispatched warriors to break Huron communications with the Onondagas and the Susquehannocks. They concerted further plans which took a little time to mature.

The year 1648 passed with inconclusive fighting. In the summer a large Huron trading fleet was brought successfully through a Mohawk blockade—with severe loss to the Mohawks. But in the autumn of that year the Mohawks and Senecas quietly sent a thousand hunters up into the woods of Ontario. At a given time, some months later, these hunters came together. At early dawn on March 16, 1649, they emerged from the snow-covered woods before the Huron town of St. Ignace, stormed and took it, and set it on fire. Three of the in-habitants escaped, making their way to St. Louis, three miles away, where they gave the alarm. But by sunrise the Iroquois were before St. Louis, and by nine o'clock it, too, was in flames.

A spirited Huron counterattack persuaded the Iroquois not to press their good fortune too far. Instead of attacking the principal Huron stronghold, Ste. Marie, they returned to their own country. But their work had been done. Behind them they left panic. The Huron people fled, burning their villages as they went. Some spent a winter of near starvation on Christian Island in the Georgian Bay. Some fled to the Petuns (Tobacco Nation), their near neighbors to the southwest. Others took refuge among the Neutrals west of Niagara. A large number made their way to the country of the Eries. Still others found shelter under the Tree of Peace, a whole Huron village seating itself among the Senecas.

More important for the subsequent history of the United States, one band made its way north to mingle with the Ottawas on Manitoulin Island. This last group of Hurons, best known now under their own name of Wyandot, in the end robbed the Iroquois of some of the hoped-for fruits of victory. These Wyandots moved to the north of Lake Superior and there continued the role of middlemen in the French fur trade. Later they came south and settled in the vicinity of Detroit and Sandusky, from which place part of the tribe moved in

1748 to establish settlements at present Coshocton, Ohio, and below present New Castle, Pennsylvania. Later in the century they transferred to the Delawares their claim to land between the Beaver, Muskingum, and Sandusky rivers.

The attack on Huronia was only the beginning of the Beaver Wars, which for the Iroquois had become a war for survival. They disposed of whole nations at a blow, not by massacring their people, but by destroying main centers of resistance and so causing their enemies' dispersion. In such manner the Petuns were overthrown in December, 1649, the Neutrals in 1650-1651, and the Eries after a more protracted struggle which lasted from 1654 to 1656.

"It is therefore a marvel," we read in the Jesuit Relation for 1659-1660, "that so few people work such great havoc and render themselves so redoubtable to so large a number of tribes, who, on all sides, bow before this conqueror." In the same connection the Relation observes, "But what is more astonishing is, that they actually hold dominion for five hundred leagues around, although their numbers are very small...."[5]

War with the Mahicans and the Susquehannocks was a different matter. The Mahicans were good for the long pull. As early as 1626 they had driven the Mohawks from their Lower Castle (as the Dutch called this palisaded village on the Mohawk River east of Schoharie Creek). The last great battle in the Mahican War, at Hoffman's Ferry, in which the Mohawks were victorious, did not come until 1669. Peace with the Mahicans was concluded in 1673.

DEFEAT OF THE SUSQUEHANNOCKS

To the Susquehannocks on the lower Susquehanna, the loss of their Huron allies was offset by an alliance made with the English in Maryland, with whom they had been enjoying a considerable trade. In 1661 Maryland made a treaty with the Susquehannocks, aimed at the Senecas, Keepers of the Iroquois' Western Door, who bore the brunt of the Beaver Wars in this quarter. Maryland sent fifty men to strengthen the Susquehannock fort.

The Seneca attack of 1663 on the Susquehannocks, though launched with what was for the American scene a very considerable army (some eight hundred men), was easily repulsed. The next year Maryland formally declared war on the Senecas.

The war dragged on for many years. The Susquehannocks seemed indestructible. They had a fort on the lower Susquehanna River,

[5] Thwaites (ed.), *Jesuit Relations*, XLV, 207.

probably at this period on the east bank, below Washington Boro, Pennsylvania. It was equipped with bastions and mounted artillery. Their warriors, who had behind them a strong military tradition, were not to be destroyed at one stroke. They not only turned back the Seneca force in 1663 but repeatedly raided the Iroquois country and for years had the best of this desolating war.

But their day passed. Continuous warfare and the ravages of small-pox ate away their numbers. Worst of all, they were deprived of their main source of arms and ammunition when in 1674 Maryland, reversing its Indian policy, made peace with the Senecas and in effect terminated its 1661 treaty with the Susquehannocks.

The next year saw their downfall. For unclear reasons they abandoned their fort on the Susquehanna and in February, 1675, were reported on the Patuxent River in Maryland. When they moved on south to Piscataway Creek, below present Washington, they were closed in by Maryland and Virginia militia and their chiefs were killed. The survivors scattered; eventually most of them were adopted by the Iroquois; others returned to the lower Susquehanna, where they were joined at Conestoga by a group of their former enemies, the Senecas. At Albany in 1679 the Oneidas thanked Maryland and Virginia for their assistance. ". . . ye Susquehannas are all destroyed," they said, "for w^h wee Return you many thanks. . . ."[6]

So it came about that, six years before the Quaker William Penn received the charter of his province, the Iroquois had established the Tree of Peace here. It was to be Pennsylvania's Indian policy to help the Iroquois tend it.

"BALANCE OF POWER"

During the first half of the eighteenth century the Iroquois performed a sustained "balancing act" between the French and the English in America. Lacking the military strength to determine the final outcome of the struggle between France and England in North America, nor desiring a victory for either, they succeeded through diplomacy and equivocation—aided by French and English reluctance to come face to face with one another—in retaining their lands and freedom in the face of white pressure.

By the Montreal Treaty of 1701 the Iroquois allied themselves, on certain terms, with the French. They adopted this policy, which marked a turning point in their history, because of the uneasiness they felt at the expansion in America not only of their old enemy, France,

* Leder (ed.), *Livingston Indian Records,* 56.

but also of their old ally, England. Against the French, who wanted a monopoly of the fur trade, and against the English, who wanted Indian lands, the Iroquois knew they were not strong enough to stand alone. They felt their safety to lie in using the one rival as a counterweight to the other. In the Montreal Treaty they made that policy open and explicit.

France was, of course, the traditional enemy and in 1701 the more immediately dangerous of the two. We must go back a little to understand this. In the year 1666 New France, in order to punish the Iroquois for their raids on her fur fleets, launched two expeditions against the Confederacy. The first, under Daniel de Rémy, Sieur de Courcelle, was a failure; but the second, under the Marquis de Tracy, though it encountered few Indians (they having wisely vanished into the woods), burned villages and destroyed the stored corn. Peace was made the following year, but it was soon broken. In 1687 the Marquis de Denonville's invasion of the Seneca country with over three thousand men caused little loss of manpower to the Iroquois, although the destruction of vast quantities of corn (excitedly estimated at 1,200,000 bushels by Denonville) was crippling, at least for the moment. In reprisal, two years later, the Iroquois secretly penetrated New France to the gates of Montreal and at a signal emerged from the woods to devastate the country for many leagues about. The incident is remembered in Canada as the Massacre of Lachine—massacre, because the Indians, being unable to reach and destroy the enemy's stores of food as the French had done, killed or captured the crop producers, which achieved the same military objective: the weakening of the enemy's economy. In 1693 and 1696, under Count Frontenac, the French launched further punitive expeditions against the Iroquois. And so the pendulum swung, from reprisal to reprisal, each side continually getting hurt, but never mortally.

What the Iroquois wanted was not war but a better share of the fur trade. "In fine," wrote Father J. de Lamberville in 1684 of their war with the Miamis in the west, "they do not wage war save but to secure a good peace."[7] What the French wanted was freedom from Iroquois terror. "An extraordinary thing," wrote Bacqueville de La Potherie, "that three or four thousand people should be able to make a whole new world tremble."[8] The Lachine affair had so frightened the Hurons and Ottawas that the French thereafter found them impossible to control.

[7] Edmund B. O'Callaghan (ed.), *The Documentary History of the State of New-York*, 4 vols. (Albany, 1849-1851), I, 133.
[8] *Histoire de l'Amérique Septentrionale*, 4 vols. (Paris, 1722), IV, 147.

By this time the situation had reached a stalemate. The French had learned that they could not destroy the Iroquois. The Iroquois had learned that it would be unwise to destroy the French: they were a good counterweight to the English. It was becoming apparent to both sides, French and Iroquois, that an accommodation was to be desired. The English, getting wind of this rapprochement, did everything they could to stop it. They reminded the Iroquois—not very wisely— that they were "subjects" of the King of England. In this the English were mistaken. The Onondaga and Cayuga chiefs, when on August 2, 1684, they said, "Wee have put ourselves under the Great Sachim Charles that lives over the Great Lake,"[9] meant only that they placed themselves under English protection in their conflict with the French, not that they surrendered either their sovereignty or their title to land. The merchants of Albany feared losing their monopoly of Iroquois trade. The province of New York feared losing Iroquois protection of her northern border. "Those Five nations," wrote Governor Thomas Dongan in 1687, "are very brave & the awe & Dread of all ye Indyans in these Parts of America, and are a better defence to us, than if they were so many Christians."[10] The middle colonies, fearing war with France, did not want to lose the support of Iroquois manpower. "If we lose the Iroquois, we are gone. . . . ," wrote James Logan, Provincial Secretary of Pennsylvania, in 1702.[11]

In the summer of 1701, what the English had feared came to pass. At Montreal the Five Nations made peace with the French and their Indian allies. The French invited the Iroquois to trade with them at Detroit. In return the Iroquois promised, in case of a Franco-British war, to remain neutral. But the Iroquois were not deserting their British allies. While one embassy was on its way to treat with the French in Montreal, another was quite honestly renewing the Chain of Friendship at Albany. By these two treaties, the Iroquois launched a new policy of armed neutrality between the English and the French as a means of holding the balance of power between them.

The importance to Pennsylvania of the Montreal Treaty was that in return for the promise of neutrality, the Iroquois stipulated that the French should *respect* that neutrality. In case of war with the English, the French were to "sit on their mats" (as far as the Iroquois were concerned) , that is, they bound themselves not to cross the Iroquois borders.

[9] O'Callaghan (ed.), *Documentary History*, I, 402.
[10] *Ibid.*, 256.
[11] Edward Armstrong (ed.), *Correspondence Between William Penn and James Logan*, 2 vols. (Philadelphia, 1870-1872), I, 88.

Let us look forward a moment to see how this worked out. During the early years of the eighteenth century, Conrad Weiser in Pennsylvania and William Johnson in New York did much to confirm the "Ancient Union" of the Iroquois and the English; while, on behalf of the French, the Joncaires, father and sons, strove to preserve Iroquois neutrality in the worsening disputes between the two European rivals. When at last the French and Indian War broke out, the Five Nations, true to their treaty with France, remained neutral. There were, it is true, some scattered acts of partisanship, as when Senecas took part in raids on English settlements or when Mohawks danced the war dance with William Johnson. But officially Iroquois neutrality was maintained, and on the whole it worked to the advantage of the English colonies. When the French in 1753 landed at Presque Isle (Erie) on their way to establish forts on French Creek and the Allegheny, the Iroquois sent an impressive embassy, "the ladies of the Council" as the French described it, to protest. A year later Tanaghrisson, the Iroquois Half King in the Ohio Valley, sent the French three successive protests—the strongest deterrent the Iroquois knew short of a declaration of war. Thereafter the Iroquois exerted judicious pressure on their wards, the Delawares and Shawnees, who had joined the French and struck the English. At the Easton Treaty of 1758, the Iroquois made peace for the Delawares over their heads and brought the Indian war in Pennsylvania to an end.

14

Indian Refugees in Pennsylvania

THE PROBLEM OF THE SUSQUEHANNA VALLEY

THE DISPERSION of the Susquehannocks by the Iroquois by 1675 left the victors with a nearly insoluble problem. The valley of the Susquehanna River, which in its north and west branches flanked the southern quarter of the Longhouse and gave access to it, lay empty and defenseless. The Iroquois knew well enough that "power abhors a vacuum." If they themselves did not quickly fill this vacuum, others would, in particular the English of Maryland, Virginia, and (after 1681) Pennsylvania. The history of the Susquehanna River for the next hundred years is largely concerned with the attempt of the Five Nations to fill the vacuum and hold the valley.

They did not throw out colonies of their own people for that purpose. Their population was too small to permit colonization on any large scale, and what colonies they did throw out were for the most part in the newly-won Ohio country. The Seneca nation, after defeating the Neutrals and Eries, had occupied the country west to Niagara and south to the upper Allegheny River and French Creek. Senecas and others of the Five Nations also sent hunting parties (some members of which settled and became permanent residents under the name of Mingoes) throughout the Upper Ohio Basin.

The Susquehanna Valley had to be filled another way. The Iroquois did it with displaced persons.

The term "displaced persons" was not in use among our forefathers in America, although the human problem it calls to mind was everywhere about them. They themselves, many of them, had suffered displacement in Europe and came to America to find freedom and security. It is one of the ironies of history that in their search for these things they should have found themselves constrained to deny them to the people "who came out of this ground." Everywhere on the frontier the Indians were being uprooted. The pressure of incoming white men—a pressure exerted sometimes through what the Indians called "pen and ink work" and sometimes by the cruder but franker method of powder and ball—forced whole tribes of Indians to leave their lands and seek refuge where they could find it.

Many of these homeless people turned to the Iroquois for help, and the Iroquois welcomed them. That was in accordance with Deganawidah's instruction to his people that aliens who traced the Great White Roots of Peace to their source should be welcomed and made to feel at home. The Confederacy offered the refugees shelter under the branches of the Tree of Peace, which extended over the Susquehanna Valley.

The placement of the refugees was not, however, a gesture of blind altruism. It was an act of enlightened self-interest. To have grateful allies in the Susquehanna Valley—at Conestoga, at the mouth of Conoy Creek, at Paxtang, Shamokin, Wyoming, Wyalusing, Sheshequin, Tioga, and the Great Bend—would help to keep the Southern Door of the Longhouse shut against white men, who were already hammering on it.

Christian Frederick Post (a Moravian missionary married to an Indian wife) understood this. In his "Observations" accompanying his second journal of 1758 to the Allegheny, he wrote of the Six Nations that:

> . . . they settle these New Allies on the Frontiers of the White People and give them this as their Instruction. "Be Watchful that no body of the White People may come to settle near you. You must appear to them as frightful Men, & if notwithstanding they come too near give them a Push we will secure and defend you against them. . . ."

109

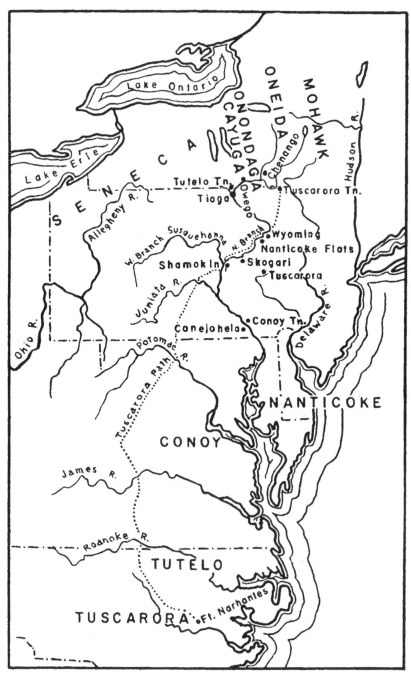

Movement of Refugee Peoples to the Iroquois Country

110

... The Chain of Union betw[n] the several Indian Nations is of that nature, that if we have War with one of them, we have also war with them all.[1]

THE CONOYS

Some confusion attends the history of the Conoy Indians, as C. A. Weslager notes, because "the word Nanticoke was loosely . . . applied to the Conoy before the Nanticoke proper made their appearance in the State."[2]

The two tribes, Conoy and Nanticoke, were closely related and may at one time have comprised one political family—as they were to do again later. But at the time of Maryland's founding in 1632, they were two distinct peoples, living on opposite shores of Chesapeake Bay; and the movements that brought them into Pennsylvania during the eighteenth century were different in time, place, and circumstance.

The Conoys or Ganawese, when Captain John Smith first visited America in 1607, were known as the Piscataway Indians. They lived in southern Maryland in the neighborhood of Piscataway Creek on the peninsula that separates Chesapeake Bay from the lower Potomac. Disturbed by the Susquehannocks, they left the Piscataway region and moved up the Potomac to an island at the site of Washington, D. C.

In 1701 they attended a treaty with William Penn at Philadelphia, and shortly afterwards, under the sponsorship of the Five Nations, they moved into Pennsylvania, settling at the old site which had been vacated by the Susquehannocks in the neighborhood of Washington Boro and naming it Conejohela, which means, according to J. N. B. Hewitt, "Kettle on a Long Upright Pole." The name survives on the west shore of the river in Canadochly Creek.

> ... our fforefathers [said their chief, Old Sack, in a message to Governor George Thomas in 1743] came from Piscatua to an Island in Potowmeck, and from thence down to Philadelphia in Old Proprietor Penn's Time, in Order to shew their ffriendship to the Proprietor; That after their return they brought down all their Brothers from Potowmeck to Conejoholo, on the East side Sasquehannah, and built a town there.
>
> That the Indians of the six Nations told 'em there was Land enough, they might chuse their place of Settlement any where about Sasquehannah.
>
> That accordingly they thought fit to remove higher up Sasquehannah to the Conoy Town [at the mouth of Conoy Creek],

[1]Dated January 19, 1759. Division of Archives and Manuscripts, Pennsylvania Historical and Museum Commission.

[2] *The Nanticoke Indians: A Refugee Tribal Group in Pennsylvania* (Harrisburg, 1948), 4.

where they now live; And on their first settling, the Indians of the six Nations came down & made their ffire, and all the great Men declared the fire of their Kindling in token of their approbation of their settling there; But that now the Lands all around them being settled by white People, their hunting is spoiled And they have been long advised by the six Nations to leave the place and go higher up the River and settle either at the Mouth of Conodogwinnet, Chiniotta [Juniata], or up at Shamokin.[3]

Once inside Pennsylvania, they continued their way northward, moving deeper into the Six Nations country. About 1718 they settled at the mouth of Conoy Creek (some two miles south of Bainbridge), a spot later made famous by Peter Bezaillon as the western terminus of Old Peter's Road. From that point, Conoy Town, they moved (about 1743) to an island at the mouth of the Juniata. We read in the Philadelphia Deed Book, I, No. 5, page 37 (under date of August 24, 1762) : "that Island Situate at the mouth of the River Juniata . . . on which Island The said Conoy Nation afterwards [i.e., after leaving Conoy Town] was settled by their Uncles the Six Nations and from whence they directly removed some years Since to their present Habitation & Settlement at Otseningo [Chenango, near Binghamton, N. Y.] on the East Branches of the Susquehanna. . . ."

Just how "directly" they had moved from the Juniata to Otseningo is not certain. There are intermediate glimpses of Conoy Indians at Shamokin, Catawissa, Wyoming, Owego, and Chugnut. But we know that by 1758 they had become "one Nation" with the Nanticokes at Chenango, as appears in the minutes of the Easton Treaty for October 8 of that year.

THE NANTICOKES

The Nanticokes, an ancient people who were said to have invented witchcraft, had a reputation also as poisoners. "I have known Indians," writes John Heckewelder, "who firmly believed they [the Nanticokes] had people among them who could, if they pleased, destroy a whole army, by merely blowing their breath towards them."[4] This reputation, which they themselves do not seem to have discouraged, may have been a protective device, like a porcupine's quills, for they were not by nature aggressive. David Zeisberger, who met them at Nanticoke in 1748, described them as "clever modest people."

They were of Algonkian stock, closely related to the Conoys and less closely to the Delawares. When John Smith saw the Nanticokes in 1608,

[3] Pennsylvania, *Colonial Records*, IV, 657.
[4] *History, Manners, and Customs*, 92.

they were living in villages on the Eastern Shore of Maryland at the mouth of the Nanticoke River and up along its reaches into Delaware. According to their own estimate, it was about the year 1680 (that is, shortly after the Iroquois conquest of the Susquehannocks) that they became "tributary" to the Iroquois. To be tributary did not mean that they were humiliated and denationalized. It meant that they accepted Iroquois protection, became loyal "Props to the Longhouse," and acknowledged that relationship by token gifts of wampum.

In the next century the Nanticokes, stung to reprisals by outrages which white men had committed against them, found themselves in trouble with the Maryland government. Looking for a way out, they sent agents in 1742 to negotiate at Shamokin with Shickellamy, the Iroquois chief, for·permission to move up into Pennsylvania, where they would be more immediately under the Confederacy's protection. Next year at Onondaga they presented their petition directly to the Great Council through Pennsylvania's Conrad Weiser as interpreter.

Already a body of them had settled at the mouth of the Juniata. At the Treaty of Lancaster in 1744, they presented a petition to the Pennsylvania authorities, asking for a safe conduct for others of their people whom they wished to bring from Maryland to Pennsylvania on the way towards the Six Nations home country. Four years later, in 1748, we find them moving in a body to the Wyoming Valley, where they settled on the Nanticoke Flats, site of the modern city of Nanticoke.

While there, they made seasonal excursions to the Eastern Shore to enjoy the sea food they were accustomed to. The Nanticoke Path may be traced today through the towns of Hazleton, Tamaqua, Reading, Honeybrook, Compass, Cochranville, Oxford, Elkton, and Calvert. It brought them to the Northeast River and the shores of Chesapeake Bay.

The Nanticoke Flats remained their home for five years. In 1753 they moved in a body—twenty-five canoe loads were seen to pass at one time—to Chenango at the southern door of the Longhouse. They were adopted into the Confederacy and accorded two chiefs to represent them at meetings of the Onondaga Council.

The Six Nations kept a paternal eye on these and all other Indians to whom they had promised asylum. During a conference at Johnson Hall in the Mohawk Valley, December, 1766, chiefs of the Six Nations spoke thus to Sir William Johnson:

> We now desire your attention on behalf of our Children the Nanticoks, Canoys, and Delawares who have lately requested of us to lay their desires before you, and begged our Interest on this occasion.—First that as their People who yet remain near

113

the Sea Side, are in a very poor Situation, and desire to come &
settle among the rest on the Six Nation's Land, we request, to
this end, you will grant them Passports, as you have done to the
Tuscaroras, and others formerly.[5]

THE TUSCARORAS

The Tuscaroras were an Iroquoian people whose towns and "castles"
were in North Carolina on streams flowing east into Pamlico Sound.
John Lawson, an early explorer and historian, knew them intimately
and described them as mild and friendly. But, it being a recognized
business among white men in those days to kidnap Tuscarora children
and sell them as slaves, the Indians at length turned savagely on the
whites and massacred them indiscriminately. John Lawson himself
was captured in 1711 and put to death. The Tuscarora War which
followed was not ended until 1713, when the last great Tuscarora fort,
Narhantes, near Snow Hill in Greene County, North Carolina, was
destroyed.

Some families headed north at once for the country of the Five
Nations, with whom the Tuscaroras had been in touch by way of what
the Iroquois called the Tuscarora Path. In 1714 the chiefs of the Five
Nations informed Governor Robert Hunter at Albany that the "Tus-
carore Indians are come to shelter themselves among the five nations
they were of us and went from us long ago and are now returned . . .
we desire you to look upon the Tuscarores that are come to live among
us as our Children who shall obey our commands & live peaceably and
orderly."[6]

The Tuscaroras were admitted to the Longhouse "on the cradleboard," as Seth Newhouse tells us, that is to say, under the sponsorship
of one of the original Five Nations, behind whose delegates they sat
at meetings of the Onondaga Council and spoke "with their voice."
At first they were protégés of the Oneidas, later of the Senecas. The
Tuscaroras are still in the Seneca country, on a reservation near Lewis-
ton at the mouth of the Niagara Gorge. Their loyalty to the Confederacy is today made plain by the lead they are taking in the Iroquois
national renaissance.

After the adoption of the Tuscaroras, the Five Nations became
known as the Six Nations. At what precise date the change was made
is not known. The first official mention of the Tuscaroras by name

[5] James Sullivan, Alexander C. Flick, and Milton W. Hamilton (eds.), *Papers of Sir
William Johnson*, 14 vols. (Albany, 1921-1965) XII (1957), 242.
[6] O'Callaghan and Fernow (eds.), *Documents Relative to the Colonial History of
the State of New-York*, V, 387.

114

as taking part in the affairs of the Confederacy was at Albany in 1722. But it is to be noted that as early as 1710 Iroquois chiefs visiting England, in their address to Queen Anne, referred to themselves as of the *Six* Nations.

It was ninety years before the migration of the Tuscaroras from North Carolina to the Iroquois country was completed. They moved in bands, at different times, at different rates of speed, and by different routes. They stopped "overnight" at points along the way. That is why their passage through Pennsylvania is marked by so many place names: Path Valley (after the Tuscarora Path) and Tuscarora Creek in Huntingdon and Juniata counties; another Tuscarora Creek in Wyoming County; a Tuscarora Post Office in Schuylkill County, and a village by that name in Juniata County; Tuscarora Mountain west of the Kittatinny; and Tuscarora Old Town, shown on early maps at the Great Bend in Susquehanna County.

We know from early documents that the Iroquois not only encouraged but actively superintended this migration. In 1765 they dispatched seven Tuscaroras south to bring away the last remnant of their people in North Carolina. These latter had sold their lands and with part of the proceeds bought horses for the long journey north. Setting out next spring, 160 or more of them under the guidance of two chiefs and an interpreter, they moved unmolested over what were now the white man's roads until they reached Harris' Ferry. There the Paxton Boys (who had murdered the Indians at Conestoga in 1763) were still operating. The Tuscaroras were plundered, losing among other things six horses. At Lackawanna (Pittston) the travelers divided into two parties, one going directly north to Tuscarora Town by the Lackawanna Path, while the other took a longer but easier route over the Great Warriors Path, which followed the Susquehanna River.

They had sent messengers ahead, in accordance with Indian custom, to let the Iroquois know at what time to expect them. The Iroquois not only made preparations to receive them but also sent agents to arrange for their comfort along the way. After the robberies at Harris' Ferry, it was necessary to provide transportation for their sick and aged. The emissaries of the Six Nations, Newallike and Aehkolunty along with others in five canoes, left a request among "the Indians everywhere along the Susquehanna," as the Moravian missionary at Wyalusing, John Jacob Schmick, noted on November 18, 1766, "to receive these poor Indians, send canoes from place to place for them, and provide them with corn so that they may get along all right. Our

115

Indians, accordingly, as soon as they hear of their arrival at Lechawachneck [Pittston] will send 10 canoes to them."[7]

THE TUTELOS

The Tutelos, described by John Lawson in their native environment as "tall, likely men," by David Zeisberger after their uprooting as "a degenerate remnant of thieves and drunkards," and more recently by James Mooney as "the most honest and bravest Indians Virginia ever knew," were a Siouan people who formerly lived in the Piedmont of Virginia and North Carolina.

During the seventeenth century, they were much knocked about by their neighbors, white and Indian. The Susquehannocks, turning south, attempted to possess themselves of the Tutelo territory. The Tutelos, aided by Nathaniel Bacon and some two hundred Virginians, drove the Susquehannocks back. Whereupon these same Virginians, attracted by the Tutelos' great wealth in beaver skins, turned upon their allies. In the battle that ensued, the Tutelos drove the Virginians off, but with severe loss to themselves.

Worse than that, their country happened to be astride the Virginia Road, a path used by the Iroquois in raids against their own and the Tuscaroras' enemies. In consequence the Tutelos, whose numbers were dwindling, found themselves much harassed. To protect themselves, they retired for a time into the mountains at the headwaters of the Yadkin, and then came east to the Roanoke and Meherrin rivers, losing something of their cultural cohesion during these migrations. When at last in 1722, after many years of wandering, they made peace with the Iroquois, they saw that under the still-standing Tree of Peace lay their best hope of survival. They moved, accordingly, into Pennsylvania.

Conrad Weiser found them in 1744 at Shamokin. Four years later some of them moved farther up the North Branch to Skogary (Lapachpeton's Town) at the mouth of Catawissa Creek in Columbia County. In 1750 they settled for a time near Tioga at "Tutelow Town" —from which comes the name of Tutelow Creek and of a suburb of Sayre formerly known as "Toodleytown." By 1771 they were established near the south end of Cayuga Lake.

Their formal adoption as "Younger Brothers," together with the Nanticokes, in 1753 at Onondaga was thought by Conrad Weiser to be a publicity stunt engineered by William Johnson of New York to increase the importance of the Six Nations; but the subsequent history

[7] The Bethlehem Diary, Archives of the Moravian Church.

116

of these "Props to the Longhouse" makes it clear that the adoption was genuine. The Cayugas, their political sponsors, promised the Tutelos freedom of religion and the preservation of their native customs. So well have they kept their word that today the Cayugas conduct an annual Tutelo Spirit Adoption Ceremony on the Six Nations Reserve in Canada, although there are no longer any Tutelo-speaking people left to fully understand its meaning.

> The political agenda of the Iroquois [writes Dr. Frank Speck] tolerated, even fostered, the retention of tribal institutions among those minority bodies of natives who voluntarily came to ally themselves with the Long House, not withstanding the circumstances that they be of alien speech-stock and extraction. The Tutelo were evidently of a temper to enjoy this form of institutional freedom with the added dignity of social and political equality accorded them.[8]

There were other refugee groups, most of them small, detached fragments of important tribes outside our area. Among these were Mahicans from the east (and Moravian converts, Mahicans and Wampanoags, from their mission at Checomeco, New York), who merged with the Delawares at Wyoming and on the Allegheny, a few Foxes who settled on the upper Allegheny and became absorbed by the Senecas, and a hundred or so Wyandot warriors under Chief Nicolas who in 1748 settled at Kuskusky (where Nicolas died in 1750) but returned to Sandusky by 1755. These and many other such bands have passed through Pennsylvania, leaving behind them here and there a few burials and perhaps a vague tradition among local white people that "there used to be Indians around here."

More important were the large Shawnee bands who for a generation or two made their home in Pennsylvania. These will be considered in the next chapter.

[8] *The Tutelo Spirit Adoption Ceremony* (Harrisburg, 1942), 2.

15

The Shawnees

ORIGIN

THE SHAWNEES were among the refugee groups in Pennsylvania, but their influence on our history has been so much greater than that of the Conoys, Nanticokes, Tutelos, and even the Tuscaroras, that it seems best to give them a chapter to themselves. They were not here long, and there were never very many of them; under these circumstances, the fact that their names have been preserved in so many different places throughout the Commonwealth is evidence of the lively impression they made upon our forefathers.

The same evidence from place names attests to the difficulty they had in settling down. When in 1697 they made their first appearance here in any great numbers, they were already known as a race of wanderers. Their movements while in this province—on the Delaware, the Susquehanna, the Allegheny, and the Ohio—confirmed that reputation. They left Pennsylvania about the time of the French and Indian War, and their subsequent history until the death of their great chief Tecumseh (the "Meteor" or "Flying Panther") in 1813 left the impression of a mettlesome people, ready to stand up for their rights (they led in the Indian defense against white encroachments in the Northwest Territory), defiant of restraint, contemptuous of white people, and (from the latter's point of view) utterly untamable.

Yet the Shawnees were not by nature drifters. The seminomadic character in which they appear in our records was forced on them by circumstances. They were manly, responsible folk and village-dwellers. The Marquis de Beauharnois spoke of them in 1728 as "a very industrious people, cultivating a good deal of land."[1] But they were unfortunate in their international contacts, and at the same time quite unsubmissive to their fate. They accepted disaster without whining, and kept moving on "for fresh luck."

Like the Delawares, they were members of the great Algonkian family, branches of which were found all the way from Labrador to the Rocky Mountains and from Hudson Bay to North Carolina. Their speech was most closely related to that of the Sacs and Foxes. Like other Algonkian tribes they called the Delawares "Grandfathers." A long time ago they had a settled homeland, but wars—Indian wars, especially with the Cherokees, Catawbas, and Iroquois—caused them to break up and scatter.

Their earliest recorded home was in western Kentucky, on the Cumberland River, identified on early French maps as "River of the Shawnees." Father Marquette, descending the Mississippi in 1673, wrote of the Ohio that

> This river flows from the lands of the East, where dwell the people called Chaouanons [Shawnees] in so great numbers that in one district there are as many as 23 villages, and 15 in another, quite near one another. They are not at all warlike, and are the nations whom the Iroquois go so far to seek, and war against without any reason; and, because these poor people cannot defend themselves, they allow themselves to be captured and taken like flocks of sheep.

This characterization contrasts sharply with the Shawnees' later reputation; but they were in fact scattered about 1680 by the Iroquois' devastating raids. Some fled to Carolina, where they had previously traded with the Spaniards; others took refuge at a French fort in Illinois but left after some disagreement with other Indian groups there.

According to their "ancient traditional history," as Alford tells us, there were five tribal divisions among them: *The-we-gi-la* (Sewickley), *Cha-lah-gaw-tha* (Chillicothe), *Pec-ku-we* (Pequea), *Kis-po-go*, and

---

[1] Quoted by Charles A. Hanna, *The Wilderness Trail*, 2 vols. (New York, 1911), I, 184.

May-ko-jay. Each of these was virtually autonomous. Yet a measure of political unity is evidenced by the acknowledged leadership of certain divisions. According to Alford, the Sewickley and Chillicothe were "the principal or national clans from either of which comes the ruler of the nation who is called principal chief. . . ."[2]

As a result of the rivalry between the Sewickley and the Chillicothe, the other divisions were constrained to take sides, the Pequea and Kispogo allying themselves with the Sewickley and the Maykojay with the Chillicothe. Shawnee villages were commonly named after the division to which most of the inhabitants belonged. Thus we find the name Pequea in many forms applied to streams and towns in eastern Pennsylvania, while Sewickley is common in western Pennsylvania.

CHARACTER AND CUSTOMS

Before we examine the Shawnees' dramatic appearances and disappearances in and from Pennsylvania, let us look for a moment at the way they lived in their own communities. To begin with, we must realize that their patriotism was conspicuous even among Indians, who are all fervent nationalists. The Shawnees' gasconading helped to preserve their national morale during several centuries of being pushed around. They never lost their arrogance nor their flamboyance. It was fortunate, too, that they seldom lost their humor. When all three of these qualities came together, they made an interesting mixture. The story of the Creation as told by one of their chiefs at Fort Wayne in 1803 will serve as an example.

> The Master of Life, . . . who was himself an Indian, made the Shawanoes before any other of the human race; and they sprang from his brain: he gave them all the knowledge he himself possessed, and placed them upon the great island, and all the other red people are descended from the Shawanoes. After he had made the Shawanoes, he made the French and English out of his breast, the Dutch out of his feet, and the long-knives [Americans] out of his hands. All these inferior races of men he made white and placed them beyond the stinking lake [Atlantic Ocean].[3]

If their contempt for foreigners was too outspoken, they made up for it by the consideration they showed for their own people. Young men, Alford tells us, made it a rule when they hunted together that each should give to his companion the first game he shot. Their elders preserved a dignity and courtesy in all their dealings. Although, as

[2] Florence Drake, *Civilization*, 200.
[3] Benjamin Drake, *Tecumseh* (Cincinnati, 1856), 21.

Alford says, they had not heard of the Golden Rule, they taught their children never to injure a neighbor, for, they said, "It is not him that you injure, you injure yourself."

For their government they had village chiefs (civil chiefs) and war chiefs.

. . . The office of the latter [said Tenskwatawa, the Shawnee Prophet, brother of Tecumseh] is considered more important & more honorable than the other & is received as the reward of great talents, exertion & bravery. To become an accepted War Chief it is necessary that a man should have led at least 4 war parties into the enemies country successively, that he should at each time take one or more scalps & that he should return his followers unhurt to their villages. If he accomplishes all this he may demand his appointment as a right, and the feast is accordingly prepared as in other cases of the kind, where the news of his acceptance is promulgated by the other chiefs and old men.

. . . .

There are female chiefs also appointed, as well for war as for peace. These are always the mothers or otherwise nearly related to the principal chiefs whose party they belong to. Their duties are not numerous nor arduous. The principal employment of the *peace woman* is by her entreaties & remonstrances to prevent the unnecessary effusion of blood; and if a War chief is bent upon prosecuting some undertaking not countenanced by the nation, the council chiefs apply to the peace woman, who goes to the War chief, and setting before him the care and anxiety & pain which the women experience in their birth & education she appeals to his better feelings and implores him to spare the innocent & unoffending against whom his hand is raised. She seldom fails to dissuade him, and in consequence of her general influence & success in such cases, is made a *dernier resort* by the village chiefs. Besides this duty these female chiefs have a general superintendence of the female affairs of the village; they order & direct the planting and the cooking & arrangement of feasts. But in the performance of the latter duty the war & peace women chiefs have separate establishments, at one of which the latter cooks the white corn & smaller vegetables & at the other the first superintends the preparation of the meats & coarser articles of food.

. . . .

There is no particular body of Counsellors or wise men, like the Lupwaaeenoawuk of the Delawares. But in important councils the aged men of the nation are invited . . . . but these old men have no authority whatever, nor any influence, other than is common to their age & experience in the national affairs.

The question of war is determined in a general council of War & peace chiefs, where, after the latter have in a few words expressed their general sentiments on the subject, the principal War Chief, who is of the Panther tribe, rises and declares the necessity of resorting to war for redress of their injuries, and then calls upon all of his own tribe to join him in raising the tomahawk. This done, is a signal of assent by all, to his proposition, the village chiefs surrender their power, the war chiefs immediately set about the preparations and the different tribes are invited to join the party. This is done by sending a tomahawk painted with red clay, through the different villages. . . .

The war dance always precedes their departure from the village and the leader declares to his followers the general order of march, the plan of attack, &c. . . .[4]

The Shawnees were famed fighters. It is a tradition, said the Shawnee Prophet, that "the Shawnees have never been in the habit of suing for peace themselves, but of receiving the propositions of their enemies." In war they were ruthless. There survived among them, as indeed among most other Indians until the eighteenth century, the practice of ritual cannibalism. The eating of human flesh was in general abhorred by Indians, but cannibalism survived as a war custom because it was believed that the virtues of a brave enemy could be transferred by this means to his captors.

The Shawnees had a curious way of determining the fate of war prisoners. It was described many years ago by the Shawnee Prophet to C. C. Trowbridge:

There existed formerly a Society among the Shawnees like that mentioned as having been known among the Miamies. This society was not formed by the Great Spirit but had its origin soon after the Indians began to wage war against each other. The members had their office by hereditary descent. The heads of the society were four women, but men also belonged to it. . . . These four old women, whenever they heard the "prisoners yell" of a returning war party painted their lips with red clay & sat out to meet the party. The peace women started from the village at the same time, and if they reached a prisoner in time to touch him before the others came up, the person was thenceforth safe and the Miseekwaaweekwaakee did not attempt to come near them. But if the latter or any one of them first touched a prisoner she immediately said to the warriors

[4] Vernon Kinietz and Erminie W. Voegelin (eds.), *Shawnese Traditions: C. C. Trowbridge's Account* (Ann Arbor, Michigan, 1939), 11-13, 17-18.

Neeauwaa	Thank you
Ne neetsharnarkee	my children
Kee peeaatarwee	you bring me
Waasar	good
Hopeekomeetaa	Broth,

and she led him off to camp. No exertions were sufficient to save a prisoner after being caught by one of these old women. His fate was irreversible. He was taken to the village & burned and afterwards cooked & eaten.[5]

A more brutal form of cannibalism was practiced by some Indians, though not by those we meet in Pennsylvania. These others cut off pieces of the prisoner's flesh while he was still alive, and roasted and ate them before his face. John Heckewelder wrote in 1793, "I could not learn that the Dellawares, Wyondotts & Shawnese had adopted this horrid act: but with the Twichtwees (or Miamis) Potawattemes, Chippuwas & Massasagues it is now a days customary."[6] Loskiel wrote: "The Delawares and Iroquois never do it. Formerly they have been known in the height of their fury to tear an enemy's heart out of his body, and devour it raw; but at present this is seldom or never practised."[7]

It was to the Chippewas and Ottawas that certain of the Iroquois, exasperated by the Moravians' pro-American activities during the Revolutionary War, offered the missionaries "to make broth of." We may hope the phrase was used in jest. Certainly, as it turned out, it was not the Chippewas and Ottawas but the Delawares and Wyandots who in the end took the Moravians prisoner and defended them from any serious harm.

Shawnee boys were physically hardened and taught to be self-reliant. When they had reached a safe age, they were trained to take a daily jump into the river—even in winter when they had to break the ice to get in. At the age of about ten, a boy underwent a test of endurance. He was sent into the woods with bow and arrows and told not to return until he had shot something to eat. Before he set out, his face was blackened with charcoal, a sign to all whom he met that he was on his test and was not to be helped. Little Wildcat Alford, when undergoing this ordeal, was two days alone in the woods without food. He became too weak to shoot straight; but he managed somehow to kill a quail and returned to his family, a man.

[5] Ibid., 53-54.
[6] Wallace (ed.), Thirty Thousand Miles with John Heckewelder, 318.
[7] History of the Mission, I, 153.

A favorite children's game, designed to develop skill in shooting at a moving object, was played with bows and arrows and a hoop. The hoop was made of a piece of wild grapevine, the ends of which were bent until they met and were then tied together. The middle of the hoop was closed tight with woven strips of bark. When the players took sides, one boy rolled the hoop, while those of the opposing side shot at it. The boy whose arrow pierced the hoop was the winner. Then those on the other side stuck their arrows into the ground just enough to make them stand up, and the winner tossed the hoop horizontally at them. Those he knocked down were his "for keeps."

Thomas Wildcat Alford's description of how the Shawnees lived when they moved to the Indian Territory (Oklahoma) in 1868 was in most particulars true of their way of living in earlier times.

It must be remembered that moving was a simple matter for our people in those days, though often it was a prolonged journey. Sometimes we camped in a locality for weeks or even months, waiting for floods to subside, or for one reason or another that suited the fancy of our leaders. Sometimes a crop of corn was planted and harvested before a journey was resumed. There was no cause for hurry; no business waited for our attention; no appointments had to be kept. Our homes, we-gi-was or cabins, could be built in a few days, and often were abandoned with little concern. We had little in the way of household effects: few clothes, a few buffalo robes, blankets, a few cooking vessels, and the crude and limited supply of utensils and implements used in carrying on the work about the camp. There were few wagons. The family effects generally were tied in bundles and strapped on the backs of horses—some were carried by the women. There was conversation and often merriment, as the groups tramped along through woods or prairie, over mountains or hills and boggy swamps. Streams were forded and when too deep or swift to wade, rafts were made to ferry across.[8]

In former days the Shawnees, like other Indians, were wise in woodcraft. Though they commonly traveled by well-trodden paths, they were not dependent on these. "Their course in unknown country," observed the Prophet, "is regulated by the sun and moon, or in cloudy weather by the moss on the trees, which is always found in greatest quantity upon the north side."

They had no newspapers, but the forest itself was full of local gossip for sharp eyes to read. Members of war parties or hunting parties, when they camped at night, often peeled strips of bark from the trees, and on the smooth surface thus exposed recorded their adventures in

[8] Florence Drake, *Civilization*, 14-15.

124

pictographs drawn with charcoal, vermilion, or other pigment. Some trails were bordered with many painted trees. A section of the Towanda Path was at one time known as "the Painted Line" because of the many peeled and painted trees along its course. Any Indian, no matter what his tribe or language, could understand these pictures. It might be said truly of Indian travelers, "He who runs may read." He could learn about the last war party that had passed: who the leader was (identifiable by his totem), the number of men in his party, what enemy scalps or prisoners they had taken, what losses they had sustained in killed, captured, and wounded.

All Indians were trained to be observant.

They can easily tell [said the Shawnee Prophet] by examining an encampment what nation of Indians the party were of who occupied it. For instance in a Shauwanoa encampment the kettle is suspended from a horizontal beam which rests upon two forked sticks placed in the ground vertically at the opposite ends of the beam. The Ottawas spread their kettle from a single stick which is placed in the earth & extends across the fire. The Wyandots also use the beam, but they always encamp between two trees, against which they lean two poles which support the beam. The Chippeways use *two* sticks, which are run into the ground & crossed at the opposite ends.[9]

MIGRATIONS

The movements of the Shawnees, even in historic times, were so complicated and so little observed by white men that they are now difficult to follow in any detail. They entered Pennsylvania by several routes and at different times. The first groups arrived by way of Maryland in response to an invitation from New York merchants who were eager to extend their fur trade in the Ohio country. Escorted by a group of Munsee Indians, they arrived at the upper Delaware River in 1692 with their chief Kakowatchiky and were reluctantly accepted by the Iroquois as neighbors. Another group settled at the head of Chesapeake Bay in Maryland, but about five years later moved up the Susquehanna into Pennsylvania. Present-day names commemorate both groups: above the Delaware Water Gap are Shawnee Island, Shawnee Run, Shawnee Lake, Shawnee-on-the-Delaware, and, in New Jersey, Pahaquarry; on the Susquehanna are Pequea Creek and, at its mouth, the village of Pequea. Both Pahaquarry and Pequea derive from *Pec-ku-we*.

[9] Kinietz and Voegelin (eds.), *Shawnese Traditions*, 48.

125

The group that moved up the Susquehanna in 1697, with their chief Opessa, met William Penn in 1701 and received his permission to live there; and in 1707 they were joined by Shawnees driven out of Carolina. In 1697, another group (or part of the same one) moved to the upper Potomac River at present Oldtown, Maryland, and in 1711 Opessa left his people on the Susquehanna and moved to this settlement, which became known as Opessa's Town. After his death this group crossed over, about 1729, to the upper Ohio, in Pennsylvania. With the Susquehanna group was also a refugee Frenchman, Martin Chartier, who had a Shawnee wife and a son Peter. Martin died in 1718, and the Indian band then moved farther up the river to the present site of New Cumberland, near Harrisburg.

The Iroquois had accepted the Shawnees reluctantly, and when a few of their young men were involved in a disturbance in 1728 the Iroquois ordered them "back toward Ohio, the place from whence you came." Kakowatchiky and his band thereupon moved to Wyoming (Wilkes-Barre); Peter Chartier's band went to the Ohio, and refused to return even though Pennsylvania reserved land for them and gave Chartier six hundred acres outright. The Iroquois appointed two Oneida chiefs to oversee the Shawnees: Swatana (better known as Shikellamy) on the Susquehanna and Scaroyady (or Monacatootha) on the Ohio.

By 1731 the Shawnees had three towns (two hundred men in all) on the Kiskiminetas and Allegheny rivers. Presumably this included the former residents of Opessa's Town on the Potomac; and they were joined about this time by a number of *The-we-gi-la* (Sewickley) Shawnees (about one hundred men) who had come from Carolina by way of the Potomac. In general the Shawnees tried to get along with everyone, Iroquois, English, and French; English traders had followed them to the Ohio, French agents had come seeking to renew friendly relations, and Peter Chartier, also engaged in the fur trade, traveled between "Chartier's Town" at present Tarentum on the Allegheny and his house on the Susquehanna. However, after an Iroquois delegation went to Kittanning in 1734 to caution the Shawnees against joining the French, the Sewickley Shawnees killed a Seneca member of the delegation and then fled back toward Carolina. English interests were strengthened when in 1744 Kakowatchiky and most of his band left Wyoming and resettled at Logstown (present Ambridge) on the Ohio; but a year later Chartier and his followers plundered some English traders and fled down the Ohio to join the French.

Kakowatchiky was one of the most colorful figures in colonial Pennsylvania. For many years—certainly since before 1709—he had been

126

chief of the Shawnees on the Delaware. To the end of his life he maintained a loyal—but by no means submissive—attachment to the Iroquois and to Pennsylvania. In 1728, when eleven of his warriors near Durham iron furnace got into a shooting affray with white men (who did not subscribe to the rule of Indian etiquette requiring neutrals to provide passing warriors with food on request), Kakowatchiky sent a polite but firm note to the governor of Pennsylvania. He regretted the fracas, blamed the white men for having provoked it, and requested the return of a gun which one of his warriors, wounded, had dropped on the field of battle.

It was in the Wyoming Valley in 1742 that Kakowatchiky had his memorable conversation with Count Zinzendorf, founder of the renewed Moravian church. As a simple statement of the Indian's attitude toward the best that European culture had to offer, Kakowatchiky's words (recorded afterwards by Conrad Weiser, who was present), are hardly to be equaled.

The old chief thanked the Count "in the most courteous manner" for proposing his conversion to the Christian faith. He said that he, too, believed in God, who had created both the Indian and the white man. But he went on to explain why, after what he had seen of white men on the frontier, he preferred Indian ways and beliefs; for, he said, the white man prayed with words while the Indian prayed in his heart.

> He himself was an Indian of God's creation and he was satisfied with his condition had no wish to be a European, above all he was a subject of the Iroquois, it did not behoove him to take up new Things without their Advice or Example. If the Iroquois chose to become Europeans, and learned to pray like them: he would have nothing to say against it. . . . He liked the Indian Way of Life. God had been very kind to him even in his old Age and would continue to look well after him. God was better pleased with the Indians, than with the Europeans. It was wonderful how much he helped them.[10]

Not all the Shawnees in the Wyoming Valley followed Kakowatchiky to the west. A few remained at the Shawnee Flats under the leadership of Paxinosa, another friend of the Iroquois and the English. The French and Indian War making neutrality dangerous in that area, Paxinosa in 1756 moved his band closer to the Six Nations, who approved his attitude. He and his people settled for a time at Tioga (Athens) among some Mahican refugees. Thence in 1760 he moved west with his family to the Ohio where he had been born, and there in the following spring he died.

[10]Wallace, *Conrad Weiser*, 144.

The Shawnee movement into western Pennsylvania was from several different directions and took a good many years to complete. For a time there were Shawnees on the West Branch of the Susquehanna at Chillisquaque, about five miles above Northumberland. There was another Shawnee town farther up the West Branch opposite the Big Island (Lock Haven). That was where Thomas McKee in 1743 nearly lost his life because the Shawnees there had been stirred up by an Iroquois war party that wanted revenge for the recent killing of some of their band by white men in Virginia. On the Juniata, Ohesson (present Lewistown) is first mentioned in 1731; Kishacoquillas, its chief, died in August, 1745, at Thomas McKee's on the Susquehanna.

It was from Allegania that five Shawnee chiefs sent a letter to Gov. Patrick Gordon and the Council, dated May 1, 1734, which ranks as one of Pennsylvania's earliest temperance manifestoes. After complaining about the malpractices of fifteen traders and commending six others, they said:

> Likewise, we beg at our Council, that no Trader above mentioned may be allowed to bring more than thirty gallons of rum, twice in a year, and no more, for by that means, we shall be capable of paying our debts and making our creditors easy; which we cannot do otherwise. . . .
> And for our parts, if we see any other Traders than those we desire amongst us, we will stave their cags, and seize their goods, likewise.[11]

In 1745 Peter Chartier's Shawnees, now deeply under French influence, robbed James Dunning and Peter Tostee, Pennsylvania traders. Next year Chartier moved his band, some three or four hundred strong, to the Wabash, leaving Chartier's Old Town as a landmark on the Traders Path to the Forks of the Ohio. Some of his Shawnees returned to Pennsylvania in 1748 and, sponsored by Scaroyady (their Iroquois overseer), asked to be accepted again as friends. When the French occupied the Ohio country a few years later, the pro-British Iroquois left and the Shawnees joined the French, who built them a new town at Logstown. Then, when the French retreated in 1758, the Shawnees also had to leave. After Pontiac's War, they agreed in 1765 to return to their former home, and some of them returned to Logstown, but in 1772, just before Dunmore's War, this last group left Pennsylvania.

[11]*Pennsylvania Archives,* 1st series, I, 425.

16

Indian Land Cessions and Delaware Migrations

LAND CESSIONS

I F THE DELAWARES, as we look back on their history, appear a restless, migratory people, we must remember that it was the white man who made them so. He acquired their lands—quietly in Pennsylvania but as inexorably as in any other colony—and pushed the Indians out. The Delawares and their Uncles the Six Nations were powerless to arrest the process. At the outset, at their first meetings with Europeans, it was in large part the Delawares' instinctive hospitality that led them to surrender their lands to strangers who wanted them. Ignorant of the white man's real estate customs, village chiefs affixed their marks to deeds conveying more rights than they were aware of. By the time the Indians had come to an understanding of what the white man's purchases involved, new pressures influenced them to continue selling. For one thing, white men swarming across the purchase bounds made it apparent to the Indians that the sale of their lands and the removal of their people was the only alternative to perpetual provocation and the risk of war.

In Pennsylvania the white man acquired Indian land not by conquest but by purchase. Indian title was recognized by the Dutch and Swedes. It was not recognized by the English (the Indians being "heathen"); but William Penn, though he accepted English title to his province, nevertheless respected the Indian right of domain and extinguished it only by purchase.

There is no certain evidence (despite claims by the Dutch) of Indian land purchases in Pennsylvania before Peter Minuit in 1638 landed Swedish colonists near the mouth of Minquas Creek and purchased land on the west shore of the Delaware as far north as the Falls (present Trenton). Thus, as George Smith writes in the *History of Delaware County, Pennsylvania,* "to the wise policy of the Swedes we are really indebted for the extinguishment of the Indian title to our lands,—a policy . . . subsequently adopted by William Penn on the score of strict justice to the natives."[1]

Although the Indians' ideas of land use and ownership were very different from ours, these Indians had had forty years' experience in land sales before William Penn arrived, and they were not so naive as they are sometimes represented. The land they had sold to Minuit in 1638 was part of the first land they sold Penn in 1683; the early sales set a precedent and prepared the way for the later ones.

The land purchased in 1638 and later had been cleared and partly settled by the Dutch and the Swedes; and although the Dutch were chiefly interested in trade and the Swedish settlers were too few in number to occupy much land, their presence undoubtedly caused the Indians to retire somewhat from these white settlements. Penn's first purchases may have seemed more like a transfer from the Dutch to the English than a further surrender of Indian land. Actually, a factor more compelling than the presence of white settlers was urging the Indians westward. The demands of the fur trade and the acquisition of firearms led the Indians to kill far more game animals than formerly; and as the game was depleted near at hand, the Indians were drawn farther and farther afield; and their westward movement facilitated Penn's peaceful acquisition of their land.

The Indians were not driven out; and in two instances Penn set aside tracts of land for groups unprepared to move westward: one along Brandywine Creek for Indians who sold him land in 1685, and one on Ridley Creek authorized in 1702 for the Okehocking or Crum Creek

[1] (Philadelphia, 1862), 24-25.

band of Delawares. White settlers infringed on the Brandywine tract, however; and the Proprietors later tried to provide greater security for some Indian communities by having tracts surveyed as Proprietary manors: Conestoga Manor in Lancaster County, in 1718; Indian Tract Manor in present Northampton County, in 1733; and Indian Manor (later named Lowther) in present Cumberland County, in 1736.

William Penn's land purchases are not easily defined on a map. Typically, they were bounded by streams on either side and extended a vague distance back into the country, and purchases overlapped one another. This was consistent, however, with the Indians' own customs. A Delaware town stood near a stream of water, and it and its cornfields occupied a definite area; the hunting grounds, however, about and beyond the village, were less well defined and might be used by several communities or even by different tribes. It was more reasonable, then, to purchase the claim of a particular band (or its spokesman) to land of indefinite extent than to purchase a definite tract of land of uncertain ownership.

On the accompanying map the landmarks of the separate purchases are shown, but the first boundary shown is that of the 1718 deed that confirmed all of William Penn's purchases. The boundary of this deed does not follow those of the individual purchases; rather, it represents an agreement about the lands actually conveyed as a result of those earlier purchases.

This procedure of purchasing rights rather than defined tracts of land leaves a strong impression that the Proprietors purchased some lands many times over. An extreme example, perhaps, is the land set off as Conestoga Manor. This had been included in a purchase from the Delaware chief Machaloha in 1683. In 1696 Governor Dongan of New York released his claim, derived from the Iroquois Indians; and in 1700 and 1701 this was confirmed by the Indians—Conestoga, Shawnee, and Conoy—actually living in the area. It was included in the Delawares' confirmation deed of 1718 (the year in which the manor was created) and in the Iroquois release of 1736. At the Fort Stanwix treaty in 1768 the Iroquois, supposing that the Conestoga Indians had had some claim to the tract, asked payment for it and were given $500. Finally, in May, 1775, eight Iroquois Indians, three of whom claimed to be the heirs of Sohaes, the former chief at Conestoga, came to Philadelphia and asked payment for his property. Governor John Penn explained that the land had already been paid for, but, in the last settlement made by the Proprietors with the Indians, he paid them $300 as consolation for their trouble.

Because purchase of Indian land was limited to the Proprietors and

PENNSYLVANIA'S INDIAN PURCHASES, 1682-1737

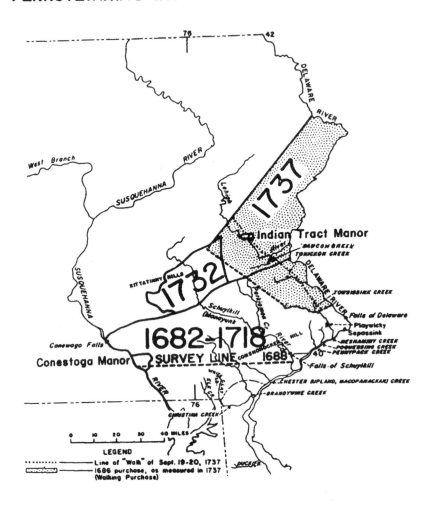

their agents, Indian deeds were not considered public records, and the early purchases were not entered in the minutes of the Governor's council except for special reason. Thus, the 1718 confirmation deed was entered in the council minutes for June 5, 1728, because there was at that time a difference of opinion about the limits of the land referred to. (It was settled in favor of the Indians.) However, a 1748 inventory of Proprietary documents in the Provincial Land Office listed the Indian deeds; and this list was checked and brought up to date in 1757, at the time of the dispute over the "Walking Purchase." At the time of the Revolution, John Penn transferred the deeds themselves to the new government, and the list—again brought up to date—was entered in the minutes of the Supreme Executive Council under date of January 3, 1783.[2]

William Penn's first purchase, dated July 15, 1682, was made by William Markham before Penn's arrival. It was for a defined tract of land (including Penn's later estate of Pennsbury) in the southeastern corner of present Bucks County. The purchase actually concluded negotiations begun by Governor Andros of New York in 1678. Thirteen "Indian Sachamakers" or chiefs signed it, three more added their marks on August 1, and two more in 1700.

Penn himself, during his first visit to Pennsylvania (1682-84), made ten purchases. The first five of these deeds, all written by the same clerk and dated in June and July, 1683, were for land fronting on the Delaware River between Neshaminy and Chester creeks—land previously bought by the Dutch and the Swedes. Two of these deeds do not specify the distance back from the river, two extend inland to Conshohocken Hill, and one "two days journey with a horse." The second group of five deeds (also by a single clerk), dated between September, 1683, and June, 1684, extend Penn's purchases. Two are for land extending to the Susquehanna River below the falls, one is for land between Chester and Christina creeks, and two are for land on Perkiomen and Pennypack creeks. The first two are especially interesting, for they lay claim to land in dispute between Penn and Lord Baltimore, and they show that some of the Delaware Indians had moved into the Susquehannocks' former land.

In the interval (1684-99) between Penn's first and second visits, his agents negotiated three purchases of additional land and obtained two deeds confirming his first purchases. Of the new purchases, one in July, 1785, covered land between Pennypack and Chester creeks and backward from Conshohocken Hill "as far as a man can go in two days."

[2]*Colonial Records*, XIII, 462-471. The texts of most of the early deeds are printed in *Pennsylvania Archives*, 1st series, I.

One dated in October of this year extended from Chester Creek to Duck Creek (in present Delaware) and inland "as far as a man can ride in two days with a horse." The third deed, in August, 1686, was for land between Delaware River and Neshaminy Creek and extending from Markham's first purchase "as far as a man can go in one day and a half."

The two confirmation deeds, in June, 1692, and July, 1697, refer to the 1683 deeds for land between Neshaminy and Pennypack creeks, and their language strongly suggests that there had been some disagreement over the extent of the Indians' release. The 1692 deed states emphatically that the release includes their claim "backwards to the utmost bounds of the said Province" and any land claimed by them "from the beginning of the world." The 1697 release is from Taminy and his brother, his designated successor, and his two sons—that is, his heirs by both Indian and English practice.

The 1697 release follows the example of earlier deeds by specifying the depth of the land as "so far as a horse can travel in two summer days"—presumably accompanied by a rider. There is no record of these travel distances actually being measured, however, except that on the basis of the July, 1685, deed a line was surveyed in 1688 from Philadelphia straight west to the Susquehanna, a distance of about seventy miles, "against the time for running the said two days journey."

During his second and last visit (1699-1701), Penn made no further purchases from the Delaware Indians, but he did wind up a rather curious claim to Susquehanna River lands. The Iroquois laid claim to these on the basis of their conquest of the Susquehannocks; however, it was understood that the Iroquois had entrusted their lands to Governor Dongan of New York. Penn had begun negotiations in 1683 to obtain Dongan's release of his claim and he obtained this in 1696. In the meantime, however, some Seneca Indians had established a settlement with some of the defeated Susquehannocks at Conestoga, and some Shawnee and Conoy Indians had obtained permission to settle near by; so, in 1700 and 1701, Penn settled matters with these groups as well. Also in 1700 he saw the law enacted that formally restricted Indian land purchases to the Proprietor and his agents. No more purchases were made during his lifetime, however, and in September, 1718, a few months after his death, his secretary James Logan obtained from "Sassoonan King of the Delaware Indians" and six chiefs associated with him, the confirmation deed previously mentioned.

Several years then passed before the Proprietorship was settled on William Penn's three sons, John, Thomas, and Richard, in 1726. That no further land purchases had been made since 1718 had proved damaging both to Indian relations and to Proprietary finances. Settlement had in fact outrun the purchases: west of the Susquehanna Maryland settlers had moved onto land in dispute between Penn and Lord Baltimore; in 1726 a group of Palatine Germans settled on the Tulpehocken lands—the last remaining land of Sassoonan's Delawares—; and on the upper Delaware settlers from New York were moving into the Minisink lands and making unauthorized purchases from the Indians.

It was hoped that one of the new Proprietors would visit Pennsylvania and put things to rights, but Thomas Penn did not come until 1732, and in the meantime Governor Patrick Gordon and Secretary James Logan did what they could. They tried in 1727 to get the Minisink country under control by having land there set aside as a Proprietary manor, but the Indians refused to allow the survey, and Logan only obtained a gift of land, in 1730, on Saucon Creek, south of the Lehigh River. A year later, however, he eased the Tulpehocken situation by persuading Sassoonan to grant land to four of the families settled there. Soon after Thomas Penn's arrival, this was superseded by Sassoonan's sale to the Proprietors of all his remaining land.

Pending a settlement with the Iroquois, Thomas Penn dealt with the trans-Susquehanna problem by directing the surveyor general, Samuel Blunston, to grant licenses, beginning in 1734, to persons who might settle, with Indian permission, on land to which they could obtain title when the Iroquois released their claim.

Of the Delawares' lands in Pennsylvania, there then remained only that in the "Forks of Delaware" (present Northampton and Lehigh counties); and Thomas Penn and Logan renewed their efforts to obtain these lands. Since it had been accepted that the "two days travel" of the 1685 purchase extended west to the Susquehanna River, it was reasonable to assume that the day-and-a-half measurement of the 1686 deed could be interpreted as extending northwest to include the "Forks"; so the negotiators set about to obtain a deed confirming this 1686 purchase. The circumstances were somewhat peculiar, however. Sassoonan's Indians made no claim to this land, and in the "Forks" the original population had been augmented or replaced by other Delawares moving across from New Jersey. Thus, the new confirmation deed would have to be obtained from Indians who had not been party to the original 1686 deed and in fact knew nothing about it. These Indians, led by Nutimus, himself from New Jersey, were therefore unwilling to grant the confirmation, but reluctantly gave it in 1737. In the meanwhile a trial "walk" had been made, and a sixty-five-hundred-acre tract, including the Indians' chief town, had been set aside as a Proprietary manor.

Popularly known as the "Walking Purchase"—though the deed does not contain the word "walk"—, this purchase was exploited twenty years later in a bitter political dispute that had more to do with partisan politics than with Indian relations, and this dispute gave the "Walking Purchase" its subsequent notoriety. It was open to criticism, however, both because the pressure on the Indians to yield land they still occupied was contrary to William Penn's philosophy and because the actual walk was pushed beyond the Blue Mountain in order to take in the irregular settlements in the Munsee (or Minisink) country above the Delaware Water Gap.

This 1737 deed completed the acquisition of the Delaware Indians' lands in Pennsylvania; for the remaining unpurchased lands were all claimed by the Iroquois on the basis of their defeat of the Susquehannocks, the Eries, and other previous occupants. Except on the upper Allegheny, where the Senecas established some towns, this vast area was little used by the Iroquois themselves except as hunting grounds; but they had permitted other Indians, Delawares and Shawnees especially, to settle parts of it under their supervision. Although Governor Dongan had transferred to Penn his ill-defined claim to the Susquehanna River lands, the Iroquois themselves still claimed a right there. In October, 1736, therefore, the Proprietors obtained two deeds from them, one for the Susquehanna lands south of the Blue Mountain, the other a release of whatever claim the Iroquois might have to the Delaware lands south of the mountain. The Susquehanna deed, the first one to include land west of the river, enabled the Blunston license holders, and new settlers as well, to become landowners in that area.

Two more purchases were made from the Iroquois before the French and Indian War: one in 1749 of land between the Susquehanna and the Delaware River, north of the Blue Mountain, and one in 1754 that, as described, included all of western Pennsylvania. The 1749 deed overlapped part of the "Walking Purchase," and representatives of the Delawares and the Shawnees also signed as residents. The 1754 (or Albany Purchase) deed was accompanied by an agreement that not all the land would be opened for settlement at once, and that an additional payment would be made when the part west of the mountains was settled. The Iroquois had second thoughts about this sale, however, and at a treaty at Easton in 1758 they requested an adjustment. The Iroquois had been instrumental in reestablishing friendly relations with the Indians who had been involved in the French and Indian War (still in progress); so the Province readily released the part of the Albany Purchase west of the Allegheny Mountain.

After this war, in 1762, the Province held a treaty with the western

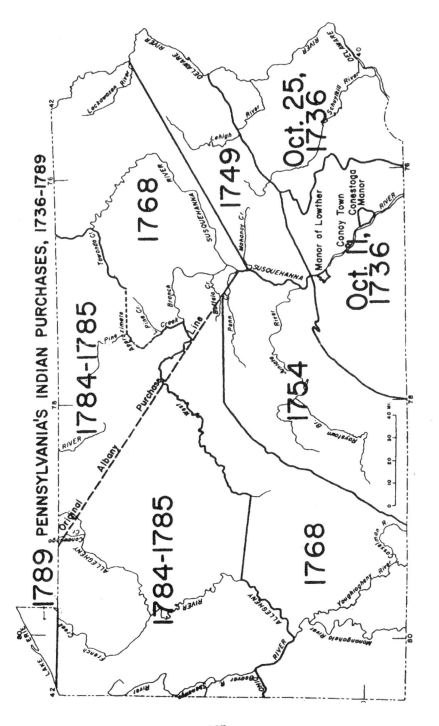

PENNSYLVANIA'S INDIAN PURCHASES, 1736-1789

1789

1784-1785

1768

1749

Oct. 25, 1736

Oct. 1, 1736

1754

1784-1785

1768

137

Indians, at Lancaster, and at this time settled the slight claims of the Shawnees and the Nanticokes and Conoys to some small tracts on the Susquehanna River. Then, in conjunction with the 1763 treaty that formally ended the war, the British government established a "Proclamation Line" following the ridge of the Allegheny Mountain, beyond which white settlement was prohibited. This was consistent with Pennsylvania's land purchases as of that date, but it further delayed the westward movement of settlers that the war had interrupted. After Pontiac's War, which broke out that same year, Sir William Johnson was instructed, as Indian agent, to draw a new "Indian boundary," which was settled at Fort Stanwix in 1768. The new line, which benefited New York and Virginia as well as Pennsylvania, gave this province a broad strip of land extending from its northeast to its southwest corner. This was the last accession of land during the Provincial period.

The last extensive purchase was made by the State in 1784 and 1785. In the former year, at a treaty held at Fort Stanwix, Pennsylvania obtained an Iroquois cession of their remaining lands in the State; and at Fort McIntosh (present Beaver, Pa.) in the following year the Delawares and Wyandots ceded their claims in the same lands. Few if any Delawares were then living there, but they had had settlements throughout the area; the Wyandots had had a town on the Beaver River, below New Castle, for a few years after 1748.

Finally, in 1789, when Pennsylvania was preparing to purchase the Erie Triangle from the Federal government (in 1792), the State purchased the Seneca Indians' right to the land. Cornplanter, a Seneca chief who assisted the State in this purchase, was rewarded in 1791 with three tracts of land on the upper Allegheny River. The "Cornplanter Tract," the only one he kept, has often been referred to as an Indian reservation, but it was in fact the private property of Cornplanter and his descendants.

DELAWARE MIGRATIONS

An account of the Delawares' migration from their homeland must take account of the bands on both sides of the Delaware River. The Indians themselves did not think of the river as a boundary. A chief from the east side of the river explained to Governor Markham in 1694 that "though we live on the other side of the river, yet we reckon ourselves all one, because we drink one water." Nevertheless, the European settlements on the lower Delaware, and the later division of the land between two different English colonies, did tend to separate the bands on the two sides of the river.

138

The bands on the Pennsylvania side were the first to leave their own country. The Dutch and Swedish settlements had occasioned some retirement westward, and as the English settlements spread inland from the river and the Proprietors purchased additional land, these people found the way open, with the Susquehannocks gone, to migrate to the Susquehanna River and, following the fur trade, to travel on to the Ohio. As their lands dwindled, these bands became more closely associated with one another and in time became known collectively as the Unami ("downriver") Indians. By 1709 their "king," Sassoonan, and the chiefs associated with him were living on the Susquehanna near present Harrisburg; and in 1718 they signed the confirmation deed for all their former lands except the northern half of present Berks County. From here a few of them moved to the upper Delaware, and a larger number to the Ohio country, where as early as 1725 they had settled at Kittanning. Sassoonan himself and some of his people then settled at Shamokin (Sunbury), where he died in 1747. Some of his followers then moved up the West Branch of Susquehanna, others joined their fellow tribesmen in the Ohio country. The period of Indian hostilities, beginning in 1755, speeded the westward migration, and by 1765, a large part of the Unamis were on the Muskingum River in Ohio. From there their chiefs, headed by "king" Newcomer, sent out invitations to scattered Delaware groups to join them in a united "Delaware Nation."

In New Jersey the more scattered pattern of white settlements and the practice of making private land purchases from the Indians permitted a slower, piecemeal emigration; and although the departure began early, there were at the time of the French and Indian War three or four Delaware communities, beside scattered families, yet living in New Jersey on their own traditional lands. In 1758, unable to settle numerous land disputes individually, New Jersey made a blanket settlement of all Delaware claims in that colony, and set up a reservation, about twenty-five miles southeast of Philadelphia, that existed until 1802.

The route of migration from New Jersey was generally from south to north, past the settlements on the lower Delaware River and then across the river into the "Forks of Delaware." Further migration up the Lehigh River then took these Indians into Iroquois-held lands on the Susquehanna North Branch. In Pennsylvania these Indians were known as "Jersey Indians" or "Forks Indians." After the sale of the "Forks" country in 1737, the Iroquois directed these Indians to Wyoming (Wilkes-Barre), where they replaced an earlier Shawnee population. The Indian wars and the Iroquois land cession in 1768 gave added weight to Newcomer's invitations to the Ohio country. Unlike the earlier migrants from southeastern Pennsylvania, these Delaware bands did not cohere into a closer association, nor receive a generally accepted group name. The Moravian missionary David Zeisberger, writing in 1769, called them Wunalachtikoks (apparently "from the waves," the seacoast),[3] a name he may have learned from the Munsees among whom he had been working; another missionary, Abraham Luckenbach, says the Unamis called them Woapannachkis ("easterners"). In spite of their different history and some slight difference in dialect, they merged easily with the Unamis into the "Delaware Nation."[4]

Among the last Delaware towns in Pennsylvania were Custaloga's Town on French Creek and Kuskusky and Shenango in the Beaver River area; Custaloga moved to the Muskingum River at the time of Pontiac's War; and when the Indians agreed, in the 1765 peace treaty, to return to their former homes, he resettled at Kuskusky instead. After this place was attacked in February, 1778, by American militia, the Delawares abandoned their remaining towns in Pennsylvania.

The Munsees (Minisinks)

The westward migration of the Delaware Indians had its counterpart in that of their relatives and neighbors the Munsee or Minisink Indians. In their homeland on the upper Delaware, above the Blue Mountain, they had found themselves hemmed in between the Iroquois and the European settlements expanding from the lower Hudson River; and by 1727, when they are first mentioned in official Pennsylvania records, they had removed their main settlement to the mouth of the Lackawanna River, above Wyoming. By this time there were some white settlers on the upper Delaware; and the Munsee lands on the Pennsylvania side of the river were arbitrarily included in the 1737 "Walking Purchase" and in the Iroquois sale of 1749.

When Indian hostilities began in 1755, the Munsees took part in the

[3]The term Wunalachtikoks (or Unalachtigo) occurs only in Zeisberger's own writings and in others derived from or repeating his statements (for example, by Loskiel in 1789 and Heckewelder in 1819). The popular idea that the Unami, Unalachtigo, and Munsee were aboriginal divisions of the Delaware people seems to derive from a misunderstanding of Zeisberger's (1780) statement that these were the major components of the "Delaware Nation."

[4]This is illustrated by an incident of 1764, when Colonel Bouquet refused to deal with Netawatwees as spokesman for the "Turtle Tribe" and ordered that lineage to choose another representative. The replacement chosen was Tapiscawen, a "Jersey Indian" who had moved from Wyoming to the Ohio only the year before. The episode illustrates not only the ready acceptance of the newcomers but also the fact that members of a given lineage (in this case the Turtle) might be found in any Delaware community.

140

destruction of Gnadenhütten, the Moravian mission north of the Blue
Mountain, and then retreated to the Chemung River, where they
established a new town, Aghsinsing, near present Corning, New York.
(The Moravians had found the Munsees a stubborn people; they received their first Munsee convert in 1742, but twenty years later they
had baptized only seven.) At Aghsinsing the Munsees were supervised
by the Senecas, who persuaded them to join in a peace treaty in 1758, at
which time they released their lands east of the Delaware to New Jersey.

In 1763 they went on the warpath again. Driven from their towns by
Sir William Johnson's raiders, they took refuge with the Senecas; then,
still under Seneca supervision, they settled at Goshgoshing on the
Allegheny River, in present Forest County, Pennsylvania. From here
they dispersed gradually through western Pennsylvania and Ohio,
where enough of them joined the Delawares for David Zeisberger to
consider them one of the three major components of Newcomer's
"Delaware Nation." By 1791 the Goshgoshing settlement itself—
possibly the last Indian community in Pennsylvania, except Cornplanter's Town—had dwindled to twenty families (of the Turkey
lineage), who then joined the Senecas in New York.

FINAL SALES OF THE DELAWARE LANDS

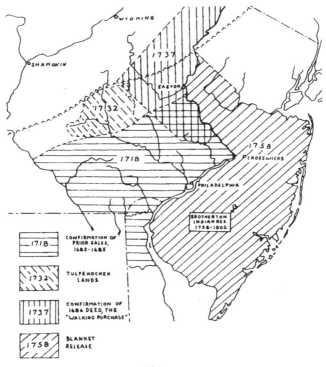

141

17

Pennsylvania's Indian Policy

WE MUST GO BACK a little in time in order to pick up the thread of this chapter, in which we follow the wise policy under which Pennsylvania conducted her Indian relations.

It should be remembered that the first contact between American Indians and white men brought wonder and delight to both parties. "They are a loving people," wrote Columbus, "without covetousness, and fit for anything. . . . They love their neighbors as themselves, and their speech is the sweetest and gentlest in the world."[1] According to Captain John Smith in 1608, the Susquehannocks took him and his white-skinned sailors for gods.

Both sides were soon disillusioned. Columbus himself started the vogue of kidnapping Indians. Reprisals produced counterreprisals, and the cycle of captivities and massacres continued for hundreds of years.

[1] Quoted in D'Arcy McNickle, *They Came Here First: The Epic of the American Indian.* (Philadelphia, 1949), 121.

142

No one can blame the Indians for fighting to preserve their country. At the same time it is difficult to blame the settlers, caught up as they were in one of the great mass movements of mankind. That does not mean that we must condone the crimes committed by those who cheated and murdered to gain their ends. It means only that we should not be unfeeling toward either side as we look back on the clash of races, remembering that there was then no way of controlling the vast migration—much like an explosion—which Columbus' discovery of America had touched off.

Pennsylvania came nearest of all the English colonies to a just and sensible handling of the problem. Until the middle of the eighteenth century, relations here between Indians and Europeans were, on the whole, cordial. There were two reasons for this. In the first place, a tradition of fair and friendly dealing, introduced on the Delaware by the Dutch and Swedes, had been reinforced by William Penn. His policy, it is true, grew somewhat worn and ragged after his death as white settlements pushed westward ahead of purchase. But the Penn tradition was never wholly lost, even in the midst of war.

In the second place, Pennsylvania had a clear-cut and well-administered Indian policy, founded on the realities of Indian and European politics. It took into account the fact that the Iroquois were, in the Indian world, the dominant power and that France was Pennsylvania's potential enemy. At the same time, the policy had behind it a good Quaker motive, the pursuit of peace, especially in those spots where it was most vulnerable: at the Forks of the Delaware, for instance, and in the Ohio country.

Pennsylvania had need of a sound Indian policy. On her western border, two dangers confronted her. One was posed by the French, who did not recognize the western bounds of Pennsylvania as laid down in the Charter of 1681. France claimed those lands for herself by right of discovery, and was engaged in persuading Pennsylvania's former Indian friends, both Shawnees and Delawares, to help her keep them. The other danger was occasioned by Pennsylvania's frontiersmen, whose encroachments on Indian lands in the Juniata Valley and elsewhere threatened to set off a train of reprisals.

Despite these dangers on the frontier, Pennsylvania was committed by a Quaker-dominated Assembly to a policy of nonviolence, and was therefore unable to set up even a minimum system of military defense. She had to find other ways of protecting herself. In this emergency, James Logan came forward with a solution. He proposed to the Provincial Council that "a Treaty should be sett on foot with the five Nations, who have an absolute Authority as well over the Shawanese as all our Indians. . . ."[2]

The course he proposed was adopted in 1731, and Pennsylvania took shelter under the Iroquois Tree of Peace, recognizing the Six Nations' claim to authority over all the Indians in the province and relying on the Confederacy to keep them quiet. As Thomas Penn, son of the first proprietor, expressed it some years later (1756) Pennsylvania's policy was "to strengthen the hands of the Six Nations, and enable them to be the better answerable for their Tributaries."[3]

Pennsylvania willingly accepted Six Nations neutrality in the Anglo-French struggle. One of the conditions of that neutrality, as has been noted, was that the French should not cross Iroquois territory to strike at the English. The neutral status of the Iroquois served as an immediate shield to the Susquehanna Valley; and in time the English came to believe that Iroquois authority in the Ohio country, which included the Allegheny and Monongahela river valleys, was as good a protection for them as a line of forts.

The formulation of Pennsylvania's Indian policy in 1731-1732 was the work of three men: James Logan, Provincial Secretary and one of the ablest students of Indian affairs the English colonies ever produced; Conrad Weiser, the erratic but brilliant "Province Interpreter" who had lived in his youth among the Mohawks; and Shickellamy, an Oneida Indian who had been sent by the Six Nations to Shamokin to superintend their southern affairs.

It was, on the whole, a good policy. It strengthened the authority of the Six Nations and so helped them to keep the peace among their tributaries. It saved Pennsylvania from any serious Indian disturbances for more than twenty years, a crucial time in the development of the province. It brought her also many particular benefits. In 1732 the Six Nations approved (through Shickellamy) a Delaware sale of lands in the Lebanon Valley. Pennsylvania acquired from the Six Nations in 1736 a release of lands on both sides of the Susquehanna River south of the Blue Mountains. In the same year the Six Nations agreed to sell no lands within the chartered bounds of the province except to Pennsylvania's proprietors. In 1737 Pennsylvania intervened successfully at Virginia's request to stave off an Iroquois war with the Catawbas, which might have involved the Old Dominion. In 1742 Pennsylvania obtained from the Six Nations an adjudication in her favor of the Walking Purchase dispute—though whether this was of ultimate benefit to the province has remained for over two hundred

[2] Pennsylvania, *Colonial Records*, III, 429.
[3] Wallace, *Conrad Weiser*, 44.

144

years a matter of controversy. The "Walk" imposed order of a sort on the troublesome "Forks" area, but it provided a deadly propaganda weapon for anyone—Quaker, Frenchman, or Indian—who wanted to attack the Proprietors and the Province. Teedyuscung in 1757, during the French and Indian War, said that while the Walk was "not the principal cause that made us Strike our Brethren, the English, yet it has caused the stroke to come harder than it otherwise would have come."[4]

Continuing our brief list of benefits received from the Iroquois alliance, we should remember that in 1743 Pennsylvania again used her good offices through Conrad Weiser at Onondaga to prevent a war between the Six Nations and Virginia. In 1744 Pennsylvania sponsored the Lancaster Treaty, at which the Six Nations released to Virginia lands "to the setting of the sun." Finally, when the French and Indian War came, although a few of the Senecas took part in it under French direction, the Six Nations as a whole restrained their Indian "nephews." At Easton in 1758 they made peace with Pennsylvania on behalf of the Delawares, and so helped to prepare the way for General Forbes' bloodless capture of Fort Duquesne.

Neither England nor France in America desired war with each other or with the Indians, but they drifted into it. To French and English alike, competing as they were for the Indian trade and also for military security, it was important to gain the support of the Indians in the Ohio-Allegheny region. The French wished to have friendly hunters around them to assure a steady supply of food for their garrisons and of furs for their traders. Montreal already had a near-monopoly of trade with the Indians north and west of the Great Lakes; but the French were anxious to stop a bad leak south of Lake Erie, where traders from Philadelphia with goods at better rates than the French could offer were getting the furs. The French wished to bring all Indians on Pennsylvania's western border under their control.

James Logan believed that one of the best ways of blocking French designs in the west was to develop Pennsylvania's fur trade. His own traders established posts on the Beaver River, in the Muskingum country, at Sandusky, and still farther west. When in 1745 the Shawnee leader Peter Chartier arrested some Pennsylvania traders and confiscated their goods (an obvious move in the trade war), the province was both angry and frightened. The Proprietors of Pennsylvania were fearful of what, if war came, Indian raids might do to the undefended back settlements which constituted the colony's breadbasket.

Out in the Ohio country (which we must remember included the Allegheny River basin, *Ohio* and *Allegheny* being respectively Seneca

⁴ Pennsylvania, *Colonial Records*, VII, 676.

and Delaware words for one stream, the Great or Beautiful River) there were large bands of Indians, such as the Ottawas and Wyandots (Hurons), who had for more than a century been France's best commercial allies, middlemen in the trade with the great northwest. There were also among them a good many Six Nations Indians (Mingoes) : hunters who had settled down with their families and made this western country their home, although the Onondaga Council still claimed authority over them.

There were also growing numbers of Delawares and Shawnees in the west, expatriates from their homelands in eastern Pennsylvania. The authorities in Philadelphia attempted by various means to bring them back out of the French sphere of influence. The Shawnees, as has been seen, were offered a reservation on what had once been their home on the west bank of the Susquehanna opposite Paxtang (Harrisburg). Pennsylvania urged the Six Nations to assert their authority and bring their "nephews"—Shawnees and Delawares—back where a British eye could be kept on them.

But the Delawares and Shawnees declined to come. They had their own interests to look after, and there was no lack of traders (it is estimated that there were about three hundred of them in the Ohio country) to supply them with blankets and ironware. French traders could not sell their goods as cheaply as the English did, but Frenchmen had greater courtesy (a quality the Indians warmly responded to) and comparative freedom from race prejudice. The French, furthermore, were less numerous than the English and their main centers were much farther away. They therefore seemed to many of the Ohio Indians to be less menacing than the English.

All in all, it seemed to the western Shawnees and Delawares that they could preserve their freedom more surely if they remained in the Ohio country in touch with the French; and Pennsylvania never succeeded in bringing them to heel.

146

18

Pennsylvania's Indian Wars

THE FRENCH AND INDIAN WAR

A PART FROM some minor local incidents and the loss of a few traders' goods during King George's War (1744-1748), Pennsylvania suffered no serious Indian disturbances for sixty-four years after William Penn received his charter. As a result, the people of the province came to believe that the peace William Penn had bequeathed to them was indestructible. When in 1753 the French brought armed forces to Presque Isle and prepared to occupy the Allegheny Valley, Pennsylvanians continued to think themselves secure behind the Allegheny Mountains and the Iroquois alliance. Washington's surrender of Fort Necessity, on July 4, 1754, seemed a matter of more concern to the Maryland and Virginia frontier than to Pennsylvania. Braddock's defeat on July 9, 1755, followed by the retreat of his army through the Cumberland Valley in August, caused anxiety that a French force might follow on its heels; but the invaders did not appear, and stories of a French army descending the Susquehanna proved false.

The massacre of settlers at Penns Creek near present Selinsgrove on

October 15, followed by other attacks in present Fulton County on November 1, one in Berks County on the 15th, and one on a Moravian mission at present Weissport, Carbon County, on the 24th, revealed the true danger to be that of Indian raids on the frontiers. It was seen at once that Pennsylvania's Indian policy was no longer sufficient. The Iroquois were not strong enough to stand alone in the west against France and her Indian allies. It was suspected (rightly) that some Seneca war parties engaged in hostilities against other Indians had been diverted from their original objectives (as Captain Jean-Daniel Dumas boasted at Fort Duquesne) and turned against the English settlements. It was feared that the Delawares and Shawnees, who knew the trails across Pennsylvania, might use them to take revenge on the settlers who had supplanted them.

Up to the last minute, the Delawares were uncertain what to do. They had not forgotten their former happy relations with William Penn, but neither had they forgotten the Walking Purchase and its Wyoming aftermath. It will be remembered that, when they were expelled from the Forks of the Delaware and from the Minisinks, the Six Nations had given them the Wyoming Valley to be their home forever. Now white men from Connecticut claimed that in 1754 they had purchased Wyoming from the Six Nations. When the French reminded the Delawares of these grievances and threatened to chastise them if they did not attack the English, they dropped their ceremonial role of "women" in the Iroquois Longhouse and lifted the hatchet.

War parties from Nescopeck on the North Branch of the Susquehanna carried gun and scalping knife into the valleys south and east of the Blue Mountains, while from Kittanning on the Allegheny River Captain Jacobs and Shingas ravaged settlements on the Juniata and Conococheague.

The policy of the French and Indians was to ruin Pennsylvania's economy by driving the farmers off the land. The province countered by raising troops and establishing a line of forts along the mountains. These stockades were placed at strategic positions, some on waterways, most of them at the junction of important trails; for it was known that Indian warriors traveled the regular highways until their objectives were approached, when they fanned out through the woods to finish the job with stealth and a final war whoop.

The Delawares and Shawnees did not often engage in pitched battles. Their numbers were too small to justify the risks that such open methods exposed them to. Instead, small raiding parties attacked individual farms, killed or captured whomever they found in the fields or the houses, destroyed the cattle, burned the buildings, and dis-

148

appeared into the forest with their prisoners. Pennsylvania's defense against these tactics was to patrol the intervals between the forts with provincial troops. This gave little enough protection to farms in the neighborhood, because raiding parties could slip easily through the cordon; but the forts and the patrols served to make any deep penetration of the settlements unsafe for the raiders. Conrad Weiser's comment on an early skirmish at Dietrich Six's in Berks County was typical of the war along this border: "The Enemy not beat but scared off."

It was known, however, that the Indians could, if they had to, fight a formal battle. While it is true that some professional soldiers looked on them as "undisciplined savages," other men knew better. Colonel James Smith, who was captured early in the French and Indian War, had a profound respect for the Indians as warriors. After being among them for some years (he was adopted by the Wyandots), he had this to say about their military capacity:

> They are under good command, and punctual in obeying orders: they can act in concert, and when their officers lay a plan and give orders, they will chearfully unite in putting all their directions into immediate execution; and by each man observing the motion or movement of his right hand companion, they can communicate the motion from right to left, and march abreast in concert, and in scattered order, though the line may be more than a mile long, and continue, if occasion requires, for a considerable distance, without disorder or confusion. They can perform various necessary manœuvers, either slowly, or as fast as they can run: they can form a circle, or semi-circle: the circle they make use of, in order to surround their enemy, and the semi-circle if the enemy has a river on one side of them. They can also form a large hollow square, face out and take trees: this they do, if their enemies are about surrounding them, to prevent from being shot from either side of the tree.[1]

It was a shock to colonial confidence when, at the end of July, 1756, Fort Granville on the Juniata, just west of modern Lewistown, was captured by French and Indian forces under François Coulon de Villiers and war chief Captain Jacobs.

To restore Pennsylvania's morale, a commando raid was led by Colonel John Armstrong against the western Delaware base at Kittanning. On the morning of September 8, 1756, the town was attacked. With the advantage of surprise and a superiority of three to one (as William A. Hunter explains in "Victory at Kittanning"[2]), Armstrong

[1] Darlington (ed.), *Life and Travels of Col. James Smith*, 150-51.
[2] *Pennsylvania History*, XXIII (1956), 376-407.

149

destroyed much of the town. Captain Jacobs at the outset ordered his women and children to flee to the woods, and then made his house the main center of resistance. When its bark covering was set on fire and he was called on to surrender or be burned alive, Captain Jacobs (according to a story repeated by James Smith) replied, "I eat fire," and fought to the death.

In the face of Indian reinforcements from across the Allegheny River, Armstrong retired. Of his force of some three hundred men, seventeen were killed, thirteen wounded (including Armstrong himself), and nineteen (some of whom got safely back) were missing.

In July, 1756, Fort Augusta had been built at Shamokin (Sunbury), where the North Branch and West Branch of the Susquehanna come together and where Indian paths converged from all directions. The establishment of a military post there served two important purposes. It gave protection to the down-river settlements, and it gave the Six Nations and other Indian friends of the English a restored confidence in Pennsylvania. The Indian world saw that the province was capable of defending itself.

The war dragged on, the Indian part of it fought as much with diplomacy as with gunfire. After Braddock's defeat, there were no further crucial engagements in Pennsylvania. At one time the province offered a bounty for Indian scalps, but withdrew it, partly in deference to Quaker scruples, partly because of the suspicion that unscrupulous scalp bounty hunters found the hair of friendly Indians (shot in the back) easier to come by than scalps taken in battle.

Indian conferences were held in which Delaware motives and objectives were explored. It would appear that fear of the French, who were strong in the west, had caused the Delawares to take up the hatchet. The desire for revenge was a contributing motive. The Indians resented not merely being cheated out of their lands but, as Teedyuscung said, being mocked for it afterwards. They wanted "a place in the sun." Teedyuscung's principal request at Easton in October, 1758, was that his people be given a deed for land to be reserved for them in perpetuity, not subject to the tricky manipulations that had hitherto kept most Indian borders in a turmoil.

In the back of men's minds was the enigma of the Six Nations. Were the Iroquois no longer able, or were they unwilling, to control the Delawares? The answer to that question came at the Easton Treaty in October, 1758, when the Six Nations, climaxing a long campaign of diplomatic pressure, brought Teedyuscung, leader of the Delawares, to heel. The Six Nations, on behalf of their Nephews, made peace with Pennsylvania over his head.

150

News of this peace treaty, which a brave Moravian, Christian Frederick Post, carried to the Ohio-Allegheny country, detached many of the Indians there from the French and helped to break French resistance in that quarter. When General John Forbes reached the Forks of the Ohio on November 25, 1758, he found that Fort Duquesne had been evacuated and burned the day before. The French continued to hold Fort Machault at Venango (Franklin) and the forts at Le Boeuf and Presque Isle for another year. On July 6, 1759, French and Indians made an unsuccessful attack at Fort Ligonier. But in the same month the British under Sir William Johnson captured Fort Niagara, a victory that cut Canada's communications with the Ohio country and caused the abandonment by the French of their remaining three forts.

PONTIAC'S WAR

Pontiac's War was a natural aftermath of the French and Indian War. The Indians in the west were as much opposed to English claims there as they had been to those of France. When the English, after driving the French from such key points as Detroit and the Forks of the Ohio, prepared to make their own occupation permanent, the Indians were alarmed. They were, moreover, infuriated by the arrogance of General Jeffery Amherst, commander-in-chief of British forces in North America. His directives (issued despite the warnings of Sir William Johnson and his Pennsylvania agent George Croghan) ignored Indian interests and disdained Indian courtesies. The camaraderie which French settlers and *coureurs de bois* (half-breed hunters and trappers) had enjoyed with the Indians was forbidden to the English. Hunting suffered because the issuance of powder and lead to the Indians was deliberately stinted. The Senecas were angry because white men who murdered Indians were seldom brought to justice, while Indians who retaliated in kind were, if surrendered according to agreement, tried in strictly English courts and hanged. Rumor spread that the English planned to exterminate them.

Pontiac, a chief of the Ottawas (who, like the Wyandots, Chippewas, and Potawatomies, lived at this time in the general vicinity of Detroit), was a moving spirit in a campaign intended to redress these grievances by driving the English out of the country. Soon the Delawares, Senecas, and Shawnees on the western borders of Pennsylvania were drawn into the struggle.

In the spring of 1763 the Indians began the siege of Detroit. They captured Fort Sandusky on May 16; Fort Miamis, May 27; Fort Ouiatenon, June 1; Fort Michilimackinac, June 2. In Pennsylvania

151

the pattern was much the same. Late in May, Senecas and Delawares began to harass Fort Pitt. On June 16 the Senecas captured Fort Venango (Franklin), and on June 18 they took Fort Le Boeuf. Four days later the Senecas, joining a party of Ottawas, Chippewas, and Wyandots, helped to capture Fort Presque Isle (Erie).

First blood at Fort Pitt was drawn when two soldiers were killed on May 29, but nothing like a regular siege began before July 27. Meantime Colonel Henry Bouquet had been sent out from the east with a relief column. The commandant at Fort Pitt, Captain Simeon Ecuyer, was confident. He had a good stockade, sixteen cannon, and 250 men. He was also ruthless. Following a suggestion made by Colonel Bouquet and approved by General Amherst, he sent the Delawares a present of blankets infected with smallpox.

Colonel Bouquet, a Swiss soldier of fortune who had entered the British service, left Carlisle on July 18 with a force of 460 men. Among them were parts of two Scottish regiments, the 77th and 42nd (the Black Watch), together with a battalion of Royal Americans and a few Rangers. This small striking force was somewhat reduced in numbers by the necessity of leaving a company at Fort Bedford. Having had no news from Fort Pitt for over a month, Bouquet left his wagons at Fort Ligonier and hurried on with 340 packhorses carrying flour for the besieged. The flour bags, as it turned out, helped to save him from a disaster like the one that had overtaken Braddock.

Believing this to be a race against time, Bouquet avoided the safe, dry, but roundabout route which General Forbes had cautiously taken on his approach to Fort Duquesne five years before. Instead, he took the more direct route which passed through the defiles of Turtle Creek, where he half expected to meet an ambush. The Indians, as it turned out, fell on him before he reached that point. On August 4, 1763, just as they were about to make camp at Bushy Run after a march of seventeen miles, Bouquet's forces were attacked by a body of Senecas, Delawares, and Shawnees. The soldiers fell back about a mile to a low hill, where they defended themselves throughout the night and part of the next day, protected by a parapet of flour bags. The horses and the wounded were kept in the center.

It is not known for certain who led the Indians in this well-directed attack. Most likely it was Mud Eater (Gaustarax), a Seneca of great influence among his own people though little known among white men. The tradition which gives the credit to the better-known Guyasuta (Kiasutha) is probably mistaken.

Bouquet had about four hundred men. He has left no estimate of the Indian forces opposing him. Sir William Johnson afterwards put their number at ninety-five, which is probably an underestimate. Bouquet's losses in the engagement were fifty killed, sixty wounded, and five missing.

"I intended to have halted to Day at Bushy Run," begins Bouquet's classic description of this battle in a letter of August 5 to General Amherst. He ended a second letter to the Commander-in-Chief next night with the solemn words, "if we have another Action, we Shall hardly be able to Carry our Wounded."[3]

He had, however, fought a more successful action on the second day than he knew at the time. By a ruse (feigning retreat in the center and, when the enemy rushed in, attacking from both flanks, first with musket fire and then with the bayonet) he inflicted such losses as the Indians could not long sustain. They disappeared in the forest, allowing him to reach Fort Pitt four days later, August 10.

Fort Pitt was thus saved, and the siege of Detroit was raised some time later. These two key points of the military line held firm, although the country between them fell into Indian hands. For months to come, the British had to guard their convoys with large forces. But in 1764 Bouquet took an army west into the Indian country and, in a treaty held at the Forks of the Muskingum, brought hostilities to an end.

At this treaty, white prisoners in Indian hands were surrendered. Some of them returned afterwards to the Indian families into which they had been adopted. In the Orderly Book of Colonel Henry Bouquet for October 29, 1764, we read:

> As there will be many among them [the white prisoners] who are very much attached to the Savages by having lived w^t them from their Infancy, These if not narrowly watched may be apt to make their Escape after they are delivered up: The Guards and Centinels therefore on this duty must be particularly attentive to prevent such accidents happening.[4]

The editor of the above passage notes that "the Shawnees were forced to bind some of the persons to be surrendered, several of the women actually escaping and returning to the savages."[5] Such things often happened at the surrender of prisoners. Major Ebenezer Denny observed in his military journal, May 14, 1786: "Several of the boys, and even one young woman of the prisoners, made their escape and returned to the Indians."[6] Conrad Richter's novel, *The Light in the Forest*, is based on such an incident.

[3] S. K. Stevens, Donald H. Kent, and Leo J. Roland (eds.), *The Papers of Col. Henry Bouquet*, 19 vols. (Harrisburg, 1940-1943), Series 21634, pp. 227, 230.
[4] *Western Pennsylvania Historical Magazine*, XLII (1959), 287-88.
[5] *Ibid.*, 299.
[6] Historical Society of Pennsylvania, *Memoirs*, VII (1860), 288.

THE PAXTON BOYS

A breed of "Indian haters" which, since the beginning of the French and Indian War, had been growing up on the Pennsylvania border, was brought to maturity by fears inspired during Pontiac's War. The Paxton Boys, so called because the core of them came from the Paxton or Paxtang (Harrisburg) district, provided the most notable example. Their guiding spirit was not the Reverend John Elder, pastor of the Paxton Presbyterian Church, though he has been blamed for the excesses committed by some of his parishioners. John Elder was no pacifist, but he tried to restrain the wilder spirits about him. The ringleader was the excitable Lazarus Stewart, an elder in the church.

On December 14, 1763, the Paxton Boys murdered six peaceable and defenseless Indians at Conestoga, where a remnant of the Susquehannocks with a few other Indians had been living quietly under the protection of the Pennsylvania government. A few days later, on December 27, the Paxton Boys entered Lancaster unopposed and butchered the remaining fourteen members of the Conestoga community, most of them old men, women, and children.

There is a tradition in Brecknock Township, Lancaster County, that one of the Conestoga Indians who had escaped both massacres was secretly given protection for the rest of his life on a farm near Alleghenyville. It is known for certain that two elderly Indians from Conestoga survived, having been living as servants on the farm of Ben Hershey's son Christian at the time of the massacres. A few months later they were given a safe conduct dated August 17, 1764. The document explained that the bearers, Michael and Mary, his wife, were "friendly Indians of the Delaware Tribe, who formerly resided with other Indians in the Conestoga Manor," and that they had for the past fifteen months or more been living with Christian Hershey at his plantation in Warwick Township, Lancaster County. All persons were called upon to treat them with civility and "to afford them all necessary assistance."[7]

By the Conestoga massacres the Paxton Boys drew attention to a new intolerance in Pennsylvania and also to a growing division between the frontier and the older settled country, a division which was not to be healed until after the Revolution and the Whiskey Rebellion. They drew attention also to the government's inability to protect friendly Indians. This last was to have unfortunate results during the Revolution, when friendly Delawares were found unwilling to come under the protection of Fort Pitt, fearing lest the government of the United States

[7] *Pennsylvania Archives*, 2d Series, II, 739.

prove as powerless as that of colonial Pennsylvania had been to protect her Indian friends from what Benjamin Franklin called "white savages."

Meanwhile Moravian Indians near Bethlehem, also threatened by local frontiersmen, were taken to Philadelphia for safety, and the Paxton Boys, reinforced by other frontier agitators, marched down with the avowed purpose of killing them too. When citizens of Philadelphia (good Quakers included) took up arms to defend these Christian Indian wards, the Paxton Boys turned back, contenting themselves for the time with a public statement of their grievances. In 1765 the Moravian Indians left Philadelphia for Wyalusing on the North Branch of the Susquehanna, where they remained until 1772, at which time they moved to the Ohio country.

The guiding spirit of the Paxton Boys, Lazarus Stewart, was officially proclaimed an outlaw. He escaped to Wyoming (Wilkes-Barre), where he joined the Connecticut forces in the Pennamite Wars. It is one of history's ironies that he died in the Massacre of Wyoming, July 3, 1778.

Wyoming

There is good reason to give the story of the Wyoming Valley a section to itself, for though it overlaps the French and Indian War, Pontiac's War, and the Revolutionary War, its parts are all bound together. There were two massacres of Wyoming, one in 1763 during Pontiac's War, the other in 1778 during the Revolutionary War; but to separate them is to break the current of history. They were but two episodes in a single theme. To understand that theme is a first necessity to any coherent view of Pennsylvania's Indian history.

From 1742 to 1779 the Wyoming Valley, always a favorite among the Indians, was the nub of Iroquois geopolitics. When in 1742 Canasatego "took the Delawares by the hair," as the Indian phrase ran, and settled the Walking Purchase dispute by ordering them out of the Forks of the Delaware and into the Wyoming Valley, he was acting in the interests of a long-range Iroquois policy.

It should be explained that the Iroquois maintained their power so late in American history, despite their small numbers, not so much by brute force (though they could still pack a wallop) as by skillful diplomacy and especially by the playing of the English and French against each other. In the contest which these two European powers were conducting in America, the Iroquois as a whole leaned toward the English; but at the same time they were aware of English encroachments. Settlers were shouldering their way up the Susquehanna.

155

The fertile Wyoming Valley on the North Branch, protected as it was on all sides by mountains or river gorges, was an outpost to be preserved at all costs. "Whoever controlled Wyoming," writes the biographer of Teedyuscung, "at once blocked white expansion northward from Pennsylvania into the Iroquois country and controlled the war and diplomatic trails from Shamokin to Onondaga."[8]

When in 1749 the proprietary government bought from the Six Nations a tract north of the Kittatinny Mountain, which turned out to contain Pennsylvania's best coal regions, the Indians were not shown a proper map of the purchase lest, as Conrad Weiser warned, on seeing how close these lands came to Wyoming, they should refuse to ratify the contract. Being unable to colonize the valley themselves yet being determined to hold it, the Iroquois made it a policy, as has been seen, to invite Indians of other nationalities to settle there. Certain bands of Shawnees came in 1701. Some Munsees came to nearby Lackawanna before 1727 and others came after the Walking Purchase.

The Nanticokes took up position here in 1748. Their removal five years later to Chenango, there to guard the more immediate approaches to the Longhouse, set in motion a series of events that led to the massacres of Wyoming.

The Nanticokes, shortly before their departure, sent a deputation across the mountains to the Moravian mission at Gnadenhütten (Lehighton) to invite the Christian Indians there—Delawares and Mahicans—to come north and occupy the Wyoming Flats. Teedyuscung, recently baptized by the Moravians (with some hesitation on their part), still felt the call of the blood. He sincerely admired the white man and desired to be a Christian; but he sympathized with the Indians' desire for independence, and he understood how important it was for the Wyoming Valley to be held by men of his race. Accordingly, with the help of the Mahican Abraham, he organized a band of some sixty-five or seventy Indians who settled themselves at Wyoming under the Six Nations shield.

Pennsylvania encouraged the move. She was aware that Connecticut was casting an eye on the valley, claiming it on the strength of her own early charter, which antedated Penn's. Pennsylvania wished to have good Indian friends settled there (under authority of the Six Nations, who had promised in 1736 to sell only to Pennsylvania) in order to forestall the New Englanders.

[8] Anthony F. C. Wallace, *King of the Delawares: Teedyuscung, 1700-1763* (Philadelphia, 1949), 48.

156

The Iroquois gave full assurance that they would not let the North Branch Valley go.

We will never part with the Land at Shamokin and Wyomink [said Chief Hendrick of the Mohawks, July 5, 1754, to John Penn and the commissioners of Pennsylvania at Albany]; our Bones are scattered there, and on this Land there has always been a great Council Fire. We desire You will not take it amiss that we will not part with it, for We reserve it to settle such of our Nations upon as shall come to us from the Ohio, or any others who shall deserve to be in our Alliance. Abundance of Indians are moving up and down, and We shall invite all such to come and live here, that so We may strengthen ourselves.[9]

That was the crucial year, 1754, in the Wyoming story, when the Susquehannah Company made the dubious Wyoming Purchase and set the stage for violence. The Six Nations announced repeatedly, at Onondaga, Albany, and Philadelphia, that the so-called purchase was a fraud: the Onondaga Council had not authorized a sale, but company agents at different times had pulled individual Indians aside, made them drunk, got them to make their marks on documents they did not understand, and announced that this was council action validating the purchase.

Conrad Weiser, early in the winter, had a conversation with Shickellamy's son John, who since his father's death had acted as the Six Nations supervisor of this area. The chief said, as Weiser reported it on March 1, 1755:

that whosoever of the white should venture to Setle any land on Wyomock or thereabout, belonging hitherto to the Indians, will have his Creatures killed first, and then If they did not desist they them self would be Killed, without distinction, let the Consequence be what it would.[10]

John Shickellamy was not fooling. Like his father, he was a friend of the English, but he knew what his own people felt about the Wyoming lands. Unhappily his warning went unheeded in some quarters, and the truth of what he said to Weiser had to be recorded in blood.

When the French and Indian War broke out, Teedyuscung, leader of the Susquehanna Delawares, after a brief period of indecision yielded to French persuasion, flouted the authority of his Uncles, the Six Nations, and attacked white settlements in Pennsylvania. When

---

[9] Pennsylvania, *Colonial Records*, VI, 116.
[10] *Pennsylvania Archives*, 1st Series, II, 260.

he found fortune deserting the French, he returned to his earlier allegiance, requesting that he be anchored in friendship with the English by receiving from them a permanent land base for his people. He proposed that Pennsylvania deed to him for that purpose some two million acres with its southern base in the Wyoming Valley.

"I sit here," he said (using the pronoun "I" correctly, according to Indian usage, for the people whom he represented), "as a Bird on a Bow [bough]; I look about and do not know where to go; let me therefore come down upon the Ground, and make that my own by a good Deed, and I shall then have a Home for Ever. . . ."[11]

The request was not granted. Teedyuscung, with his band of Susquehanna Delawares, remained at Wyoming for some uneasy years, keeping an eye on the trail from Cushetunk on the upper Delaware, where armed Connecticut "settlers" were assembling in a body for an advance into the disputed valley.

The trouble came to a head in 1762, when the New Englanders began to cut a wagon road from Cushetunk and prospecting parties arrived at Wyoming. Teedyuscung warned them off. He was offered pay if he would join them in surveying the land. He refused. They stole his horse. He threatened to arrest them and take them to the governor in Philadelphia. They gave him a new horse and decamped, saying, however, that they would return in the spring with thousands of armed men. The Six Nations stood behind him and in March, 1763, promised the New Englanders war if they attempted to seize the valley.

On April 16 of that year Teedyuscung was burned to death in his cabin. His death may well have been accidental, but to a community depleted by the previous year's epidemic (in which Teedyuscung's wife and others had died) and faced with the New Englanders' threat, it must have seemed the last straw. In June the survivors abandoned their town and removed to the West Branch of Susquehanna.

Two or three weeks after Teedyuscung's death, Connecticut families took up residence in the valley. On October 15, 1763, there occurred the first Massacre of Wyoming. That was when Captain Bull, a son of Teedyuscung, swept through the valley with a Delaware war party and left no white people alive in it. Some were tortured and killed. About twenty were led into captivity. Three or four escaped.

Soon after the conclusion of Pontiac's War, Connecticut settlers were back again in the Wyoming Valley. Thereafter the quarrel, climaxing in the Pennamite Wars, was waged for the most part among white men rather than between white men and Indians. But the

[11] Pennsylvania, *Colonial Records*, VIII, 203.

Iroquois continued to keep a jealous eye on the valley. The Moravians at Friedenshütten (Wyalusing) noted in their diary on June 14, 1768: "Two Mohawks arrived, sent by the Six Nations to the Yankees: 'that if they did not leave Wyomick, they would come down and *strike their heads.'* "[12]

The Fort Stanwix Treaty of November 5, 1768, at which the Iroquois were induced to cede lands on the North Branch south of Towanda (including the Wyoming Valley), did not end Indian resentment. John Heckewelder observed that after the treaty the Six Nations sent the Christian Indians at Wyalusing "two Spanish dollars. . . . as *their* share of the money for the land sold by them to the English"; and he added this significant note: "By sending the two dollars to the Christian Indians, the Six Nations meant to say, that thus they had been cheated by the English in the purchase made; for every five miles square they received 2 dollars."[13]

THE REVOLUTIONARY WAR

The years immediately preceding the American Revolution found Indian relations in the colonies deteriorating. The governments of New York, Pennsylvania, and Virginia were unable to restrain their border populations, who murdered Indians wholesale and with impunity. George Croghan, known as "Prince of Traders," complained in 1768 of "the Repated Murders on those Fronteers and y[e]. Want of power in y[e]. Goverment to bring y[e]. Murdreres to punishment. . . ." Benjamin Franklin observed, "It grieves me to hear that our Frontier People are yet greater Barbarians than the Indians, and continue to murder them in time of Peace."[14] In the Yellow Creek massacre of April, 1774, on the Ohio, thirteen members of Logan's (i.e., John Shickellamy's) family were killed. "There runs not a drop of my blood in the veins of any living creature. . . . Who is there to mourn for Logan?—Not one!" So ends "Logan's Lament," as reported to John Gibson and presented to the world by Thomas Jefferson.

At first, after the Revolution had broken out, both Americans and British advised the Indians to "sit still." But before long that policy was abandoned by both sides. The British, in order to divert American forces from the more crucial areas of conflict in the east, opened a

---

[12] *Now and Then*, V (1936), 62.
[13] *A Narrative of the Mission of the United Brethren Among the Delaware and Mohegan Indians . . .* (Philadelphia, 1820), 108.
[14] Sullivan, Flick, and Hamilton (eds.), *Papers of Sir William Johnson*, XII, 425, 178.

new front in the west. Agents from Detroit—Matthew Elliot, Alexander McKee, and Simon Girty—went among the Indians reminding them of their grievances and stirring up their fears. Some Americans, on the other hand, at one time played with the idea of forming a fourteenth (Indian) state, if the Indians would support them in the war.

Unhappily, the militia of Pennsylvania and Virginia gave some substance to the Indians' distrust. Friendly Delawares were alienated by the "Squaw Campaign." That was in February, 1778, when a body of militia, failing to reach their objective—some British stores at Cuyahoga—because of the heavy rains, satisfied themselves with shooting up and plundering friendly Delaware camps on the Shenango River near present New Castle, Pennsylvania, and on Mahoning Creek at the Salt Spring (Niles, Ohio). They killed several women and a small boy, wounded and captured the mother of an eminent Delaware chief, Captain Pipe, and killed his brother (the only grown man in the two Indian camps), whom George Morgan declared to be "a noted friend to the United States."[15] A wave of anti-American sentiment swept over Delaware councils. Captain Pipe demanded war. It was with difficulty that Captain White Eyes, who was resolutely favorable to the Americans, managed to keep the Delawares neutral for a few more months.

Meanwhile the Iroquois had come into the war, disunited. For two years they had resisted solicitation from both sides, English and American. They were resolved to keep out of the white man's quarrel. But in the end they were sucked in. "You can't live in the woods and stay neutral," was an Iroquois saying that had come down from the French and Indian War.

The Confederacy as such took no action. Each of the Six Nations was left to choose its own course. Four of them—Mohawks, Onondagas, Cayugas, and Senecas—decided for the British, but the Oneidas and a large part of the Tuscaroras decided for the "Thirteen Fires." Lafayette's bodyguard was a Tuscarora, Nicholas Cusick. Near Valley Forge, a body of Oneidas performed a gallant action that should be better remembered in American annals.

Lafayette, with over two thousand men, had crossed the Schuylkill to observe the movements of the British, who were preparing to leave Philadelphia. On May 20, 1778, finding himself about to be cut off by superior British forces, he barely managed to reach Matson's Ford at Conshohocken, a little ahead of the enemy. To save his men from

[15] Morgan to the Board of War, July 17, 1778, quoted in Louise Phelps Kellogg (ed.), *Frontier Advance on the Upper Ohio, 1778-1779* (Madison, Wisconsin, 1916), 113.

disaster as they waded the chest-deep ford, he posted the Oneidas as a rear guard. General Peter Muhlenberg, whose troops held advanced lines at Valley Forge, described the incident to his father, the Reverend Henry Melchior Muhlenberg, who put it all down in his diary:

> The Indians were the last to get over, and they were surrounded in a small thicket by the English light cavalry, but they retired behind the trees in accord with their custom and let loose their usual hideous war whoops, which threw the horses and riders into confusion and sent them flying; whereupon the Indians shot several of the cavalrymen and gathered up their lost cloaks.[16]

As encouragement to the pro-American party among the Delawares, United States commissioners in a treaty at Pittsburgh, September 19, 1778, offered the tribe admission to the Union as part of a fourteenth Indian state. At about the same time White Eyes was made a colonel in the American army. Unfortunately, both gestures came to nothing. Colonel White Eyes died (murdered by the militia, according to George Morgan), and Congress did not ratify the treaty.

Most of the Delawares joined the British. Small war parties struck at American settlements. The only set battle in this western campaign of terror was at Upper Sandusky, Ohio, in June, 1782. That was when Colonel William Crawford, who had taken part in the Squaw Campaign, was defeated, captured, and burned at the stake by Captain Pipe's warriors.

Meanwhile in central Pennsylvania during the summer of 1778, a series of heavy raids, mostly from the Seneca country, had been directed against the Susquehanna Valley above Shamokin. A captured prisoner reported that it was the intention of the Indians to murder all the inhabitants on both branches of the river. Ownership of the land between Lycoming Creek and Pine Creek on the West Branch was a matter of continuing dispute. As for the North Branch, memory of the "Wyoming Purchase" still rankled.

The "Great Runaway" of May, 1778, which emptied the West Branch Valley of its settlers, was described by Lieutenant Samuel Hunter at Fort Augusta (Sunbury) in a letter to John Hambright of the Supreme Executive Council, which was then in Lancaster:

> We are Really in a Meloncoly situation in this County at present, the back inhabitants has all Evacuated their habitations and Assembled in different places; all above Muncy to Lycoming is come to Samuel Wallises, and the People of Muncy has

[16] Theodore G. Tappert and John W. Doberstein (trans.), *The Journals of Henry Melchior Muhlenberg*, 3 vols. (Philadelphia, 1942-1958), III, 156.

161

gathered to Captain Bradys, all above Lycoming is at Antis's Mill & the mouth of Bald Eagle Creek, all the inhabitants of Penn's Valley is gathered to one place in Potters Township, the Inhabitants of White Dear Township is assembled at three Different places, and the Back setlers of Bufaloe is come down to the River, Penn's Township likewise has moved to the River, all from Muncy Hill to Chilisquake has assembled at three Different places, Fishing Creek and Mahoning Setlement has all come to the River side; . . . to think what a pannick prevails in this County; it is really Distressing to see the inhabitants flying away and leaving their all. . . .[17]

Settlement in the North Branch Valley came to an end with the Battle of Wyoming. That engagement was the climax of one of the great tragedies, in the classical sense, in American history. The defenders of Forty Fort were fighting for their homes and for the survival of a great humanitarian ideal embodied in the new nation to whose cause they committed their lives. They were unaware of the dark forces ranged against them: not only a three-to-one superiority in numbers but also the revival among the Indians of old memories coupled with a determination to recover their lost valley.

The massacre of prisoners that followed the Battle of Wyoming shocked the world and brought deep sympathy for the American cause. The name *Wyoming* became a synonym in men's minds for patriotic devotion and martyrdom. The English poet Thomas Campbell (after whom Campbell's Ledge, overlooking the Susquehanna above Pittston, has been named) has given the traditional view of the battle and its aftermath in *Gertrude of Wyoming*.

How did the engagement look from Indian eyes? Dr. Arthur Parker, former New York State Archaeologist, whose Seneca ancestors fought at Wyoming, has told us that the tactics employed by the Indians in that battle had been mapped out months before in consultation with the British. At a meeting of the whole Iroquois Confederacy at Onondaga (so we are informed by Daniel Claus in a manuscript preserved in the Canadian Archives at Ottawa), it was decided to undertake a campaign against the Wyoming settlement. The Mohawk Colonel Joseph Brant (principal promoter of the scheme) hoped by this means to offset the "Shock of Gen[l] Burgoyne's Disaster." It was arranged that Brant should create a diversion in the north while Sakayengwaraghton, a Seneca chief, led his warriors into the Susquehanna Valley. Details were worked out in a conference at Montreal. Next spring at Niagara and later at Canadesaga (where Sakayeng-

[17] *Pennsylvania Archives*, 1st Series, VI, 570.

waraghton assembled his forces) it was made known to the British that the Indians wanted to do this thing alone. When, nevertheless, Colonel John Butler attached himself to the expedition with some of his Rangers, the Indians found a way to push them aside. At the last moment, when his forces were about to be engaged, Sakayeng-waraghton warned Butler to keep his men out of sight lest the Indians mistake them for enemies.

> Sakayengwaraghton [wrote Claus] . . . put his plan in Execution making every preparation Disposition & Manoeuvre with his Ind[ns]. himself and when the Rebels of Wayoming came to attack him desired Col[o] Butler to keep his people seperate from his for fear of Confusion and stood the whole Brunt of the Action himself for there were but 2. White Men [Rangers was crossed out in the original] killed; and then destroyed the whole Settlement without hurting or Molesting a Woman or Child w[ch] these 2. Ind[n] Chiefs [Brant and Sakayengwaraghton] (to their honor be it said) [had] agreed upon . . . in the Spring.[18]

During the course of the battle, the Indians used tactics similar to those employed by Colonel Henry Bouquet at the Battle of Bushy Run. Early in the fighting, they appeared to give way, but, when the Americans pressed forward in pursuit, the Indians closed in on them from both sides and the rear. No quarter was given. The few men who were taken alive during the battle were killed that same night.

By an ironical twist of fate it appears to have been Lazarus Stewart, former ringleader of the Paxton Boys, who unwittingly gave victory to the Indians. Colonel Zebulon Butler, who was in command at Forty Fort, had not desired an engagement. He expected reinforcements, and he believed he could hold out until they arrived. He decided, therefore, against risking his inferior forces in open battle. But the excitable Lazarus Stewart so stirred up the men about him that they pressured the unwilling commander into making a sortie. Lazarus Stewart was among the slain.

Folklore has been hard at work on the Battle of Wyoming and has produced a number of distortions that should be corrected. In the first place, Joseph Brant has been blamed, mistakenly, for the killing of the prisoners. He was not at Wyoming but up in the Mohawk Valley. It is doubtful if Queen Esther was present at the massacre although tradition identifies her with the Indian woman who killed the prisoners at what is now known as "Queen Esther's Rock." The tradition is out of key with her known character. She treated the Strope

---

[18] Anecdotes of Captain Joseph Brant, by Daniel Claus, Niagara, 1778, Claus Papers, II, 61, Public Archives of Canada, Ottawa (microfilm).

family, who had been her prisoners since May of that year, with great kindness. The "Narrative" of Mrs. Whittaker (Jane Strope) makes that clear. It is possible that at the time of the massacre Queen Esther may have been confused with Catharine Montour (wife of a Seneca chief), who, it is commonly thought, was her sister. Catharine's name, instead of Esther's, appears in several early accounts of the massacre as that of the "priestess" who presided at it. On the other hand, we know that Queen Esther, whatever her normal character, may have been inflamed to avenge the death of her son, who had been killed by American scouts the day before the battle.

Another tradition is that some three hundred persons, including women and children, were killed at Forty Fort after its surrender. There was no such massacre. The terms of capitulation were honorable. Some Indians got out of hand, and their chiefs were unable to restrain them from looting, but they did not injure the occupants of the fort, soldiers or civilians. A British deserter, Sergeant Boyd, was formally executed, but no other lives were taken. There were a few isolated cases of violence on the outlying farms when houses were burned and settlers expelled (as all were) from the valley. But the Massacre of Wyoming occurred on the battlefield, not among the refugees in Forty Fort.

The American reply to the Great Runaway and the Battle of Wyoming came in three parts, led by Colonel Hartley, Colonel Van Schaick, and General Sullivan. In September, 1778, Colonel Thomas Hartley led a reprisal raid over the Sheshequin Path to the Forks of the Susquehanna (Athens), where he destroyed a number of Indian settlements, among them these three: Tioga, Queen Esther's Town, and Old Sheshequin (Ulster).

In April, 1779, Colonel Goose Van Schaick invaded the country of the Onondagas, burned their principal town with its stores of corn, killed their cattle, and took a few prisoners.

Late in the summer of the same year, General John Sullivan, General James Clinton, and Colonel Daniel Brodhead, in a concerted movement, ravaged the Seneca country. On July 31 Sullivan set out from Wyoming for Tioga. Meanwhile Clinton had assembled his force at the foot of Otsego Lake, which he dammed to raise the level. On receiving word from Sullivan, he broke the dam and on the flood waters floated some of his men down the river in bateaux to Pennsylvania. At Fort Sullivan (Tioga) he joined General Sullivan's main force. The combined armies, amounting to some four thousand five hundred men, entered the Seneca country by way of the "Forbidden Path"—forbidden, that is, to white men. A body of about six hundred

Indians with a few British attempted to stop them in the narrows near Newtown (Elmira, New York); but Sullivan, with the help of an Oneida guide, outflanked and defeated them on August 29. Advancing, Sullivan burned towns, cornfields, and orchards, and drove many of the Indians back on the British base at Niagara for subsistence.

Among the forty Indian towns Sullivan destroyed were Canadesaga (Geneva) —a beautiful town of eighty houses, some of stone, some with window boxes filled with flowers—and Canandaigua, described as "a very pretty town." Sullivan reported also that he had destroyed 160,000 bushels of corn. His men were amazed at the Iroquois cornfields, superior to anything of the kind they had seen before.

While this was going on, Colonel Brodhead had set out from Fort Pitt with six hundred men on a diversionary raid against the Senecas' western flank. He had a skirmish at Thompson's Island nine miles below Conewango (Warren), burned Cornplanter's Town, destroyed some five hundred acres of corn, and then pulled out fast—before the Indians should have time to get themselves together. Contrary to popular tradition, he did not get as far into the Seneca country as Bucktooth (West Salamanca). Some western Senecas still say, "We won the war."

The Senecas were far from being knocked out, as may be gathered from their subsequent devastation of Westmoreland County and particularly the destruction of Hannastown, July 13, 1782. Indeed, the Sullivan Expedition drew them more furiously into the conflict. Hitherto they had sent out only scattered and occasional war parties. They were "dragging their feet" in the British service. But now they felt themselves committed as a nation.

Sullivan has been much criticized because he did not capture Fort Niagara, took only a very few prisoners, and failed to destroy the Iroquois war potential. Yet the expedition was by no means a failure. Sullivan had thrown many of the Iroquois back on Niagara, which was expensive to the British. He had destroyed vast fields of corn on the Chemung River, and, by the establishment of Fort Sullivan at Tioga, had made sure that this Indian food base should never again be used against the United States. The very fact that such a raid had been undertaken at all against the fabled Iroquois had done much to restore American morale.

After the Revolutionary War the United States made peace of a kind with the Indians in a series of treaties: in 1784 at Fort Stanwix with the Iroquois; in 1785 at Fort McIntosh with the Delawares and Wyandots; in 1786 at Fort Finney with the Shawnees; and in 1789 with all four of them again at Fort Harmar. The difficulty—as William Penn had found—was to make sure that the right Indians (that is, chiefs with authority to speak for the various divisions of their people) attended the treaties and signed the documents. The commissioners were too often ignorant of Indian protocol. Only a few chiefs signed at Fort Stanwix in 1784, and the right of these to sign was afterwards contested. Of the Fort Harmar Treaty, John Heckewelder (who had lived for many years among the Indians) observed that he did not find among the signatures the name of even one great chief. For some years the Indians defeated attempts to overawe them by military force, as was seen in the overwhelming defeat administered to Major General Arthur St. Clair near Fort Wayne on November 4, 1791, by Indian confederates under the Miami, Chief Little Turtle.

White men—settlers, land speculators, and the United States government—sought to extinguish Indian land rights beyond the Ohio, which river had been established at the Fort Stanwix Treaty of 1768 as the permanent boundary between the races. The Indians of the Wabash and Maumee rivers—Miamis, Weas, Delawares, Shawnees, Wyandots, and others—had come together in a loose confederacy, not unlike that organized by Pontiac twenty years earlier, to resist encroachment on Indian land. They were successful for a time. The Iroquois sympathized with them, but sought for compromise. In 1794 the United States made a settlement with the Six Nations at Canandaigua, largely through the influence of Cornplanter and the women of the Confederacy. After Anthony Wayne's decisive victory on August 20 of that year at Fallen Timbers on the Maumee, the western Indians made a firm peace with the United States at the Treaty of Greenville, August 3, 1795. Pennsylvania's Indian wars were over.

19

The Cornplanter Grant

CORNPLANTER

DURING THE NINETEENTH and twentieth centuries, Pennsylvania's main link with the Indians has been through the Cornplanter Grant, a small tract of land on the Allegheny River just south of the New York state line.

Cornplanter (Gyantwahia), after whom the tract was named, was one of the Seneca war chiefs who fought against the United States during the Revolutionary War. Born about 1750, he was known sometimes as John Abeel (O'Bail), for he was the son of a Dutch trader and a Seneca woman of chiefly lineage. His uncle was Guyasuta. Cornplanter, rejected by his father, identified himself wholly with his mother's people.

After the war, he was spokesman in Iroquois councils for a policy of reconciliation with the United States. He helped to keep the Senecas from assisting the Miami confederacy, which defeated Brigadier General Harmar in 1790 and Major General St. Clair in 1791, but which was defeated by Anthony Wayne at Fallen Timbers in 1794.

In response to Cornplanter's friendly attitude, as shown at the Fort Harmar Treaty in 1789 and on his visit to Philadelphia in 1790, the legislature of Pennsylvania on January 29, 1791, granted to him and his heirs "in perpetuity" three tracts of land on the upper Allegheny. One of these, "Richland," near present West Hickory, he sold to his friend General John Wilkins, Jr. Another, the "Gift," was at what is now Oil City. It is said that when Cornplanter sold it in 1818, he was paid in worthless money and notes. Attempts by him and his heirs to recover the property or to get proper payment for it met with no success.

The third tract was some six hundred acres in extent, most of it on the west bank of the Allegheny just south of the New York state line. It included his own town of Jenuchshadego and two islands in the river.

Cornplanter was an Indian patriot of the best kind. He was generous, forward-looking, constructive. In 1798 he brought in Quaker teachers, established schools, made roads, built good houses, developed agriculture, bred large herds of cattle, and, in a word, turned the Cornplanter Grant into a model community. In his later years he became disillusioned with white men, closed the schools, broke his sword, and destroyed all other gifts received from white friends such as George Washington and Thomas Mifflin. He died February 18, 1836.

HANDSOME LAKE

Cornplanter's half brother Handsome Lake (Skaniadariyo) is remembered for the decisive influence he exerted in restoring Iroquois morale after the Revolutionary War. Handsome Lake himself suffered the moral and mental collapse that came to many Iroquois at the turn of the nineteenth century as they watched the breakup of their national home and saw the end of the Six Nations' heroic role in North American affairs.

Proud, frustrated, drunken, Handsome Lake lay on his pallet for years, expecting and hoping to die. But there came to him a series of visions in which, as he reported, he traveled the Sky Road and received from the Creator (through the Three Messengers) instructions on how to revitalize the Iroquois. He was to preach, not the old ideal of self-expression, but a new and puritanical self-control.

Recovering his health, he presented the Creator's message—*Gaiwiio*, the Good Word or Gospel—first at Cornplanter's Town, then at Cold Spring, and later at Tonawanda. All these were Seneca communities. At the last place his teaching took such deep root that Tonawanda remains today the principal stronghold of what the Indians call the

"New Religion." In response to urging from the Three Messengers, he took the Good Word to Onondaga, capital of the Six Nations, that men might know the message was intended by the Creator not only for Senecas but for the whole Iroquois Confederacy. At Onondaga he was well received, but on August 10, 1815, a few days after his arrival, he died and for the last time journeyed (in company with the Fourth Messenger) over the Sky Road—the Milky Way—to the Land of Happy Spirits and the dwelling place of the Creator.

His followers launched a religious movement which spread throughout the Iroquois world, preaching the same strict morality and restoring a deserved pride in their race. The religion of Handsome Lake is today undergoing a strong revival. The Prophet's adherents constitute a large part of the Iroquois population in the United States and Canada. Their "Keepers of the Faith" conduct periodical meetings which last three, four, or even five days. Public worship consists of prayers of thanksgiving and intercession, exhortation, confession, religious dancing, the burning of sacred tobacco, and the recitation of the "Code of Handsome Lake"—the story of his career and a collection of his sayings.

According to Handsome Lake, there are four great sky trails leading to "the Land of Happy Spirits," one for each of the four great races of the world. The ethics of his code are essentially Christian. An Indian observer, Chief Joseph Montour (a Methodist preacher on the Six Nations Reserve), described the religion of Handsome Lake as "Christianity without the Redeemer."

The following selections from the code will serve to illustrate Handsome Lake's main purposes: to root out evils that threatened to destroy his people, to restore pride of race and confidence in the future, and to preserve the best of the beautiful old Iroquois customs.

1. The Creator made one-ga [oh-nay-ga, whisky or rum] and gave it to our younger brethren, the white man, as a medicine but they use it for evil. . . . No, the Creator did not make it for you.

44. You have had the constant fear that the white race would exterminate you. The Creator will care for his On-gwe-o-we [Iroquois].

60. It is a custom for thanksgiving to be made over the hills of planted corn. Let the head of the family make an invocation over the planted hills that the corn may continue to support life.

64. Let this be your ceremony when you wish to employ the medicine in a plant: First offer tobacco [sprinkling a little on the glowing embers of a fire]. Then tell the plant in gentle

169

words what you desire of it and pluck it from the roots. It is said in the upper world that it is not right to take a plant for medicine without first talking to it.

67. . . . Our grief adds to the sorrows of the dead. . . . Ten days shall be the time for mourning and when our friends depart [the soul leaving the earth on the tenth day] we must lay grief aside. . . . you can journey with the dead only as far as the grave.[1]

Brooks Redeye, a Seneca Keeper of the Faith, on September 22, 1843, delivered a prayer, recorded at the time, of which the following is the substance:

God hear us. This rising smoke represents our faith in Thee. We thank Thee for our creation and for our enjoyment of the world Thou hast given us.

We also thank the Four Angels who are placed over us to guide us day and night.

We also thank the Thunders, servants of God, who nourish the earth.

We also thank the Sun that God put in the sky to give us light.

We also thank the Moon that God put up there.

We also thank the Waters that God meant to keep us from thirst.

We also thank the Earth that God has given us to walk upon.

We also thank the Trees that God placed on the land.

We also thank the Grasses and Herbs that God placed here for our medicine.

We also thank Silverlake [Handsome Lake], our prophet, who communicated with God's servants, the Four Angels, and who has now returned to Heaven and lives by the side of God.

We owe thanks to God for all the wonderful works he has done for us and for all the things he has given us to see day and night; and we pray God to continue these in return for our pure faith and for our proper and joyful performance of the worship songs and dances and games.[2]

Handsome Lake and his followers were largely responsible for the regeneration of the Iroquois, both as individuals and as a nation, in the early nineteenth century. The present Iroquois renaissance also owes much to the same influence.

[1] See Arthur C. Parker, *The Code of Handsome Lake* (Albany, 1913).
[2] Prayer of Brooks Redeye, September 22, 1843, Draper MSS, 22 F, 138 (Joseph Brant Papers), State Historical Society of Wisconsin (microfilm). The version in the text is a paraphrased version of the original manuscript.

20

Envoi

THE DELAWARES as a people have long since disappeared from Pennsylvania. Some bands moved north to the protection of the Iroquois Longhouse. Descendants of Pennsylvania's Moravian Indians, Delawares and Mahicans, now live in a community (the former Fairfield or Moraviantown) situated on the Thames River between London and Chatham in Kent County, Ontario, where their annual agricultural fair has won much praise. There is a large band of Delawares on the Six Nations Reserve near Brantford, Ontario. Numbers of Munsees live at nearby Muncytown, where they keep alive their traditional reputation of a lively and aggressive people.

The greater number of the Delawares removed to Ohio during the middle years of the eighteenth century, and there enjoyed some years of national prosperity under Netawatwees (Newcomer) and White Eyes. In 1830 a considerable body moved west to a reservation in eastern Kansas at the forks of the Kansas and Missouri rivers. After suffering much distress from white marauders, a large part of the Kansas Delawares moved south into the Indian Territory (Oklahoma) where they may still be found.

Other Delaware bands moved even farther afield. Those, for instance, who now live among the Caddo in Oklahoma had at one time wandered as far south as Mexico. A few Delawares are in Wisconsin. But it is the Delawares now settled among the Cherokees in Oklahoma who have longest preserved their native culture. Some of the ancient rites of the Big House Ceremony are still practiced among them.

The Iroquois, who planted the Tree of Peace in Pennsylvania before William Penn received his charter, are now a divided people, scattered over many reservations in the United States and Canada. But they are by no means broken. They still retain, whether on their reservations in New York, Wisconsin, Ontario, or Quebec, a strong national consciousness. "The Six Nations," they say, "will never die."

At the same time they are loyal supporters (whether or not they accept the citizenship offered them) of the American and Canadian

171

governments under whose aegis they live. During the Second World War they put into the field, in the armies of the United States and Canada, over two thousand men—a greater number of warriors than they had ever assembled at one time during the Beaver Wars and the days of their greatest national glory.

In Pennsylvania, however, the Cornplanter grant—and, with it, the last Indian community in the State—has now vanished:

> Cornplanter's descendants and other Indians continued to live on the tract. The community had its own school and its Presbyterian Church. Eventually, however, the population dwindled as residents moved to the adjacent, larger, and related Allegany Reservation of New York. Residence became largely seasonal, and in late 1964 the last inhabitant left, permitting Kinzua Dam to be closed and the reservoir flooded. The Cornplanter Indians would no longer call Pennsylvania their home.[1]

[1]Merle H. Deardorff, "Chief Cornplanter," Historical Pennsylvania Leaflet No. 32 (Harrisburg, 1972).

Therefore let it be a Part of the present Agreement that We shall treat one another as Brethren to the latest Generation, even after We shall not have left a Foot of Land.

—Chief Hendrick of the Mohawks to the Pennsylvania Commissioners, Albany, July 5, 1754.

Famous Indians of Pennsylvania

ALLIQUIPPA. A Seneca woman (though her name is a Delaware word, "hat" or "cap"), best known as the acknowledged head of an Indian community near present Pittsburgh. She may have been among the Senecas settled at Conestoga; for she was among the Indians who bade William Penn farewell at New Castle in 1701, and Governor Morris gave her son the name Captain Newcastle in commemoration of that event. She was living in western Pennsylvania by 1731. Conrad Weiser in 1748 visited her on the Allegheny a short distance above the mouth of the Monongahela. In 1752 she was found living near the mouth of Chartier's Creek. George Washington in 1753 called on her at the mouth of the Youghiogheny. "Queen Aliquippa's Cornfield" is the name of a field by the Youghiogheny at Robbins Station (North Huntington Township, Westmoreland County) where Alliquippa's Indians are said to have come in the summer to raise corn. She died, 1754, at Aughwick, whither she had retired with other Indians friendly to Pennsylvania after Washington's surrender at Fort Necessity.

ALLUMAPEES (OLUMAPIES). See SASSOONAN.

BALD EAGLE (WOAPALANNE). There is uncertainty about the career and even the identity of the Indian after whom Bald Eagle's Nest (now Milesburg), Bald Eagle Creek, Bald Eagle Mountain, and Bald Eagle Township (Clinton County) were named. It is known that a friendly and respected Indian named Bald Eagle was murdered by white men on the Monongahela in 1773. There is also a tradition that during the Revolutionary War a Munsee Indian chief named Bald Eagle led war parties from "the Nest" against settlements in the West Branch Valley. He is said to have killed James Brady near Williamsport in August, 1778, and to have been killed himself by James' elder brother Sam near Brady's Bend (Clarion County) on the Allegheny in June, 1779.

BEAVER (TAMAQUA). A leading man of the Delawares, a nephew (sister's son) of Sassoonan, after whose death he moved to the Ohio country, where he was recognized as a chief of the Delawares in that area. He lived at McKee's Rocks until the French invasion in 1754, at Kittanning until Armstrong's attack in 1756, and at Kuskusky until 1759, when he moved to Tuscarawas (near present Bolivar, Ohio). During the French and Indian War the Iroquois designated him as "king" or spokesman to seek peace with the English, and in that capacity he negotiated with Christian Frederick Post in 1758. He was recognized as principal chief of the Turkey lineage in Netawatwee's "Delaware Nation." He died in 1769 at the site of present Gnadenhutten, Ohio, and was succeeded by Welapachiken (Captain Johnny).

CANASATEGO. Onondaga chief, member of the Six Nations' Great Council. He is remembered in Pennsylvania as the principal speaker for the Iroquois at Philadelphia, 1742, when Delaware complaints against the Walking Purchase were examined. Canasatego, presenting the Iroquois decision, ordered the Delawares to leave the Forks of the Delaware and Minisinks and to move to the Susquehanna at Wyoming (Wilkes-Barre) or Shamokin (Sunbury). He attended Indian conferences at Lancaster, 1744, and Philadelphia, 1742 and 1749. Conrad Weiser visited him at Onondaga, 1743 and 1745. He died in 1750.

CHARTIER, PETER. Son of a French Canadian father and his Shawnee wife, Peter Chartier came to Pennsylvania with the Shawnee band that moved up the Susquehanna from Maryland in 1697. Like his father, who died in 1718, he engaged in the Indian trade, in which he continued after the Shawnee band moved to the Ohio about 1728. In an effort to retain the friendship of these people, the Proprietors in 1740 gave Chartier 600 acres of land at present New Cumberland, which he forfeited five years later when he and his Indian associates plundered some Pennsylvania traders. The French then settled this band on the Wabash, but Chartier removed to Alabama, where he remained until 1759, when they returned to the Cumberland River in Kentucky. His further history is unknown.

CORNPLANTER (GYANTWAHIA). Influential Seneca leader, though not a *royaner* or hereditary chief; half brother of Chief Handsome Lake (founder of the Iroquois "New Religion") and nephew of Guyasuta. His mother was a Seneca woman of chiefly lineage and his father was a Dutch trader from Albany named John Abeel. Cornplanter was born about 1750 at Ganawaugus (Avon) on the Genesee River. In 1780 he became Head Man of that town. In later years he made his home at Jenuchshadego (Burnt House), better known as Cornplanter's Town. From this center he supervised alien Indians on the Allegheny-Ohio for the Iroquois Confederacy. During the Revolutionary War he fought for the British, but after its conclusion he urged reconciliation and helped to keep his people from joining in the Indian war for the Northwest Territory. For his many conciliatory acts, Pennsylvania gave him deeds for three tracts of land, only one of which he kept, the Cornplanter Grant, submerged in 1967 by the Kinzua Dam. He died in 1836.

CUSTALOGA (PACKANKE). A Delaware chief whose first known residence was on French Creek. The Senecas reportedly had given him and his followers the land between French Creek and the Beaver River and regarded him as spokesman for the Delawares in councils at Venango (present Franklin), where George Washington met him in 1753. He was on friendly terms with the French during their occupation of western Pennsylvania until 1759, but afterwards made peace with the English. He was the principal chief of the Wolf lineage in Newcomer's "Delaware Nation." He joined the hostile Indians in Pontiac's War and moved to a site near present Coshocton, Ohio. When peace was concluded and the Indians were instructed to return to their former places, Custaloga resettled at Kuskusky, near present New Castle. On his invitation the Moravians established a mission at present Moravia, Pennsylvania, in 1770. He died in 1776 and was succeeded by his nephew, Captain Pipe.

DELAWARE GEORGE. *See* NENACHEEHUNT.

ESTHER, QUEEN. Supposed, on doubtful evidence, to have been a daughter of French Margaret, she lived at a settlement known as Queen Esther's Town, opposite Tioga Point. She protected white settlers at the beginning of the Revolutionary War, and treated the Strope family, her prisoners, with great kindness. It is debatable whether it was she or another Indian woman who killed the prisoners taken in the Battle of Wyoming. Tradition assigns her that role, but Jane Strope (Mrs. Whittaker, whose "Narrative" has been published) did not think Queen Esther was at Wyoming at the time. Being warned of the approach of Colonel Hartley's raiders in the fall of 1778, she took her people with their livestock into hiding, possibly in the ravine still known as Esther's Glen. After the war she is said to have married a Tuscarora chief named Steel Trap and to have moved north with him to Cayuga Lake.

FRENCH MARGARET. A niece (sister's daughter) of Madam Montour, married to an Iroquois chief, Katarionegha (Peter Quebec). She is first mentioned, with her aunt, in 1727, then living at Shamokin (present Sunbury), but by 1745 she and her husband had moved to the Hocking River, near present Lancaster, Ohio, from which place they brought twenty horse loads of deerskins to Philadelphia. By 1753, however, they were

174

back on the Susquehanna West Branch, near present Montoursville; and from there, in July, 1754, they arrived at Bethlehem, by way of Nescopeck, on their way to New York with two grandchildren, an Irish servant, and eleven horseloads of peltry. When the upper Susquehanna was vacated by the Indians in 1755, Margaret moved to the Chemung River, near present Elmira, New York, and her family are last mentioned there in 1763. Margaret had two daughters, Mary (Molly) and Catharine (Kate) and a son, Nicholas Quebec. Another Indian woman, Queen Esther, has also been identified as a daughter, but on rather weak evidence.

GAUSTARAX (OSCOTAX, "MUD EATER"). Seneca chief at Geneseo; a man of great influence in the Indian world but little known among white men. For years he headed the Genesee River division of the Senecas, which was anti-League and anti-English. Although he signed the Six Nations release to Pennsylvania of the Susquehanna lands in 1736 and of lands north of the Kittatinny Mountains in 1749, he bitterly opposed the encroachments of the settlers on unpurchased Indian lands and inspired a policy that for many years kept the Genesee-Allegheny region closed to white men. It was probably Gaustarax, not Guyasuta, who led the Indian forces against Colonel Bouquet at the Battle of Bushy Run in 1763.

GLICKHICAN. Famous Delaware warrior (his name means "gun sight") and principal advisor to Custaloga, principal chief of the Wolf lineage. In 1769 he was sent to drive the Moravians from their new mission at Lawunakhannek (East Hickory) on the upper Allegheny. After hearing David Zeisberger preach, however, Glickhican decided to become a Christian. He was baptized under the name of Isaac on Christmas Eve, 1770, and soon became a "National Helper" or Native Elder. He arranged for the establishment of Moravian towns in the heart of the Delaware nation, first at what is now Moravia on the Beaver River and later at Schönbrunn and Gnadenhütten on the Tuscarawas. During the Revolutionary War he on several occasions persuaded hostile war parties to return without striking their intended blow at American settlements. On March 8, 1782, he was among the ninety Christian Indians killed by Pennsylvania and Virginia militia at Gnadenhütten.

GUYASUTA (KIASUTHA). A Seneca chief of the Wolf Clan, born about 1720 among the Genesee River Senecas. His name, Ki-ä'-sut-ha, means "Crosses Standing in a Row." His sister was Cornplanter's mother. All his life, although he was not a hereditary chief, he exerted vast influence among his own people and among the whites. He was for many years the League deputy or "half king" on the Allegheny-Ohio. "Able, prudent, and wise," as Merle Deardorff of Warren describes him, he tried to adjust peacefully the differences that arose between Indians and white men. He tried to prevent Pontiac's War. He did not, as commonly supposed, lead the Indians (though he may have been present) at the Battle of Bushy Run, 1763. Without being disloyal to his own people, he greatly helped Colonel Bouquet at the conference in 1764 that ended hostilities. George Washington, who met him in 1770, recognized him as "the Hunter" who had accompanied him to Fort Le Boeuf in 1753. In 1776 the Americans offered him a colonel's commission. When in 1777 the Senecas entered the war on the British side, he accepted his people's decision but did not take a very active part. It was not he but Farmer's Brother who led the Senecas in the destruction of Hannastown in 1782. After the war he worked with Cornplanter for friendly relations with the United States. He died, 1794, in Cornplanter's house and was buried on the Cornplanter Grant.

HALF KING. A title, devised by Europeans, best known as applied to Tanaghrisson (d. 1754) and his successor Scaroyady (d. 1757), who were spokesmen for the Iroquois resident on the upper Ohio. The fact that the title occasionally is used without the personal name has sometimes led historical writers into error; and it should be noted that there was also a Huron (Wyandot) chief known as the Half King.

European attempts to apply their own terms of rank to Indian personages were awkward at best, and usage varied in different places and times. In Pennsylvania, by mid-eighteenth century, "king" (as distinguished from "chief") meant a spokesman representing a body of Indians in dealing with some other party. Thus "king" Sassoonan represented certain Delaware bands in treaties with Pennsylvania officials; and Teedyuscung, authorized by several Indian groups to conclude peace with Pennsylvania, could boast that he was "king of ten nations."

HANDSOME LAKE (SKANIADARIYO). A Seneca chief of the Turtle Clan, half brother of Cornplanter. In 1799 and 1800 on the Cornplanter Grant in Warren County, during the course of a long illness, he had a series of visions. In these, messengers from the Creator appeared to him. They led him up the Sky Path, showed him the punishments of the wicked and the rewards of the righteous. They transmitted to him *Gaiwiio*, the Good Word from the Creator, and told him how to save his people from the evils that threatened their national existence. The movement he initiated, known as the "New Religion," and the practical solutions he proposed for his people's problems contributed much to the Iroquois renaissance in the nineteenth century. Today his sayings, "The Code of Handsome Lake," are devoutly preserved by his followers, who constitute a large part of the Iroquois in the United States and Canada. Most of his work was accomplished at Cornplanter's Town, Cold Spring, and Tonawanda. He died on a visit to Onondaga, August 10, 1815.

JACOBS. A Delaware war chief, or "captain," who joined Shingas in raids on Virginia and Pennsylvania settlers in the French and Indian War; in consequence both colonies offered rewards for his head. Although reported killed in January, 1756, in Northampton County and in April in Cumberland County, Jacobs led the Indians in Captain de Villiers' capture of Fort Granville (near Lewistown, Pa.) on July 31, 1756. He was in fact killed at Kittanning, on September 8 of this same year in Colonel Armstrong's surprise attack. A nephew, also called Captain Jacobs, survived this attack (though reported killed); the Mason and Dixon surveying party met him in August, 1767.

KAKOWATCHIKY. A Shawnee chief of the Pequea division. It is possible that it was he who led the Shawnees from the Illinois country to the upper Delaware in 1694. Certainly he was chief of the Shawnees at the Pechoquealin towns above the Delaware Water Gap as early as 1709. About 1728 he moved with his band to the Shawnee Flats on the North Branch of the Susquehanna (just below the present town of Plymouth), the general area being known then as Wyoming. There Conrad Weiser and Count Zinzendorf visited him in 1742. About 1744 he moved with his band to Logstown on the Ohio, where Conrad Weiser met him in 1748. John Patton found him bedridden at Logstown in 1752.

KIASUTHA. *See* GUYASUTA.

KILLBUCK. The popular name of two Delaware leaders, father and son. The father (identified as Bemineo in a 1765 treaty) had lived near the Lehigh River, and his aunt was the wife of one of Teedyuscung's "brothers," Joe Evans. He participated in raids with Shingas and Captain Jacobs in 1755, but in 1758 was living at Sawcunk (present Beaver, Pa.), where he was Netawatwees' counselor of the Wolf lineage (as White Eyes was for the Turkey lineage). He later moved to the Tuscarawas. He was one of the deputies sent to make peace with Sir William Johnson in 1765, after Pontiac's War, and was also at the Fort Stanwix Treaty in 1768. He visited Philadelphia in 1771, and as a counselor took a pro-American stand in the Revolution. Although then blind, he went as far as Pittsburgh in 1779 with a delegation on its way to Philadelphia. He died not long afterward.

The son, whose Indian name was Gelelemend, was, like his mother, of the Turtle lineage. Born near the Lehigh in 1737, he was taken to the Ohio country by his parents. He accompanied his father to Philadelphia in 1771, and became like him a prominent counselor. He was the designated successor to Netwatwees, who died in 1776. He wished to join the Moravians, who however advised him to delay this action because of his ability as chief to help them and to preserve good relations between the Delawares and the Americans. He headed the Delaware delegation that in 1779 went to Philadelphia to meet General Washington and the Continental Congress. When relations with the Americans broke down in 1781, Gelelemend and a few other Delawares took refuge at Pittsburgh. He was baptized in 1789, as William Henry (after William Henry of Lancaster), but he and his descendants have continued to use Killbuck as a family name. He died in 1811 at Goshen mission, on the Tuscarawas River.

KISHACOQUILLAS. A Shawnee chief living at Ohesson or Kishacoquillas' Town (Lewistown) on the Juniata. He was reported in 1731 to be chief man of that town, which then contained twenty Shawnee families and sixty warriors. In 1739, on behalf of "the Shawnee nation," he signed a treaty of friendship with Pennsylvania, to last "while the Sun, Moon, and Stars endure." He died at Captain McKee's, August, 1754. His death was formally "condoled" by Conrad Weiser at Aughwick (Shirleysburg) a few days later.

LAPAGHPETON. A Unami Delaware Indian, one of Sassoonan's associates. According to Conrad Weiser, he was born about 1700. When payment was made in 1733 for the Tulpehocken lands, which Sassoonan's people had sold the year before, one of the signers of the receipt was "Lapahpaton in behalf of (his Father so called) Elalapis." He probably was Elalapis's nephew, and he may have been Sassoonan's nephew as well; for on Sassoonan's death in 1747, Weiser described Lapaghpeton as "an honest, true-hearted man," best qualified to succeed him. He preferred a quieter life, however, and settled at present Catawissa, commonly referred to as "Lapachpeton's Town." In the French and Indian War, when the Indians vacated this region, he retired to Secaughcung (Canisteo, New York). He attended the 1757 treaty at Easton, held to make peace between the Indians and Pennsylvania; and when Teedyuscung, the Indians' spokesman, digressed into a complaint about land, Lapaghpeton rebuked him publicly. In 1758 his son set out to the Ohio with Christian Frederick Post, but turned back when news came of the British defeat at Ticonderoga. He later moved to the Ohio country, where Post and John Heckewelder met him at Tuscarawas in 1762, when he expressed his apprehension that the arrival of missionaries might herald such troubles there as the Indians had experienced on the Susquehanna.

LOGAN (TAGHNEGHDORUS). John, son of Shickellamy (or Swatana, the chief at Shamokin), was one of the ten Cayuga sachems or council chiefs of the Iroquois. He came to be known as "John Logan" through false analogy with the name of his younger brother "James Logan," and then simply as "Logan." Like his father, he was a friend of the English. He helped Pennsylvania make the Albany Purchase of 1754. Some of his people were killed by the Paxton Boys at Conestoga in 1763, but he took no revenge. When, however, in 1774 Daniel Greathouse's men murdered thirteen members of his family at Yellow Creek on the Ohio, Logan helped to bring on the Shawnee War (Lord Dunmore's War). At the Battle of Mount Pleasant, he is said to have taken thirteen scalps. His message to Lord Dunmore at the close of the war, dictated to Simon Girty, put on paper by John Gibson, and transmitted to the public by Thomas Jefferson, has become famous as "Logan's Lament." David McClure described him in 1772 as "the most martial figure of an Indian that I had ever seen." John Heckewelder called him "a man of superior talents but of deep Melancholy," to whom life "had become a torment." The tradition that he was murdered by white men is mistaken. On orders from some of the elders among his own people, he was killed about 1786 by his nephew, who explained afterwards to John Adlum that Logan had become presumptuous, "too great a man to live," and that he, the nephew, expected to inherit Logan's greatness.

MONTOUR, MADAM. Born at Three Rivers, Canada, in 1667, of a French father, Pierre Couc, and his Algonkin wife, she led an adventurous life on the French and English frontiers, and for several years before 1709 lived at Mackinac and Detroit, where relatives were engaged in the Indian trade. In that year her brother Louis was murdered while conducting western Indians to Albany to trade there. Madam Montour, who had accompanied him, then remained in New York, where she was employed by Governor Robert Hunter as an interpreter and became the wife of an Oneida chief, Carandowana. In 1727, when the Oneida chief Swatana (Shickellamy) came to Pennsylvania, Madam Montour and her family came also; and here too she served for a few years as an interpreter. Carandowana was killed in 1729 in a raid on southern Indians; and Madam Montour thereafter lived at various times at Shamokin and near present Montoursville, with her son Andrew and her niece French Margaret. In 1748 she was with Andrew near present Harrisburg, but her last years are obscure. She is reported to have died in 1753. She was a person of distinguished bearing and engaging personality. Witham Marshe, who interviewed her in 1744, at the age of 77, wrote that "She has been a handsome woman, genteel, and of polite address," and he was easily convinced that her father had been a French gentleman and a governor of Canada. In addition to her son Andrew and niece Margaret, her youngest brother Jean also lived in Pennsylvania for a few years after 1727 and had a Delaware Indian wife; and another son, Louis, lived here for some time in the 1750's.

MONTOUR, ANDREW (SATTELIHU, EGHNISERA). Presumably the "little son," mentioned in 1730, of Madam Montour and her Indian husband; prominent in Indian affairs from 1742 until his death thirty years later. Count Zinzendorf, who met him on the West Branch of Susquehanna in 1742, has left a vivid description: "This man had a countenance like another European but around his whole face an Indianish broad ring of bear fat and paint, and had on a sky-colored coat of fine cloth, black cordovan neckband with silver bugles, a red damask lapelled waistcoat, breeches over which his shirt hung, shoes and stockings, a hat, and both ears braided with brass and other wire like a handle on a basket. He welcomed us cordially, and when I spoke to him in French he replied in English. His name is André." He performed numerous diplomatic errands for both Pennsylvania and Virginia and journeyed to both New York and the Ohio country. He held a captain's commission from Virginia in 1754 and captained one of Sir William Johnson's raiding parties in 1764. He received (but did not keep) land in Pennsylvania in present Mifflin County and at present Montoursville, and Montour's Island near Pittsburgh. He was killed near Pittsburgh in 1772 by a Seneca Indian. He had a brother, Louis or Tan Weson, who spent several years in Pennsylvania. The best known of his children was a son John, born about 1744, who during the Revolution served with American troops at Pittsburgh. Andrew was sometimes called Henry, probably from the similarity between the French names André and Henri.

NENACHEEHUNT (DELAWARE GEORGE). A chief of the "Delawares of Shamokin," he accompanied Sassoonan to the 1742 treaty at Philadelphia, and was a witness to the treaty with the Miami Indians signed at Lancaster in 1748. He afterward moved to the Ohio, where he was associated with Shingas, whom he accompanied to treaties at Winchester and Carlisle in September, 1753. Through the French and Indian War he continued friendly to the English. In July, 1755, he journeyed east to give warning of French attacks on the frontiers, and he was at Shamokin when the first of these attacks took place, at nearby Penns Creek on October 15. He lived later at Kuskusky. In August, 1757, Teedyuscung reported an inquiry from him and Netawatwees about peace negotiations; and in June, 1758, a visit by him at Wyoming. Post met him at Kuskusky in August. He was frequently at Pittsburgh after the French defeat, and, with the Beaver and Netawatwees, headed the Delawares at General Monckton's peace treaty in 1760. He and his followers settled at Kuskusky (Shingas and the Beaver having moved to Tuscarawas), where he expected Monckton to build him a council house. In the spring of 1762 his people brought him to Pittsburgh, very sick, and he died there three days later, on April 30, "much Lemented [wrote Croghan] by his own Nation & Likewise by yᵉ white pople as he was a Stedy frend to yᵉ British Intrest. . . ."

178

NETAWATWEES (NETOTWELEMET, NEWCOMER). A Delaware chief of the Turtle lineage. Presumably he is the "Nedawaway or Oliver" who witnessed the 1718 confirmation deed and the "Nectotaylemet" who witnessed the 1737 "Walking Purchase" deed. Otherwise nothing is known of him until 1754 when at Logstown he and six other Indian leaders gave George Croghan a request for Virginia and Pennsylvania to build "strong houses" on the Ohio. His role in the French and Indian War is obscure, but in 1757 he and Delaware George sent messengers to inquire about peace negotiations. A year later a message sent to the Ohio was delivered to "the great man of the Unami nation," then living at the mouth of Beaver River. When Christian Frederick Post arrived at Kuskusky later that year, Netawatwees sent messengers (Killbuck and White Eyes) inviting him to his town. Following British victory, he retired to Cuyahoga, and although he attended the 1760 treaty at Pittsburgh he maintained a reserved, noncommital attitude. He and Custaloga (chief of the Wolf lineage) only sent deputies to the 1762 Lancaster treaty which the Beaver (the Turkey chief) attended. About 1764, during Pontiac's War, he moved to the site of present Newcomerstown, Ohio; and afterward, when Colonel Bouquet marched his troops to that place, Newcomer was so tardy in meeting him that Bouquet ordered the Turtle lineage to choose another spokesman. His sustained efforts for Delaware unity, freedom, and welfare led to the creation of the "Delaware Nation," in which each of the three lineages had its own chief but Netawatwees, as "king," spoke for all. To this end he invited the scattered Delaware communities in New Jersey and Pennsylvania, and some of the Munsees as well, to join him; inviting the Moravian mission Indians, he accepted their teachers also, but he discouraged sectarian divisions. In the Revolution he aimed at friendly neutrality toward the Americans and rebuked one of his counselors, White Eyes, for favoring closer ties. In 1776 he established a new "capital" at the site of present Coshocton, Ohio; but later that year he died at Pittsburgh, on October 31, while attending a treaty. Killbuck (Gelelemend), his designated successor, replaced him, but the subsequent strains and consequences of war contributed to the decline of the "Delaware Nation" thereafter.

NEWALLIKE (NEOLEGAN, "THE FOUR STEPS"). A Munsee chief from the Minisinks who, as pressure from white men increased, moved from the Delaware Valley to Tunkhannock Creek, then to the North Branch of the Susquehanna at Sheshequin, thence to the West Branch, later to the Muskingum, and at last to Sandusky. In 1766 he was sent by the Six Nations to notify the Indians living on the Susquehanna that certain bands of Tuscaroras and Nanticokes were moving north toward the Iroquois homeland and to request that food and transportation be made ready for them. For some years he was chief at the Big Island (Lock Haven). In 1774 he moved with all his family to the Moravian mission town of Schönbrunn on the Tuscarawas branch of the Muskingum. There he built a house, and on May 12, 1774, was baptized. The Revolutionary War disturbed him, and in February, 1777, he renounced the Moravians and joined the pro-British party among the Delawares.

NUTIMUS. A Delaware chief, born in New Jersey, though he appears to have had some right to land on the west side of the Delaware River as well. When he moved into what is now northern Bucks County, he probably was unaware that this land had been included in the 1718 confirmation deed. About 1727 he sold land here to James Logan for his Durham ironworks. When in 1732 Thomas Penn resumed negotiations for the purchase of Indian land rights, Nutimus became the protagonist of the Indians who opposed acceptance of the 1737 "Walking Purchase" confirmation deed. He settled thereafter at Nescopeck with his family and five slaves, "a negress and four children," who worked on his plantation. After the French and Indian War broke out, he removed to Canisteo, on the Chemung River; and after the war he and his family lived at the Big Island (near Lock Haven, Pennsylvania). He is last mentioned there in 1763, and he probably died not long afterward. Members of his family removed later to Ohio; and the missionary John Heckewelder, confusing a son Isaac (a blacksmith) with his father, has credited the older man with having lived until about 1780.

OLUMAPIES (ALLUMAPEES). *See* SASSOONAN

OPESSA. Chief of the band of Shawnees who came up from Maryland about 1697 and settled at Pequea in what is now Lancaster County. He represented his people at the treaty held by William Penn at Philadelphia in April, 1701, with the Five Nations, Susquehannocks, Conoys, and Shawnees. In 1707 he received a visit at Pequea from Governor John Evans. In 1711, after some difficulty, he left his people and "went hunting." He visited Philadelphia in 1715, but then resumed his hunting, in fact settling on the upper Potomac at Opessa's Town (Oldtown, Maryland). Here, apparently, he died; and after an attack by southern Indians in 1729, the Shawnees moved from that place to the Allegheny River.

PAPOONHAN. A Munsee preacher who before the French and Indian War lived at a town at the mouth of the Lackawanna River. Here, about 1752, he founded a religious group that—remarkable for Munsees—took a pacifist stand that earned them the nickname of "Quaker Indians." They moved at the outbreak of hostilities, and in 1758 were living above Tioga Point. Later that year they moved down to Wyalusing. Papoonan visited Bethlehem the following year, and Christian Frederick Post stopped at his town in 1760. David Zeisberger baptized him in 1763 as a Moravian convert, named John. He and his Munsee followers went with the other Moravian Indians to Philadelphia for safety during Pontiac's War, after which he enabled the Moravians to establish a mission (Friedenshütten) at Wyalusing. In 1772 he moved with this Moravian colony to the Tuscarawas River, and was the speaker for the embassy sent to announce their arrival before the chiefs' council at Newcomer's Town. He died in May, 1775.

PAXINOSA. A Shawnee born in the Ohio country. When the Shawnee settlement at Wyoming broke up in 1744, most of them going to the Ohio with Kakowatchiky, Paxinosa (whose Delaware wife was a Moravian convert) became the leader of those who remained at Wyoming. He was a strong friend of the English. In 1756, soon after the outbreak of the French and Indian War, he moved north with his band to Tioga (Athens, Pa.). He attended the Easton treaty of 1757, bringing with him a company of fifty-seven Indians. About 1758 he moved up to Secaughcung (Canisteo) in New York; and in the spring of 1760 he went with his family to the Ohio, where he died a year later. The Moravians later met one of his sons and a daughter in Ohio. The famous Shawnee chief Cornstalk was his grandson.

PIPE, CAPTAIN (HOPOCAN, "tobacco pipe"; KOGESHQUANOHEL). A Delaware Indian of the Wolf lineage. During the French and Indian War the Shawnees, having lost some of their own war captains, "borrowed" him to lead them. Christian Frederick Post met him at Kuskusky in 1758, and he attended later peace treaties, including the 1765 meeting at Pittsburgh after Pontiac's War. He was the designated successor to Custaloga, on whose death in 1776 he became the head of the Wolf lineage. In the Revolution he was friendly toward the Americans until 1778, when militia from Fort Pitt, on the so-called "Squaw Campaign," attacked Delaware Indians at Kuskusky, where they killed Pipe's brother and wounded his mother. Pipe thereafter headed the pro-British Delawares. In 1781 he removed the Moravians from the Tuscarawas River to Upper Sandusky. When, however, the missionaries were put on trial by the British at Detroit, Pipe defended them and got them released. At the Battle of Upper Sandusky, in 1782, he took prisoner Colonel William Crawford, who had been on the "Squaw Campaign," and permitted him to be tortured to death. After the war Pipe advised the western tribes to maintain friendly relations with the United States. He moved to the Miami in 1791. Hokingpomska succeeded him as head of the Wolf lineage.

SASSOONAN (ALLUMAPEES) remembered that as a boy he had seen William Penn at Perkasie (in upper Bucks County)—probably in May, 1683, when Penn was negotiating the land purchases made later that year. By 1709 Sassoonan was living at Paxtang (near present Harrisburg) and was one of the Delaware chiefs who then visited Governor Gookin. A few years later he was the recognized spokesman ("king") for the Delaware bands known collectively as the Schuylkill Indians; and in this capacity he signed the 1718 deed that confirmed all of William Penn's land purchases. This left Sassoonan's people only the Tulpehocken lands, which he and the other chiefs sold in 1732. Many of his people had by then gone to the Ohio country, and the Iroquois settled the rest at Shamokin (Sunbury). Here Sassoonan spent his last years. Since his people had no land of their own, and the Iroquois had their own representative, Swatana (Shickellamy), at Shamokin, they considered Sassoonan as a person of no importance; but Pennsylvania continued to treat him as "king" for the sake of relations with his people in the Ohio country. When he died, in September, 1747, the naming of a successor was delayed. In June, 1752, finally, Shingas (his nephew and so eligible to succeed), who had removed to the Ohio, was designated and accepted as "king" of the Delawares of that area.

SCAROYADY ("side of the sky"; MONACATOOTHA, by which he was also known, is a Shawnee translation). A famous Oneida warrior and chief who, according to his own pictographic "memoir," had fought in thirty-one engagements, killed seven warriors, and taken eleven prisoners. About 1747 he was appointed by the Iroquois Confederacy to supervise the Shawnees at the Forks of the Ohio. On the death of Tanaghrisson in 1754, he succeeded him as "half king" with general "Direction of Indian Affairs," as Richard Peters wrote, in the west. At Logstown Conrad Weiser met him in 1748, and George Washington met him there in 1753. After Washington's defeat at Fort Necessity in 1754, Scaroyady moved to Aughwick to escape the French. In that year he journeyed to Onondaga to protest the so-called Wyoming Purchase. A strong friend of the English, he campaigned with Washington and Braddock. In the months that followed Braddock's defeat, he tried to enlist Pennsylvania's military aid for the Delawares living on the Susquehanna, who were under pressure from the French to take up the hatchet against the English. "You can't live in the woods and stay neutral," he said. On behalf of the Province, he made a dangerous journey through the Delaware country to find out just what the situation was. As a result of his report on the widespread hostility, the Pennsylvania Governor declared war on the Delawares. He died at Lancaster in June, 1757, while attending a treaty.

SHICKELLAMY. See SWATANA.

SHINGAS ("bog meadow"). One of several nephews of Sassoonan, and brother of Pisquitomen and the Beaver. Sassoonan's death in 1747 left the Delawares without a designated spokesman or "king." Two nephews, designated in turn, had died previously; Pisquitomen, eldest of the three brothers, seems to have been his uncle's next choice but was unacceptable to James Logan, the Provincial Secretary. The Iroquois were in no hurry to name a successor, possibly because the Delawares had sold all their land and had in great part moved to the Ohio. Pennsylvania and Virginia, because of their interests in the Ohio country, were more concerned and, Sassoonan's nephews having moved to the Ohio, took steps to settle the matter. In 1752, when Virginia held a treaty at Logstown, Tanaghrisson formally designated Shingas as the Delaware "king," promptly approved by Virginia and Pennsylvania. His participation in frontier attacks in 1755 terminated his "kingship," however, and elicited the offer of rewards by the two colonies for Shingas' and Captain Jacobs' heads. Jacobs was killed a few months later at Kittanning, but Shingas lived to join in the restoration of peace between his people and the English. James Kenny wrote of him in 1762 that "its generally said by yᵉ White people that he shows them the most kindness & generossity of all yᵉ Indians thereabouts." He died during the winter of 1763-1764.

SWATANA ("enlightener"; SHICKELLAMY is an Algonkian equivalent). An Oneida chief who, according to the naturalist John Bartram, who met him in 1743, was "a Frenchman born at Montreal, and adopted by the Oneidas after being taken prisoner." Delegated about 1727 to oversee the Shawnees settled on the Susquehanna, he lived until sometime after 1737 near one of their towns about twelve miles north of Shamokin (Sunbury). In contemporary accounts he appears as an able and intelligent man, dignified but pleasant, industrious and dependable. Pennsylvania officials soon became aware of his usefulness in Indian affairs, which they placed largely in his and Conrad

Weiser's hands. By 1742, the Shawnees having migrated, Swatana moved to Shamokin itself, where Weiser supervised the building of a house for his use. Here he oversaw Sassoonan's Delawares and also became a friend of the Moravians, who eventually regarded him as one of their followers, but did not baptize him, because he said a priest had baptized him as a child. His wife, who was of the Cayuga tribe, died in 1747, in the same epidemic that carried off Sassoonan; and Swatana himself died on December 6 of the following year. He was survived by two daughters and three sons, best known as John Shickellamy (later as LOGAN), James Logan, and John Petty.

TAMANEND ("the affable"). Chief of a Delaware band, who in 1683 sold William Penn a tract of land between Pennypack and Neshaminy creeks, was one of the witnesses to a sale of land north of Neshaminy in 1686, and in 1692 and 1697 gave deeds confirming his original sale. He is noteworthy chiefly for the legends that have grown up around his name, perhaps arising from the fact that his was the first sale negotiated by William Penn personally. He has been portrayed as chief of all the Delaware Indians who met Penn in a legendary "Great Treaty" held under the "Treaty Elm" at Shakamaxon. In 1772 a secret society, the Sons of King Tammany, forerunner of the Improved Order of Red Men, was named for him; and so also was the Society of St. Tammany, forerunner of Tammany Hall.

TANAGHRISSON. A Seneca chief, resident after 1747 on the upper Ohio, presumably to oversee the Iroquois dispersed through the region and also the Indians, mostly Delawares, resettled there under Iroquois supervision. The Iroquois council at Onondaga regarded its dispersed people as "hunters," without authority to hold formal councils. However, Virginia and Pennsylvania, with special interest in the region, found it tedious to deal through Onondaga and preferred direct negotiations. They therefore lit a council fire at Logstown (present Ambridge), with Tanaghrisson as the designated speaker or "king"—"half king" in this case, presumably because he represented a segment of his people—; and at a treaty held in 1748 Conrad Weiser provided Tanaghrisson the wampum and other goods required for Indian diplomacy. When in 1753 the French built Fort Presque Isle (Erie) and Fort Le Boeuf (Waterford), he sent three successive messages (the strongest Iroquois protest short of a declaration of war), calling on the French to remove their military forces from Iroquois territory. In December of that year he accompanied Washington to Fort Le Boeuf with a similar summons from Virginia. These efforts to stop the French failing, he invited Virginia to build a fort at the Forks. He was present, April 17, 1754, when that fort, half finished, was surrendered to the French. Before sunrise on the morning of May 28 he conferred with George Washington at the Half King's Rock (near Summit, east of Uniontown). With his warriors about three hours later, he supported Washington in the skirmish at Jumonville Rocks, an incident which set off the French and Indian War. Against Tanaghrisson's advice, Washington erected palisades (Fort Necessity) at the Great Meadows, which he was soon obliged to surrender. After this disaster, the Half King moved his headquarters east to Aughwick (present Shirleysburg). He died October 4, 1754, at John Harris' (present Harrisburg) and was buried there.

TEEDYUSCUNG (HONEST JOHN). One of the best known Pennsylvania Indians, but born about 1705 near Trenton, New Jersey. His life is obscure until 1750, when he and his wife were baptized by the Moravians as Gideon and Elisabeth. Three years later, however, he left the mission, on an Iroquois invitation to settle at Wyoming; and in the spring of 1755 he visited Philadelphia as one of three Delaware chiefs at that place. On the outbreak of hostilities later that year, he led one small attack on white settlers in the Minisink country and then retreated to Tioga. Urged by Sir William Johnson, the Iroquois directed him to make peace; and his acceptance by local bands of Delawares, Shawnees, Mahicans, and Munsees as spokesman for this purpose provided the basis for his bizarre claim to be "king of ten nations." An observer at Easton at this time described him as "a lusty, raw bon'd man, haughty, and very desireous of respect and command." A basis for peace was established at the Easton treaty of 1757, but Teedyuscung's role was complicated by a Quaker faction's effort to use him in creating a controversy over the

1737 "Walking Purchase" and Governor Morris' attempt to use him as a messenger to the Ohio Delawares who did not recognize his "kingship." As a practical encouragement to reconciliation, the Province built Teedyuscung a new home at Wyoming. The end of military hostilities in Pennsylvania and Sir William Johnson's closing of the "Walking Purchase" case in 1762 virtually ended Teedyuscung's public career. His wife died in an epidemic in this same year, and Teedyuscung himself died on April 16, 1763, when his house caught fire, probably accidentally. Threatened by arriving Connecticut settlers, the rest of the Wyoming community abandoned the place two months later and moved to the Long Island (near Jersey Shore) in the Susquehanna West Branch. The only member of his family to attract later notice was the son best known as Captain Bull, who joined the hostile Indians in Pontiac's War. Teedyuscung was not a "hereditary chief," and he had no designated successor.

WHITE EYES (COQUETAGEGHTON; also known as Grey Eyes and Sir William Johnson) was so called, we are told, because of "not having black eyes, like other Indians." In 1758 he and Killbuck were sent by Netawatwees to invite Christian Frederick Post to Sawcunk (present Beaver, Pa.). He remained at Sawcunk after the town was abandoned in 1759, and had there "a good shingled house & several stables & cow houses under one roof." Post described him in 1762 as "one of the cleverest Indians," and the missionary David Jones, who met him in 1772, said "He was the only Indian I met with in my travels, that seemed to have a design of accomplishing something future." He resettled at "White Eyes' Town," a few miles west of Newcomerstown, Ohio, about 1770. As a counselor he was a party to numerous treaties and embassies. He worked to prevent Dunmore's War in 1774, and to support the Americans in the Revolution; but his initiative and boldness raised some opposition. In a 1774 treaty at Pittsburgh, Iroquois and colonial representatives chose him, as a "captain," to replace Netawatwees as their spokesman to the Delaware Indians (but being of the Turkey lineage, he could not have replaced him as chief, as is sometimes stated). In the following year, however, he offended the Iroquois by a speech at Pittsburgh; and his appeals to the Continental Congress in 1776 brought him a rebuke from Netawatwees for going beyond what had been authorized by the Delaware council. He received a colonel's commission from the Americans in 1778 to lead Indian allies, but he died suddenly, not far from Pittsburgh, on November 10, reportedly of smallpox and an old ailment; but George Morgan, the Indian agent, later asserted that he had been killed by American militiamen.

NOTE

There are no established rules for spelling Indian names. The aim is to present them in a form reasonably accurate and also agreeable to the reader. Indians themselves rarely undertook to write their names, which were often recorded by poorly educated traders or by officials ignorant of the Indian language. In general the names were most carefully recorded by missionaries who learned the Indian language for their own work. This is true of the Moravians in Pennsylvania, who used a German system of spelling; where we have followed them we have therefore altered *sch* and *ch* (the gutteral) to *sh* and *gh*.

The difficulty of settling on a spelling is illustrated by some of the recorded versions of White Eyes' Indian name:

Cochquacaukehlton	Koquethagechton
Coquactogahowhay	Kuckquekakechiton
Coquataginta	Kuckquetackton
Coquetakeghton	Kuckquetakeckton
Goquedhakechton	Quequedagaytho
Goquethagechton	Quequedegatha

Bibliography

GENERAL REFERENCE

Donehoo, George P. *Indian Villages and Place Names in Pennsylvania* (Harrisburg, 1928). This book remains, on the whole, a handy and valuable reference.

Kent, Barry C. *Discovering Pennsylvania's Archeological Heritage* (Harrisburg: Pennsylvania Historical and Museum Commission, 1981). A booklet survey of Indian cultures and archeology.

Kent, Barry C., Ira F. Smith III, and Catherine McCann, eds. *Foundations of Pennsylvania Prehistory* (Harrisburg: Pennsylvania Historical and Museum Commission, 1971). A collection of major studies in Pennsylvania Indian anthropology, 1931-1971.

Trigger, Bruce G. ed. *Handbook of North American Indians,* Vol. 15: *Northeast* (Washington: Smithsonian Institution, 1978).

Underhill, Ruth. *Red Man's America: A History of Indians in the United States* (Chicago: University of Chicago Press, 1971). A good introduction to Indian cultures in their historical setting. Printed in paperback.

HISTORY

Brandon, William. *Indians* (New York: American Heritage, 1985). Paperbound.

Downes, Randolph C. *Council Fires on the Upper Ohio: A Narrative of Indian Affairs on the Upper Ohio Valley until 1795* (Pittsburgh: University of Pittsburgh Press, 1940). In paper covers.

Hunt, George T. *The Wars of the Iroquois: A Study in Intertribal Trade Relations* (Madison: University of Wisconsin Press, 1960). Paperbound available.

Jennings, Francis. *Empire of Fortune: Crowns, Colonies, and Tribes in the Seven Years' War in America* (New York: Norton, 1988).

——————— . *The Ambiguous Iroquois Empire: The Covenant Chain Confederation of Indian Tribes with English Colonies from Its Beginnings to the Lancaster Treaty of 1744* (New York: Norton, 1984). Available in paper.

Kupperman, Karen Ordahl. *Settling with the Indians: The Meeting of English and American Cultures in America, 1580-1640* (Totowa, N.J.: Rowan and Littlefield, 1980).

Norton, Thomas Elliot. *The Fur Trade in Colonial New York, 1686-1776* (Madison: University of Wisconsin Press, 1974).

Wainwright, Nicholas B. *George Croghan, Wilderness Diplomat* (Chapel Hill: University of North Carolina Press, 1959). Pennsylvania's foremost Indian trader and his influence among the Indians of the Ohio country.

Wallace, Anthony F. C. *King of the Delawares: Teedyuscung* (Philadelphia: University of Pennsylvania Press, 1949). A biography of the most prominent Delaware Indian of the mid-eighteenth century, with a background study of Delaware social and political organization.

Wallace, Paul A. W. *Conrad Weiser, Friend of Colonist and Mohawk* (Philadelphia: University of Pennsylvania Press, 1945). The career of Pennsylvania's Indian ambassador, the Province's Indian policy, and the men who administered it from 1732 to 1760.

184

_____, ed. *The Travels of John Heckewelder in Frontier America* (Pittsburgh: University of Pittsburgh Press, 1985). Originally published as *Thirty Thousand Miles with John Heckewelder;* a Moravian missionary's travels among the Delaware and Mahican Indians. In paper.

Washburn, Wilcomb E. *The Indian in America* (New York: Harper and Row, 1975). Published in Torchbook paperbound edition.

DELAWARES

Gray, Elma E. *Wilderness Christians* (Ithaca: Cornell University Press, 1956). A study of Moravian missionaries among Delaware and Mahican Indians in Pennsylvania, Ohio, Michigan and Ontario.

Kraft, Herbert C. *The Lenape: Archeology, History and Ethnography* (Newark: New Jersey Historical Society, 1986). Available in paper edition.

Newcomb, William W. Jr. *The Culture and Acculturation of the Delaware Indians* (Ann Arbor: University of Michigan Museum of Anthropology, 1956). A study of old Delaware customs and beliefs and the changes that have occurred during assimilation.

Speck, Frank G. *The Celestial Bear Comes Down to Earth* (Reading, Pa.: Reading Public Museum and Art Gallery, 1945). The Delawares' Big House Ceremony, its history, rites and symbolism.

Tantaquidgeon, Gladys. *Folk Medicine of the Delaware and Related Algonkian Indians* (Harrisburg: Pennsylvania Historical and Museum Commission, 1972). Based on information from a Delaware Indian of Oklahoma. Paperbound.

Weslager, C. A. *The Delaware Indians: A History* (New Brunswick, N.J.: Rutgers University Press, 1972).

IROQUOIS

Graymont, Barbara. *The Iroquois in the American Revolution* (Syracuse: Syracuse University Press, 1972). Available in paperback.

Parker, Arthur C. *Parker on the Iroquois,* edited by William N. Fenton (Syracuse: Syracuse University Press, 1968). A collection of three Parker studies, *Iroquois Uses of Maize and Other Food Plants; The Code of Handsome Lake, the Seneca Prophet;* and *The Constitution of the Five Nations.* Published also in paperbound edition.

Richter, Daniel K., and James H. Merrell, *Beyond the Covenant Chain: The Iroquois and Their Neighbors in Indian North America, 1600-1800* (Syracuse: Syracuse University Press, 1987).

Wallace, Anthony F. C. *The Death and Rebirth of the Seneca* (New York: Alfred A. Knopf, 1970). Subtitled "The history and culture of the Great Iroquois nation, their destruction and demoralization, and their cultural revival at the hands of the Indian visionary, Handsome Lake." In paper.

Wallace, Paul A. W. *The White Roots of Peace* (Philadelphia: University of Pennsylvania Press, 1946). The foundation legend, based on original sources, of the Five Nations (Iroquois). Paperbound reprint by Chauncy Press, Saranac Lake, New York.

185

Index

Long Island (near Jersey Shore, Pa.), 183
Longhouse (dwelling), 12, 29
Longhouse, Props to the, 113, 117; *see also* Iroquois Indians
Lord Dunmore's War, 128, 183
Loskiel, George Henry, 22, 24, 30, 31, 34, 49, 56, 64, 85, 123
Lower Sandusky, 64
Lowther, Manor of; *see* Indian Manor
Luckenbach, Abraham, 140
Lupwaaeenoawuk (Delaware Council), 121
Lycoming Creek, 45, 161

McClure, David, 177
Machaloha (Delaware Indian), 131
Machault, Fort, 151
McIntosh, Fort (Beaver, Pa.), 136, 138, 165
McKee, Alexander, 160
McKee, Capt. Thomas, 128, 177
McKee's Rocks, 173
Mackinac, 178
Macungie, Pa., 37
Mahican Indians, 18, 59, 100, 103, 117, 127, 156, 171; *see also* Abraham Mahican War, 103
Mahoning Creek, 160
Mahoning settlement, 162
Manito (guardian), 40, 63, 79
Manitoulin Island, 102
Maple sugar, 28, 33-34
Margaret; *see* French Margaret
Markham, Gov. William, 133, 134, 138
Marquette, Father, 119
Marriage, 64
Marsh, Witham, 178
Mary (Delaware Indian), 154
Mary (Molly, daughter of French Margaret), 175
Maryland, Eastern Shore of, 113
Mask Being, 63, 68
Mason and Dixon Line, 44, 176
Massasagues; *see* Missisauga Indians
Massawomekes (Indians), 11
Matson's Ford, 160
Maumee River, 166
Mayer-Oakes, William J., 14
May-ko-jay (Shawnee tribal division), 120
Medeu (conjurors), 39
Medicine, 30, 38-40, 76, 97, 169
Medicine Bundle, 40, 74

Meherrin River, 116
Meteor (Tecumseh), 118
Methodist preacher, 169
Metoxon, Emerson (Oneida Indian), 4
Miami Indians, 105, 122-23, 167, 178; *see also* Little Turtle
Miami River, 180
Michael (Delaware Indian), 154
Michael (Munsee Indian), 25
Michilimackinac, Fort, 151
Mifflin, Gov. Thomas, 168
Mingoes, 9, 12, 13, 15, 16, 109, 146; *see also* Iroquois Indians
Minisink Path, 42
Minisinks, 135, 136, 148, 173, 179, 182
Minquas; *see* Susquehannocks
Minquas Creek, 130
Minsi, John; *see* Papoonhank
Minuit, Peter, 130
Miseekwaaweekwaakee (Shawnee society), 122
Missisauga Indians, 123
Mississippi River, 119
Missouri River, 171
Moccasin game, 85
Moccasins, 21, 32, 85
Mohawk Indians, 56, 75, 89, 90, 91, 93, 94, 96, 101, 102, 103, 107, 144, 157, 159, 162, 172; *see also* John Fadden, Hendrick, Kiotsaeton, Peter Quebec, Sharenkhowane
Mohawk River, 10, 103, 113
Mohawk Valley, 163
Molly (daughter of French Margaret); *see* Mary
Monacatootha; *see* Scaroyady
Monckton, General, 178
Monongahela People, 10, 13-15, 29
Monongahela River, 12, 42, 44, 144, 173
Montour, Andrew (Henry), biographical sketch of, 178
Montour, Madam, 174; biographical sketch of, 178
Montour, Catharine, 164, 175
Montour, Jean, 178
Montour, John (Andrew Montour's son), 178
Montour, Louis (Madame Montour's brother), 178
Montour, Louis (Madame Montour's son, Tan Weson), 178
Montour, Pierre, 178
Montour Creek, 176

Montour's Island, 178
Montoursville, Pa., 175, 178
Montreal, Que., 49, 100-101, 105, 106, 145, 162, 181
Montreal Treaty (1701), 104-106
Mooney, James, 116
Moravia, Pa., 174
Moravian church (Unitas Fratrum), 127
Moravian Indians, 155, 159, 171, 175, 177, 179, 180, 182; massacre of, 51
Moravian missionaries, 23, 25, 33, 36, 68-69, 73, 84, 109, 115, 141, 148, 154, 159, 174, 175, 177, 179, 180, 182, 183
Moraviantown (Fairfield), 171
Morgan, George, 160, 161, 183
Morgan, Lewis, 33
Morris, Gov. Robert Hunter, 173, 183
Mortimer, Rev. Benjamin, 84
Mount Pleasant, Battle of, 177
Mount Union, Pa., 24
Mud Eater; see Gaustarax
Muhlenberg, Rev. Henry Melchior, 161
Muhlenberg, Gen. Peter, 161
Muncy, Pa., 25, 161
Muncy Creek, 42
Muncy Hill, 162
Muncytown, Ont., 171
Munsee Indians, 9, 18, 25, 36, 39, 58, 60, 70, 84, 125, 136, 140-41, 156, 171; see also Bald Eagle, Michael, Newallike, Papoonhan, Wangomen
Mushemeelin (Delaware Indian), 24
Music, 84
Muskingum Country, 145
Muskingum River, 25, 103, 139, 140, 153, 179
Muskrat, 74
Myths, 73-75, 81-84; see also Legends

Naked Bear, 63
Naming a child, 62
Nanticoke Flats, 113
Nanticoke Indians, 18, 40, 111, 112-14, 118, 156, 179; in the Iroquois Confederacy, 116
Nanticoke Path, 113
Nanticoke River, 113
Narhantes, Fort, 114
Nashville, Tenn., 45
Nassau, Fort, 20

Natchez Trace, 45
Nearing, Helen and Scott, 33
Necessity, Fort, 147, 173, 181, 182
Nekatcit (Delaware Indian), 71
Nemacolin, 47
Nenacheehunt (Delaware George), 178, 179
Neolegan; see Newallike
Neolin, 55
Nescopeck, 148, 175, 179
Neshaminy Creek, 133, 134, 182
Netawatwees (Newcomer, head chief of the Delawares), 54, 58, 139, 140, 141, 171, 174, 176, 177, 178, 179, 183; biographical sketch of, 179
Neutral Indians, 13, 16, 100, 102, 103, 108
New Castle, Captain, 173
New Castle, Del., 173
New Castle, Pa., 60, 103, 136, 138, 160, 174
New Cumberland, Pa., 126, 174
Newallike (Munsee chief), 115; biographical sketch of, 179
Newcomb, William W., Jr., 29, 57, 66
Newcomer; see Netawatwees
Newcomer's Town, 180
Newcomerstown, Ohio, 179, 183
Newhouse, Seth (Mohawk Indian), 114
Newtown (Elmira, N.Y.), 165
Niagara, 13, 102, 108, 162, 165
Niagara, Fort, 151, 165
Niagara Gorge, 114
Nicholas; see Quebec, Nicholas
Nicholas (Wyandot chief), 117
Niles, Ohio, 160
Nootamis; see Nutimus
Northeast River, 113
Northumberland, Pa., 128
Northwest Territory, 119, 174
Nutimus (Delaware chief), 135; biographical sketch of, 179
Nutimus, Isaac (Delaware Indian), 179

O'Bail; see Abeel
Ohesson (Kishacoquillas' Town), 128, 177
Ohio (State), 141, 179, 180
Ohio country, 13, 29, 108, 125, 128, 137, 139, 140, 143, 145, 146, 149, 155, 173, 177, 178, 180, 181, 183
Ohio Indians, 132, 146, 176

194

Ohio River, 9, 41, 44, 100, 109, 118, 119, 126, 127, 128, 137, 139, 143-44, 151, 157, 159, 166, 174, 175, 176, 177, 178, 179, 180, 181, 182
Ohio Valley, 13, 14, 42, 107, 109
Oil City, Pa., 168
Okehocking, 130-31
Oklahoma Delawares, 68, 82, 124, 171
Old age, respect for, 64-65
Old Peter's Road, 112
Old Sac (Conoy chief), 111
Old Sheshequin (Ulster); see Sheshequin
"Old Town," 36
Oldtown, Md., 44, 126, 180
Olumapies; see Sassoonan
Oneida Indians, 90, 93, 102, 114, 126, 142, 160-61, 165; see also Carandowana, Emerson Metoxon, Scaroyady
On-gwe-o-we (Ongwe-Honwe); see Iroquois Indians
Onondaga, 11, 89-90, 113, 145, 156, 157, 162, 169, 173, 176, 181, 182
Onondaga (Six Nations) Council, 90-93, 113, 114, 146, 157, 173
Onondaga Indians, 90, 93, 101, 102, 106, 160; see also Atotarho, Canasatego, Hiawatha, Swatana
Onondaga Lake, 94
Ononharoia (Dream Festival), 97
Ontario, Lake, 13, 89, 95
Opessa (Shawnee chief), 126; biographical sketch of, 180
Opessa's Town (Oldtown, Md.), 44, 126, 180
Opies; see Wappinger Indians
Orange, Fort, 100
Oregon Trail, 45
Orite of Adequentaga, 88
Ornaments, 21
Oscotax; see Gaustarax
Otsego Lake, 164
Otseningo; see Chenango
Ottawa, Ont., 162
Ottawa Indians, 102, 105, 125, 144, 146, 152; see also Pontiac
Ottawa River, 101
Owego, 112
Oxford, Pa., 113

Packanke; see Custaloga
Pahaquarry, 125
Paint, uses of, 24-25, 55, 122, 124-25

Painted Line, on the Towanda Path, 124-25
Painted Post, N.Y., 55
Palatine Germans, 135
Pamlico Sound, N.C., 114
Panther Tribe (Shawnee), 122
Papoonhan (Munsee prophet), biographical sketch of, 180
Parker, Arthur, 162
Pastorius, Daniel, 20
Path Valley, 115
Paths; see Indian paths
Patton, John, 176
Patuxent River, 104
Paxinosa (Shawnee chief), 127; biographical sketch of, 180
Paxtang (Harrisburg), 44, 109, 146, 154, 180
Paxton; see Paxtang
Paxton Boys, 115, 154-55, 163, 177
Paxton Presbyterian Church, 154
Peace pipe, 76, 86
Peace Women, Shawnee, 121
Pechoquealin towns, 176
Pechstank; see Paxtang
Pec-ku-we; see Pequea Indians
Peixtang; see Paxtang
Penn, John, 131, 133, 134
Penn, Richard, 134
Penn, Thomas, 134, 135, 144, 179
Penn, William, 29, 53, 54, 57, 58, 88, 104, 111, 126, 131, 133, 134, 135, 136, 143, 147, 148, 165-66, 171, 173, 180; describes the Delawares, 19-20, 53; Indian policy of, 129-33, 181, 182; land purchases of, 133-34.
Penn Wampum Belt, 56-57
Pennamite Wars, 133, 155, 158
Penns Creek, 147, 178
Penns Valley, 162
Pennsbury, 133
Pennypack Creek, 133, 134, 182
Pequea (Shawnee town), 125, 180
Pequea Creek, 125
Pequea Indians (Shawnee tribal division), 119, 120, 176
Perkasie, 180
Perkiomen Creek, 133
Peter's Road; see Old Peter's Road
Peters, Nicodemus (Delaware Indian), 71
Peters, Richard, 181
Petroleum, 22
Petty, John (Cayuga Indian, Sugtana's son), 182

195